John Hitchman

Christianity v. Ecclesiasticism

Parochial parleys on the ecclesiastic creeds and ecclesiastics

John Hitchman

Christianity v. Ecclesiasticism
Parochial parleys on the ecclesiastic creeds and ecclesiastics

ISBN/EAN: 9783337261993

Printed in Europe, USA, Canada, Australia, Japan

Cover: Foto ©Lupo / pixelio.de

More available books at **www.hansebooks.com**

CHRISTIANITY v. ECCLESIASTICISM

OR

PAROCHIAL PARLEYS

ON THE

ECCLESIASTIC CREEDS AND ECCLESIASTICS

(*KEBLE, PUSEY, NEWMAN*),

ON

BIBLICAL INSPIRATION AND OTHER KINDRED SUBJECTS

BETWEEN THE

Rev. HUGH HIEROUS, M.A., M.C.U.,

AND

His Parishioner, THEOPHILUS TRUMAN

EDITED BY J. H.

PRO AMORE DEI.

'Force never yet a generous heart did gain;
We yield on parley, but are storm'd in vain.'—*Dryden.*

'Beloved, while I was giving all diligence to write unto you of our common salvation, I was constrained to write unto you exhorting you to contend earnestly for the faith once for all delivered unto the saints.'—*Epistle of Jude* 3.

'Reason is the only faculty whereby we have to judge of anything, even revelation itself.'—*Bishop Butler.*

'At last he beat his music out,
There lives more faith in honest doubt,
Believe me, than in half the creeds.'—*Tennyson.*

'I shut my grave Aquinas fast
The monkish gloss of ages past,
The schoolman's creed aside I cast.

'And my heart answered, "Lord, I see
How Three are One, and One is Three;
Thy riddle hath been read to me."'—*Whittier.*

'I say, that in God's own good time you will know all things.'—*The last words of a loving and beloved wife.*

WILLIAMS AND NORGATE,
14, HENRIETTA STREET, COVENT GARDEN, LONDON, AND
20, SOUTH FREDERICK STREET, EDINBURGH.

1887.

In Memoriam

OF

M. A. H.,

THE BELOVED.

MARCH 24th, 1884.

'SHE OPENED HER MOUTH WITH WISDOM
AND IN
HER TONGUE WAS THE LAW OF KINDNESS.'

PREFACE.

To soothe a deep sorrow, to cherish a beloved memory, and to vindicate within a special circle, a departure from old associations, creeds, and practices this book has been written. It lays no claim to literary distinction. The great storehouse of biblical literature and religious biography has been searched for materials to sustain and enforce his arguments, but the Writer's obligations are too many and too great to admit of individual references, except, it may be, to Archbishop Tillotson, Bishops Bull, Warburton, and Watson, to the Cardinal Newman, and the Rev. Thos. Mozley, M.A. of Oriel College, and the Rev. G. Vance Smith, B.A., Ph.D.

It is, perhaps, right to state that *italics* have been employed frequently in the text, even in quotations from Authors who had not so used them. They have been used, indeed, with greater freedom than literary taste could approve; but, since the book has been written for the special purpose of pointing out the fallacies deduced by many from the words of Scripture; written, in short, to vindicate a departure from a Creed, and to exhibit a more rational and scriptural theory based on a correct reading of the biblical text, the graces of composition and of type have been foregone, in the wish of arresting attention, especially of persons who have passively accepted 'scriptural texts' without a full consideration of their true meaning. For a similar reason, and from a strong desire to rouse and fix the reflective faculties of the Reader, the repetition of important matter, in various forms, or even in identical phrases, has not been avoided, but rather has the counsel of Isaiah, of 'precept upon precept, precept upon precept, line upon line, line upon line; here a little, and there a little' (Isaiah xxviii. 10), been followed.

To avoid local misapprehension, it is right to

state that the character of the Rev. H. Hierous is intended to be generic, and that the personality and the conversations are wholly imaginary. The wish of the Writer has been, through Mr. Hierous, to state most honestly and fully all that could possibly be said in support of the tenets in which he (the Writer), as a Member of the Church of England, had been educated—to which for many years he had been attached with unquestioning devotion; but which tenets he is now compelled by facts—and by intellectual and conscientious convictions—to abandon as unsound.

The Writer feels most strongly that if the Reader will, in a judicial spirit, ponder on the facts and arguments brought forward in this volume, he too will likewise think that such tenets ought to be abandoned — abandoned as untrue and dishonouring to the Most High, who hath declared, 'I am the Lord, and there is none else; beside me, there is no God: I will guide thee, though thou hast not known me; that they may know from the rising of the sun, and from the west, that there is none beside me: I am the

Lord, and there is none else' (Isaiah xlv. 5, 6); abandoned and forgotten, as being mistrustful of our blessed Lord, who has so emphatically declared, 'This is life eternal, that they should know thee the only true God, and him whom thou didst send (even) Jesus Christ' (John xvii. 3).

J. H.

PAROCHIAL PARLEYS

ON THE

ECCLESIASTIC CREEDS AND OTHER KINDRED TOPICS.

INTERVIEW THE FIRST.

Vicar (the Rev. Hugh Hierous). I am glad to have met you in this cool and secluded spot, for I have been longing to speak to you on a subject of some delicacy—a topic, indeed, which has given me great anxiety, and which, even now, I would not broach to a person of your age and intelligence were it not that I feel bound by my ordination vows to do so.

Parishioner (Mr. Truman). My dear Vicar, you somewhat startle me; but I am sure that your motives are kindly, and as I have found this small and beautiful flower (*Parnassia palustris*) —the object of my search—I have abundance of time before me, and am quite curious to know what in me has given you anxiety.

Vicar. Well, I have been concerned to observe that during the five years I have been the vicar of this parish you have never once attended the Holy Communion, although you are a very regular attendant at church; and my appeals to the parishioners on the vital importance of this sacred rite have been most earnest and frequent. Even these circumstances *per se* would not have caused me to intrude on you, because I feel that my strong appeals from the pulpit exonerate me from responsibility in this matter—*liberavi animam meam;* but an intimate friend of yours has informed me that you absent yourself because you hold erroneous doctrine, and that you cannot enunciate the 'Belief,' which is an essential preliminary to the participation of the Holy Sacrament; that, in brief, you disbelieve in the doctrine of the Blessed Trinity, and are even unwilling to address our Lord Jesus Christ as 'God of God, Light of Light, very God of very God.'

Parishioner. Your informant is correct as to the reasons which preclude my presence, but I am not willing to admit that I hold 'erroneous doctrine'; on the contrary, I think it is the faith which was 'once delivered to the saints,' and that it becomes me 'to contend' for it on those rare occasions when I can do so without danger of wrecking the simple faith of others in still more important particulars; and as this appears to be one of those occasions, I invite you, my dear Pastor, to speak freely, and I assure you that I shall accept with becoming reverence your admonitions. In these solemn matters my one sole, prayerful wish is to be guided to what is true, and when, as the Premier Apostle puts it, I am unable 'to give an answer to every man that *asketh* me a *reason* of the hope that is in me' (1 Peter iii. 15), then will I bow with thankfulness to him who has shown me the better way.

Vicar. Your frankness relieves me of all embarrassment. I felt it to be my duty, at whatever cost, to admonish you, on hearing what I did from Mr. H. B., inasmuch as, with a solemnity equivalent to an oath, I had promised the Bishop 'to use both publick and *private* monitions and exhortations,' and 'to be ready with all faithful diligence to banish and drive away all erroneous and strange doctrine contrary to God's Word.' And that these views, which you now acknowledge to me, are so, the Church plainly, strongly, yea, most emphatically, teaches in the grandest of her utterances, and in words which no man living can by possibility mistake. She says: '*Whosoever* will be saved, *before all things* it is necessary to hold the Catholick Faith; and the Catholick Faith *is this*: That we worship one God in Trinity, and Trinity in Unity; that the Godhead of the Father, of the Son, and of the Holy Ghost is all *one*, the glory equal, the majesty *co-eternal;* the Father is God, the Son is God, the Holy Ghost is God; and yet they are not three Gods, but one God;' and she closes her amplifications of this ancient Creed with the awful words, '*This is the Catholick Faith, which except a man believe faithfully* HE CANNOT BE SAVED!'

Parishioner. Yes, sir; no honest man can say that it is *not* the teaching of the Church of England. She received this metaphysical creed from her venerable mother the Church of Rome, and has given it a conspicuousness and a power in her services higher than does the older Church, dealing out its damnatory clauses with a frequency and an audacity which her parent seems to regard as imprudent. Indeed, it is a very surprising thing that the Church of England should retain only one day in the ecclesiastic year, and that the first day in Lent, on which to pass a formal 'Commination' on great moral crimes, such vile sins as idolatry, adultery and murder, cursing parents and 'causing the blind to go out of his way,' and the like : one day in twelve months, and one day only (and that day oftentimes a week-day, when comparatively few persons are in the church), on which she officially proclaims that 'Cursed is he that taketh reward to slay the innocent,' and yet that she should appoint no less than fourteen high festival days, on each of which her priests should formally proclaim that '*without doubt*' .... '*he shall perish everlastingly*' who is unable to comprehend—or unwilling to confess—the 'Catholick Faith' in all its entirety—'whole and undefiled'—and to 'worship one God in Trinity, and Trinity in Unity, neither confounding the persons nor dividing the substance'! Thus placing the man who is intellectually embarrassed by a metaphysical paradox, in the same position as a wilful murderer; and announcing with ten times greater frequency in the public services of the Church, that 'without doubt he shall perish everlastingly.' Surely, it is the deadening influence of habit alone which enables sane individuals to listen to, and approve of, such anathemas! One would suppose that on the principles of equity, not to say anything of Christian charity or ' love,' the said services ought to be in the reverse order of frequency. The venerable Church of Rome is more reserved in her utterances respecting this mysterious ecclesiastic dogma. Canon Oakley of that Church informs us, that in their 'liturgical systems the Athanasian Creed occupies a place which secures it against the risk, and our people against the temptation, of criticism. It forms part of an office which is *rarely* recited in public except in cathedral chapters, colleges, and religious communities.' Our own Church is more demonstrative—and the creed is unmistakably, as you say, ' the teaching of the Church of England,' and the teaching is clear, bold, and unmistakable; it is almost her characteristic mark among the three great Churches of Christendom — the

Roman, the Greek, and the Anglican—for she alone proclaims it aloud as a creed in the *public* services of the Church at several great and distinct festivals in the course of one year. The 'Holy Orthodox Eastern Church' never uses it; she could hardly do so, for she, with her tens of thousands of followers in Syria, Palestine, Russia, and elsewhere, falls under the condemnation equally with myself; she also is unable to discover any apostolic authority for the statement that 'the Holy Ghost is of the Father *and* of the Son,' and because of this incapacity, all the myriads who do, or have, accepted her teachings, '*without doubt* shall perish everlastingly.' The Church of England decrees this appalling sentence, and every priest in her pay is bound *as an honest man* to sing or say it at Morning Prayer on thirteen distinct and separate Feasts, among which, as I have already said, stand out prominently the very greatest and most solemn of her festivals—Christmas Day, Easter Day, Ascension Day, and Whitsunday. Yes, sir, I accept all that you state as to the teachings of your Church; I recognize with full reverence that you are simply performing your duty, as one of her consecrated priests, to bring this fact before me as a parishioner and an attendant at your church. Yet, with all this, I fail to perceive that in not accepting such teachings I am espousing 'erroneous and strange doctrines contrary to God's Word.'

Vicar. We are distinctly told in God's Word that 'There are three that bear record in Heaven —the Father, the Word, and the Holy Ghost; and these three are one' (1 John v. 7). And as to the damnatory clauses so called, which evidently excite your indignation, St. Athanasius in asserting them is simply following the very words of Scripture, for in Mark xvi. 16, it is stated distinctly that 'he that believeth not shall be damned.'

Parishioner. Certainly your quotations are very clear and explicit, and no one who accepts the Bible, *as we have it*, as the undoubted Word of God, can do other than bow with reverence to the statements and be silent evermore. I was once in that happy condition. In common with tens of thousands of my countrymen, I accepted without question all the religious statements made by my teachers. I heard them as others hear them—at an age and under circumstances which caused them to be received as 'a matter of course;' and moreover, they did not rouse sufficient feeling to make it a question of *anxious* inquiry. I am sure that in these particulars I formed no exception to my fellows—that is, I had no doubts, *because* I had no continuous or anxious thought upon the subjects, one way or the other.

Vicar. I hope that I am not to understand that you do not NOW accept the Bible as the

Word of God, and that those clear statements which I have given to you are no longer esteemed by you as of Divine authority.

Parishioner. The solemnity of your question demands that I should give it the fullest thought, and that my statements should be so simple and clear as to leave no erroneous impression on your mind; and that I may not unduly excite your indignation, or your pity, I should like to give a slight sketch of the history of my opinions, or, to use a well-known sentence, my 'phases of faith.'

Vicar. There is scarcely need for this, and it would occupy too long a time, to the exclusion of more essential matters; and I must frankly tell you that I have no other, and desire no other, arguments in defence of my position than the plain statements of the written Word. The opinions of the Fathers and the decrees of the Church are weighty, most weighty; but, in our respective positions, I shall not refer to them, as I have reason to know that the Scriptures will have greater weight with you than even the decrees of Councils.

Parishioner. Yes. You understand me. Like the Puritans of the Commonwealth, I prefer the opinion of the 'grandfathers' to that of the 'fathers'; although even Cardinal Newman has assured us 'that Tertullian is heterodox on the doctrine of our Lord's Divinity,' 'Origen is at the very least suspected,' 'and Eusebius was a semi-Arian.' 'The creeds of that early day make no mention in their letter of the Catholic doctrine at all. They make mention, indeed, of a Three; but that there is any *mystery* in the doctrine that the Three are one, that they are co-equal, co-eternal, all increate, all omnipotent, all incomprehensible is not stated, and never could be gathered from them.'* And as for 'Councils,' their decrees have been so contradictory, and have been so often influenced by State or secular motives that they fail to inspire my reverence. I have spent much time, unprofitably, in reading the long and tedious discussions, spread almost over centuries, by the Polemics of various dogmatic theories, which were often decided by the secular Power. I prefer, however, to give the statements of learned theologians rather than my own, and will again repeat the Cardinal : 'There is one, and one only, great doctrinal Council in ante-Nicene times. It was held at Antioch in the middle of the third century, on occasion of the incipient innovations of the Syrian heretical School. Now, the Fathers there assembled, for whatever reason, *condemned*, or *at least withdrew*, when it came into the dispute, the word 'Homoousian,' which was afterwards received at Nicæa as the special symbol of Catholicism against Arius.' And, as to Councils,

* *Development of Christian Doctrine,* p. 16.

even your great St. Athanasius, my dear sir, has been disapproved by Councils at Tyre, Antioch, Milan, Constantinople, and elsewhere. The command of an emperor has more than once decided a dogma or creed, and set aside the statements of bishops avowedly made after study, meditation, and prayer. In the fourth century, even at the great Council of Nice, where, and when, the Nicene Creed itself was fixed, the final issue was dependent on the will of the Emperor Constantine; and by what carnal weapons that incomprehensible creed was enforced may be seen in his decree, in which he commanded not only that all the treaties of Arius should be burnt, but, further, imperiously, nay ruthlessly, proclaimed that 'if anyone shall be detected concealing a book compiled by Arius, and shall not instantly bring it forward and burn it, the penalty for his offence shall be *death*.' The learned historian Gibbon has written truthfully on this subject—'the decrees of Heaven were enforced by the *sword* of the *soldier* rather than by the *arguments of an apostle*,' and another great historian of Christianity, the pious and venerable Dean Milman, tells us that the Roman world was ordered to believe in a 'co-equal Holy Trinity upon the authority of two feeble boys and a rude Spanish soldier.'

Vicar. This is lightly spoken on the part of

the Dean; but this is not of much moment, since, by whomsoever it may have been originally enforced, it is NOW emphatically *the creed* of the Church—*the* creed which '*before all things*' is necessary to be holden, and of which our Holy Church most solemnly declares, 'which Faith, except every one do keep *whole* and undefiled, *without doubt* he shall *perish everlastingly.*'

Parishioner. You have made a most appalling statement, but as a consecrated priest of the Church of England, bound by promises, nay by solemn vows, to recite this creed, it would be dishonest in you *not* to do so. Those awful words do not appal me as they once did. In the present age of the world they alarm very few indeed, because they can no longer 'be enforced by the sword of the soldier.' The 'Anathemas' of the Church *now* merely excite a smile among thoughtful and intelligent men in England, Germany, and France, however deterrent they may be among the uneducated classes of these countries. The Church of England blundered (as ecclesiastic bodies usually blunder in their policy when matters of 'faith' are discussed) in 1872, when even so 'orthodox' and pious a man as the seventh Earl of Shaftesbury petitioned in vain for the removal of the 'damnatory clause only'—a petition got up in haste; and yet it contained between five and six thousand signatures, among which were ten judges, two hundred and thirty-six barristers and solicitors, one hundred and eighty justices of the peace, some eighty-one peers, and members of the House of Commons, besides mayors, doctors, officers, and churchwardens 'too numerous to mention.' 'Reformed' Church as she is sometimes called, she yet clings as tenaciously as Rome herself to every word and tittle of this mediæval creed, even to assigning ' *everlasting*' perdition to those whose reason and conscience are unable to accept it. It has survived through all the stormy conflicts of the Reformation, and her bishops and clergy resolve that 'it shall be retained, and be in use by the Authority of Parliament.' But, although 'retained,' and although 'in use,' the 'anathema' has become a mere sound, almost resembling

> a tale
> Told by an idiot, full of sound and fury,
> Signifying nothing.

It is received by nearly all, except the illiterate, with indifference, because it is so generally felt that it is not true.

Vicar. Not true ! No one who dares to say this ought for a single moment afterwards to call himself a member of the Church of England. She teaches no doctrine so plainly, so unequivocally as she teaches this, and to none other does she as a Church declare with more emphasis that it 'may be *proved* by *most certain warrants* of

Holy Scripture,'* nor can I at this moment recall any other matters of faith which she places so distinctly and categorically before her people in the solemn moments of Divine worship, and declares so authoritatively, '*which* Faith except every one do keep whole and undefiled, WITHOUT DOUBT he SHALL PERISH *everlastingly.*'

Parishioner. I honour you for your honesty, your consistency, and your courage. This is a time of equivocation, unreality, and untruth. Men tamper with their consciences; and to hide, if possible, even from themselves the falseness of their position, they give to words what is called a 'non-natural' sense; they invent 'theories of development;' they 'darken counsel by words without knowledge;' and after pledging themselves by vows and prayers so to 'minister the *doctrine* and Sacraments and the discipline of Christ as the Lord hath commanded, and *as this Church and realm hath received the same,*' they proceed to explain them away, or, as Archbishop Tillotson said of the Athanasian Creed, they 'wish they were well rid of them;'† and as hundreds of the 'Evangelical section' of former days said of the plain words of the Prayer Book in reference to baptismal regeneration and the Supper of our Lord. This treachery to language,

* Article viii.
† In a Letter to Bishop Burnet from Lambeth House, October 23rd, 1694.

this 'mental reservation,' is observable in clergymen to a degree unknown among other men, and lessens them much in the esteem of the cultured classes. The effeminate puerilities, genuflexions, and millinery of the High Church party are less offensive (and must be less mischievous in their result) than is the subtle perversion of words, terms, and incidents observable in the preachings and writings of the more enthusiastic members of the 'Low' and 'Broad' sections in the Church of England; for widely as these two classes differ on doctrinal points, they resemble each other in giving a 'non-natural sense' to words and a fictitious meaning to plain incidents. Your courage and consistency in adhering to the common sense meaning of the lucid words of the Prayer Book please me much, and I thank you.

Vicar. It would seem that I must accept your praise for courage and honesty at the expense of being puerile in my tastes and formal in my worship; but I do not own the soft impeachment. I belong to no party, for I know *who* it was that said, 'Every kingdom divided against itself is brought to desolation, and every city or house divided against itself shall not stand.'

Parishioner. Although you stand apart from party squabbles and profess to have 'no views,' yet it is in vain to disguise the fact that there are at least three distinct 'parties' in the Church of

England, with 'views' as divided and distinct as the Wesleyans from the Church of England, or as the 'Independents' in contrast with the 'Baptists,' or as either of these with the National Church. For general purposes, or in defence of the 'Church' in her connection with the State, the clergy may, and do, assemble as one body; but between the respective parties in their daily work, in their ministrations, and in their pulpit teachings, it would seem 'there is a great gulf fixed.' In private intercourse with their flocks each describes the other as 'unsound,' or weak, or wicked. In one day I have heard the good Dean Stanley called 'that wicked man' by a member of the 'Evangelical' section, and, worse still, charged with 'profligacy' by a clergyman of the 'High Church' party; the 'profligacy' consisting in his pleading for a 'hearing' on behalf of an absent bishop charged with 'heresy.' In short, the 'divisions' in the 'Church' are well marked, conspicuous, nay rampant; and unfortunately for the Church as a national institution, two of these 'parties' have their own *special newspapers* to support and disseminate their special 'views.' The 'record' which these respective 'religious papers' give of their 'brethren' is as damnatory as the early and closing sentences of the Athanasian Creed itself. If a portrait of the Church of England were drawn from the description given by the 'High

Church' division of the 'Low,' or from the description of the 'Low Church' of the 'High,' and the people believed what their clergy said of each other in these rival papers, the National Church would become, like Babylon in the days of Jeremiah, 'an astonishment and an hissing,' yea, 'men would clap their hands at her and would hiss her out of her place.'

Vicar. You speak strongly, but I cannot gainsay your statements. The writings of the so-called religious papers are a disgrace to our age. There is not a trace of practical Christianity in their columns. When writing of a clergyman of opposite views to their own, they seem to read all the instructions of our Lord in a contrary sense, and to rebuke the things He praised, and praise the things which He rebuked. The party spirit of John appears to possess them in a frantic form, and they loudly and proudly proclaim that 'they saw one casting out devils' and 'we forbad him *because he followeth not us.*' I am astonished at their virulence, but not so much astonished at this as at the little effect their writings appear to have on the *public* mind. Party zeal and hate are thereby intensified in the special party, and the *odium theologicum* is vivified among the priests. But despite all the theological thunders of the 'religious' press each individual parish seems content with its own clergyman, even in places where he has been

RELIGIOUS NEWSPAPERS.

preceded by an incumbent of opposite 'views.' In a neighbouring parish, where 'Evangelical views' had been preached and enforced in all their gloomy intensity for nearly fifty years, a minister of the opposite school, or rather clergyman of sound Church principles, holding up the Prayer Book in all its integrity (as I strive to do), fills his church with *the same* congregation which listened with like reverential calm while 'apostolical succession,' 'baptismal regeneration,' and 'priestly absolution' were *denounced* with the same fervour as they are *now* upheld and enforced as the true teachings of the 'Catholic Church' and of the Book of Common Prayer.

Parishioner. As regards the scornful contumely and the reckless assertions of the 'religious' newspapers, it is a fortunate thing for the 'Church of England,' nor less so for the nation, that the secular law enforces that each priest should have his own distinctly defined local area of action, within which no other priest of his own Church can exercise priestly functions except by permission. Hence theological strife is lessened, if not removed, in the individual Church, and the general moral tone of the incumbent, and his social courtesy, and his friendly interest in the secular affairs of the parish make each one popular, or at least accepted with grace by his own parishioners. Mankind (at least those who dwell in villages) are as a class passive and apathetic on the matters the newspapers wrangle over. They may incidentally hear at their market table that *The Church Times* or *The Record*, as the case may be, has painted their respected vicar in very black colours; but when they learn that it was not because of 'a matter of wrong, or wicked lewdness,' he had done, but that the paper had fiercely assailed him because, as it said, ' this fellow persuadeth men to worship God contrary to law,' they at once conclude that it ' is a question of words and names,' of which they will be no judge; like the prudent Gallio of old, ' they care for none of these things' (Acts xviii. 7). If he preach 'contrary to law,' they know that he has been placed over them by the ordinary custom, and *mos pro lege* is their axiom in all things. He has become '*their parson*'; he occupies the same house or 'parsonage' as his predecessor; they hear the same chimes, on the same day, from the same place, and at the same hour, calling them to prayer; they go to the same church, and to the same spot in the church, as heretofore; the same words are addressed to them at the opening of the service, and the old familiar prayers follow; and, provided that their *senses* are not offended by the sight of new robes, new sounds, and new formalities, or be grieved by the *omission* of something, however trivial, which they have been long accustomed to, the old weekly routine of conduct will be followed, and they will walk contentedly along the old paths to the old church in which their forefathers worshipped. But both these things must be observed. Country folk are not given to change, and, as a rule, any change is distasteful— whether of commission or of omission. The Hon. J. Russell Lowell, American Minister, and the author of the brilliant satire *The Biglow Papers*, tells a story which illustrates perfectly the principle to which I have been referring : he says, 'My father remembered the last clergyman in New York who continued to wear a wig ; but the time came when he thought it desirable to leave it off. When he did so it was lamented by some of his parishioners, and an old woman waylaid him as he came out of church, and said, " Ah ! dear doctor, I have always listened to your sermons with the greatest edification and comfort, but now that the wig is gone all is gone." ' On the other hand, the turning to the east when the 'Belief' is read, and the wearing of a white surplice in the pulpit, have excited the greatest commotion. Most true is it, that if in an ordinary country congregation the *senses* are not appealed to, there will be no desertion of the ' parish church'; for I speak from the long-accumulated experience of years, when I say that in our small towns and rural parishes the bulk of the congregation would be equally content whether the sermon preached was taken from the pages of Cardinal Newman, of Dr. Pusey, of John Wesley, of Charles Simeon, or of Francis W. Rice. Only let the sermon not be too long, and the incumbent take care not to wear any robes strikingly distinct from those worn by his predecessor, and then the slumbers of his hearers will be equally sweet at night, whether he faithfully observed the charter of his Church, and taught them that in baptism 'they were made members of Christ, children of God, and inheritors of the kingdom of heaven,' or whether, deserting this authority, he courageously declared, as did the Rev. F. W. Rice, Vicar of Fairford, that such statements 'lead men to mistake nature for grace, to fancy themselves spiritual whilst they are carnal, and to *assume* that they are the children of God whilst they are in *reality* children of the wicked one.'* As I have already said, it would be all the same to such parishioners. The elder ones, if appealed to, would probably say, 'I be noa scholar,' and conclude that this solved their responsibility, if indeed they thought at all on such a subject. In the secluded villages of the Cotswold Hills, during my youth, few, if any, of the older farm-labourers could read, and I knew not one who was forty years old and could write. As a class, they are apathetic or most passive in religious matters. Religion with them is a senti-

---

* *Reply to Mr. Dodsworth on Baptismal Regeneration*, by Rev. F. W. Rice, p. 3.

ment with which the intellect has little to do. They trouble not themselves about 'creeds' or 'doctrines,' but retain a general reverence for the Bible—a kind of 'fetish' worship or awe difficult to describe, but manifest in times of sickness or sorrow; *then* 'the Bible' is resorted to, and, if not read beyond the verse or two which may first fall under the eye, is kept near to them, feeling, if not expressing, that it imparts a protective influence or support, and to have it *near* to them was a good thing, a religious act acceptable to God, regarding it, in fact, with the same emotion or sentiment as an unlettered but a devout Papist would regard the presence of a picture of 'the Virgin,' a crucifix, a rosary, or a bottle of holy water. Whenever I found in this class of people any special interest in religion, they were usually 'chapel-folk'—descendants of men who in the long past had suffered from the 'Act of Uniformity,' the 'Mile Act,' and such unwise legislation. They were 'dissenters' by birth, and for the same reason as their more numerous neighbours were Churchmen. It was an hereditary custom, which had become instinctive. As a peasant once said to me, 'Why, zur, it be our way; vathear and granvathear did it afore.' It was a habit which had become confirmed by continuous hereditary transmission, an act prompted by an impulse apart from *mental* convictions of any kind, a habit produced by long-continued antecedents, almost as much as the features of their faces.

Vicar. This is a very dangerous deduction of yours. It strikes at the very roots of moral responsibility, and makes men the creatures of circumstances.

Parishioner. It may be a dangerous statement, but the *consequences* of any *truth* should not deter us from seeking it. To broach an 'hypothesis' may be wrong, but it never *can* be wrong to state a *fact* in nature, for *God* has made it. His word and His works *cannot* contradict each other. We may be in doubt as to His *alleged* word ; we may be deceived by the statements of history, more especially when that history comes down to us through long ages, through various nations with all their complexities of language, with all the possible errors of translators, and with all the bias of conflicting religious creeds ; but a *natural fact* stands before us in its integrity, and is as new at *this* moment—as *recent*, that is—as the words of Moses were recent when spoken at Sinai three thousand three hundred and seventy-five years ago, or by Paul and Peter one thousand eight hundred and twenty-four years ago.

Vicar. Time cannot affect these statements ; and you seem to forget that St. Peter distinctly states that 'holy men of God spake as they were moved by the Holy Ghost' (2 Peter i. 21).

Parishioner. I will not now pause to say that the second Epistle of Peter is one of those epistles whose authenticity is questioned by many pious men and ripe scholars, nor will I espouse wholly the statement of the distinguished biologist Lawrance, or of the great Lord Brougham (who, by-the-bye, edited with much ability an edition of Paley's *Natural Theology*), to the effect that a 'man was no more responsible for his creed than for the colour of his skin,' but I am not able to forget that one who was as much inspired as Peter (even if the text you quote be genuine) has said, 'Can the Ethiopian change his skin, or the leopard his spots? then may ye also do good that are accustomed to do evil' (Jeremiah xiii. 23); and another (the most distinguished of all the apostles), in an epistle whose authenticity has never been questioned by the most sceptical of historians, distinctly asks, 'Nay, but, O man, who art thou that repliest against God? Shall the thing formed say to him that formed it, Why hast thou made me thus? Hath not the potter power over the clay of the same lump to *make one* vessel unto *honour* and *another* unto *dishonour?*' (Romans ix. 20, 21.) And sure am I that I have seen men so organized that in their cranial and facial configurations they appear to approximate the brute creation, and again and again in visiting a prison have I been able to 'pick out' the 'confirmed criminals' from these characteristics alone, and have gone away saddened by the solemnity and the truth of the words spoken amid 'thunders and lightnings, and a thick cloud upon the mount, and the voice of the tempest exceeding loud,' at Sinai some three thousand years ago, to this awful effect : ' I the Lord thy God am a jealous God, visiting *the iniquity of the fathers upon the children* unto the third and fourth generation of them that hate me ' (Exodus xx. 5). Here are statements made by Jeremiah, by Paul, and by Moses, more startling in themselves than the statements made by Tyndal, by Darwin, and by Spencer, which have roused the indignation and evoked the censure of many pious divines. That some persons have been distinctly created and specially ordained to be *vessels of dishonour* is affirmed by Paul ; that you may as reasonably expect the 'Ethiopian' to 'change his skin' as to think that a certain class of habitual wrong-doers will 'do good,' is implied by Jeremiah, and that *the innocent suffer* not from any iniquity of their own doing, but from the iniquity of their fathers committed before they were born, is pronounced by Moses to be the decree of the Almighty Himself. Moreover, any person of observation may see *proofs*, actual, positive, *living proofs, of the truth* of each one of the statements if he will look for them in the society around him, in the gaols of our land, or in the hospitals and lunatic asylums of the kingdom. It is as true in the nineteenth century after Christ as it was in the seventh century before Him, that 'the fathers have eaten a sour grape and the children's teeth are set on edge' (Jeremiah xxxi. 30).

Vicar. You use that passage very wrongly. The prophet quotes the saying, expressly to declare that it shall be said ' no more.'

Parishioner. The 'Bible' being a collection of many books, poems, histories, and essays, written in different places, in ages far apart, and by people of various positions, differing in age, station, education, and knowledge, it often happens that one statement or 'text' is in apparent contradiction to another; but in this particular instance there is no discrepancy either as to fact or inference. Ezekiel, who wrote somewhat later than Jeremiah, still called the above saying a 'PROVERB.' Now, a proverb is always the fitting record of *experience*, if it be long current as a 'proverb' among an intelligent people. Jeremiah speaks as a prophet (*pro*, before ; *phemi*, to speak) concerning something which is *to come*, and not of what IS. 'Behold the days *come*'; and then, in reference to that coming time, Jeremiah added : ' *In those days* they shall say no more the above proverb.' So that I do not feel that I have used the passage 'wrongly': although the time foretold has not yet arrived in Europe. Moreover, I remember that even when using this figurative language the prophet distinctly enunciates that the event foretold is to be brought about in strict accordance with the same Divine law which had previously ordained that the 'sour grape' *should* produce special results, that the 'iniquity of the father *should* be visited upon the child; for, as a necessary preliminary to the disappearance of the proverb, a '*new covenant*' had to be made, and 'the house of Israel and the house of Judah had to be *renewed*,' the promised law that 'whatsoever a man *soweth* that shall he also reap' had to be acted upon, and the great Eternal resolved 'to sow' them with 'the seed of man, and with the seed of beast,' and that as heretofore they had been surrounded by agencies (environments) 'to pluck up and break down, to destroy and to afflict,' so henceforth should they be watched over 'to build and to plant' (Jeremiah xxxi. 27, 28, 29), to become, in the words of Oriental poesy, figs—'very good figs, even like the figs that are first ripe' (Jeremiah xxiv. 2).

Vicar. These are deep mysteries, into which I do not at this moment desire to enter. I am not able to contradict you as to the unhappy divisions which beset our Church. You have yourself admitted that there are good men who hold each of the various 'views' which you have taken such pains to set forth; and I think you must admit that when individuals have given

THE CHURCH PRAYER BOOK.

their solemn pledge to uphold the teachings of the Church, they are bound as honest men *so to uphold them*, or to cease to take the pecuniary endowments of that Church, and to resign the office the duties of which they have failed to fulfil. '*Scripta litera manet*'—the written words remain. The Prayer Book is the charter of the Church. All its formulas are simple, clear, and intelligible, so that 'he may run that readeth it' (Habakkuk ii. 2). Individually I cannot accept the special pleadings and the ingenious subtleties by which many of my fellow-priests attempt to explain away, by 'non-natural' verbiage, the simple and lucid statements of that book. It has come down to us sanctioned and hallowed by the practice of ages; its creeds and its formulas are the creeds and the formulas of the Church long before it was distracted by divisions—before the monk Luther of Erfurt violated his vows, or the lustful arrogance of Henry VIII., or the imperious will of Queen Elizabeth, or the immature mind of Edward VI., influenced by vile, ambitious, and political priests, had attempted to 'explain,' dilute, modify, and change them, or to nullify their import by 'Acts of Parliament' and by an appendix of 'articles,' which for decency's sake, however, is not intruded into the orders for Morning and Evening Prayer, and which articles are not heard of until the exigencies of party strife drag them into the controversy. That book distinctly tells us that there are two sacraments '*necessary to salvation,*' 'that is to say, baptism and the supper of the Lord'; and it emphatically and unmistakably declares that in the latter 'the Body and Blood of Christ *are verily* and *indeed* taken and received by the faithful.' The Church, as if it prophetically foresaw that in the 'latter days' some doubters or even 'scoffers' may arise, was not content simply to state that the Body and Blood of Christ were taken in that blessed Sacrament, but to place her decree beyond all possible honest 'cavil,' *emphasized*, nay reiterated her emphasis, by two of the strongest, clearest, and most unmistakable words our language possesses, and added, 'are *verily* and *indeed taken and received.*' To controvert these words is wilfully to trampel her language and her meaning under foot, and practically to affirm that words were meant not to *express* thoughts and wishes, but to *conceal* them. And it grieves me, more than I can tell, to observe the prevalence of such casuistry—such torturing of words, to wrench out a meaning, which shall conceal, or palliate, a distinct departure from the primitive teachings of the Church. It is one of the worst evils of the day, is this vile verbal legerdemain, and it is spreading all too rapidly, both among Ritualistic-Anglicans, and 'Broad Churchmen' or Latitudinarian 'Liberals,' by which they, respectively, contrive to translate miracles into 'sensory illusions,' and the solemn anathemas of the Athanasian Creed into jubilant words of praise and joy. Even, in moments of solemn debate, one is absurdly reminded of the speech of the clown in Shakespeare's *Twelfth Night*, when asked for the reason of something he had said. 'Troth, Sir, I can yield you none without words, and words are grown so false I am loath to prove reason with them' (Act iii. scene 1). This playing with words is very shocking. It is a crime against the distinguishing characteristic of humanity; that faculty of speech, which at once elevates man above all other terrestrial creatures; but the words of the Church are too clear to be travestied, even by such sophistry. And this brings me to the object of my interview with you, from which we have too long departed, namely, to speak respecting your absence from the Holy Communion, and to remind you that the Church expects, nay demands, your presence, for in one of the most prominent of her rubrics she says, 'and NOTE that every parishioner *shall* communicate *at the least* three times in the year, of which Easter to be one.'

Parishioner. I am glad that you have returned to it, although I do not feel that a sentence has been spoken by either of us which is irrelevant to that subject. I know that as a 'Churchman' I have failed in fealty to her commands; but I have done so in obedience to a *higher* law, and could, I think, justify the act—as a very large number of 'Evangelicals,' clergymen even, justify *their* corresponding procedure, in other departments of her liturgy—by quoting the twentieth clause in her 'Articles of Religion,' to the effect that although 'the Church hath power to decree rites and ceremonies' . . . 'yet it is *not lawful* for the Church to ordain *anything* that is contrary to *God's Word written*, neither may it so expound one place of Scripture that *it be repugnant to another*'; but I shall not do so, because I think it is subtle sophistry on their part so to manipulate and parry with her plain instructions, and because, moreover, I regard this particular 'rite' as one clearly commanded to be observed by our Divine Master. My reverence and love for Jesus of Nazareth are sincere and profound, and I remember that on that august occasion when He last partook of bread and wine with His disciples, He said, 'This do ye as oft as ye drink it in remembrance of me' (1 Cor. xi. 25), and in the most tender and touching of all His speeches to His disciples He added, 'If ye love me keep my commandments' (John xiv. 15). I yearn to partake of that hallowed festival, but the Church precludes me by the additions, and conditions, and prefaces with which she surrounds it, and by which she converts the sweet Memorial of a dear Friend and great Deliverer into a theological dogma against which my mind and my conscience alike rebel.

Vicar. I am sorry to hear that you again revert to this difficulty, because I had hoped that the distinct Scriptural authority which I had given to you from the words of the inspired apostle John, that 'there are *three* that bear record in heaven—the Father, the Son, and the Holy Ghost—and that these three are *one*,' would have removed your objection, would have caused you to abandon your position, and compelled you to forsake the vain suggestions of a feeble reason and to bow to the supreme authority of the Divine Word. Moreover, I would add (and the awful consequences involved compel me to forego the shallow amenities of social life) that the entire Christian world, north, east, west, and south, with the exception of a small, cold, and singular sect, numbering units among tens of thousands, adopt this creed, and that it implies something of arrogance and self-conceit in any individual to withstand such a testimony, such 'a cloud of witnesses'; and to think himself *wiser* than the Fathers, wiser than the great Churches of west and east, wiser (although it is certainly lowering the standard) than all the Nonconformist bodies—Wesleyans, Presbyterians, Baptists, Independents—and the shoals of sectaries, who, however schismatic, rebellious, and heretical in *other particulars*, accept *this* Divine tradition, and make the rebellious reason to bow before the sublime authority of the Word of God.

Parishioner. The solemnity of these facts impressed me so deeply, that, as I have already said, it made me tremble to depart from the teachings of my early life, and all the associations which clung around an ardent Church-membership of many years' duration. Having a deep reverence for the past, all these influences peculiarly and powerfully affected me. Old ruins, stately ancient edifices, chronicles, customs and traditions appealed, and still appeal to my feelings and imagination with intense force; and there was a time when 'Councils' and 'Fathers' possessed an authority with me only short of direct inspiration. These things bound me like a spell until assiduous and honest research revealed to me the true nature of 'Councils' and their decrees, and the fallacy of the 'Fathers.' When I read in the writings of a 'canonized' saint the general character of 'Councils' and of the 'Bishops' and soldiers and civilians which composed them, spiritual awe and reverence passed away. When Gregory could write, as Dean Stanley tells us, of Councils, 'as tho' a herald had convoked to them all the gluttons, villains, liars, and false swearers of the empire,' as men who were 'time servers waiting not on God but on the rise and flow of the tides, or the straw in the wind,' 'angry lions to the small, fawning spaniels to the great,' 'affecting manners not their own'—'the long beard, the downcast look, the head bowed, the subdued voice, the slow walk, the got-up devotee.' And declares further, elsewhere, 'I will not sit in one of these councils of geese and cranes.' 'I fly from every meeting of Bishops, for I *never saw a good end of any such*, nor a termination, but rather an addition of evils.'* Their true nature becomes revealed, common sense assumes its sway, and we perceive that these ancient 'Councils,' around which ecclesiastics have thrown such seeming holiness and wisdom, were precisely like the stormy conventions of our own times, when interested parties meet to discuss polemics or politics. I am almost ashamed to confess to you that the facts mentioned at the close of your remarks kept my judgment in suspense for several years, and even now, at this moment, it is to me one of the most stupendously astounding facts in the history of mental thought, that the great majority of men 'who profess and call themselves Christians' should acquiesce in the wild, mystic theory of the Trinity. The thought *did weigh*, and weigh heavily, upon me, as to whether it was *not* presumptuous in one so unlearned as myself to differ in opinion from the Fathers and the Councils of the Church, from the teachings of the National Establishment of the Church of England, and *more especially* from the tenets of the

* Ad. Episc., 206. De Rt. i., 855.

tens of thousands of 'Nonconformists' who are so clamorous and so combative in respect to other religious opinions and practices, which appear to me so *small* and *insignificant* compared with this *momentous* question; for, as the eloquent and learned Rev. Henry Melville once said, in a sermon which became the 'momentum' to my mind, and fixed its conclusions for ever: 'It is a *fundamental doctrine.* It is not a mere abstruse and speculative matter on which your judgment may be safely suspended'; and he added, 'Take away the doctrine of the Trinity from the creed of Christendom, and there is no resting-place for guilty sinners.'*

Vicar. In thus preaching, that learned divine was faithfully enunciating the doctrines of the Church, was honestly fulfilling his ordination vow, was, in simple truth, reiterating the doctrine of that holy, ancient, and august Creed, which, as I have already told you, the Church of England in the solemn moments of Divine worship places so distinctly and categorically before her people, and respecting which she declares more authoritatively than she does of any other belief, or rite, or sacrament, that 'except every one do keep whole and undefiled, WITHOUT DOUBT he shall PERISH EVERLASTINGLY.' The eloquent clergyman expressed no more than the Athanasian

---

* Preached at Camden Chapel, Camberwell, May 29th, 1831. Published by Sherwood, Gilbert, and Piper, 1838.

Creed does, or ought to do, and would do thirteen times a year, and especially on the high festivals, the great *epochs* of Christian history— the celebrations of the Birth, the Resurrection, and Ascension of our Lord, and the descent of the Great Comforter, the Illuminating Spirit and Guide of the Church : that is on Christmas Day, Easter Day, Ascension Day, and on Whit-sunday —if all her priests did their duty faithfully and fearlessly. But how *could* such a statement as this by Mr. Melville have become a 'momentum' to your mind and have brought about such sad conclusions as those you now unhappily hold ?

Parishioner. It *did so.* No enthusiastic Wesleyan is more conscious and more positive of the birth-moment of his 'conversion' and spiritual life than am I of the cause, or 'momentum' and of the 'start-point' of those readings, researches, and prayers which have ended in *demonstrating the fallacy of my former views* — of those 'teachings' which I accepted in childhood, nurtured in youth, and kept unquestioned in manhood until the moment Mr. Melville's statements aroused my attention and demonstrated the fallacy of my former views, revealing to me the eternal truth as spoken by Moses—'Hear, O Israel : The Lord our God is *one Lord*'; and as reiterated, and confirmed by Jesus in one of the latest and most tender and impassioned of His prayers—'And this is life eternal, that they might know THEE, THE ONLY TRUE GOD, AND Jesus Christ, *whom* THOU *hast sent*' (John xvii. 3). Until that memorable day, I had passively received the '*incomprehensible*' statement which declares 'the Father incomprehensible, the Son incomprehensible, and the Holy Ghost incomprehensible : the Father uncreate, the Son uncreate, the Holy Ghost uncreate : the Father eternal, the Son eternal ; the Father is God, the Son is God, the Holy Ghost is God, and yet there are not three incomprehensibles, nor three uncreated, nor three eternals, nor three Gods, but one incomprehensible, one uncreated, one eternal and one God.' This extraordinary paradox of words had been accepted by me with the same simplicity as a good 'Catholic' accepts the '*fact*' of the flight of the Virgin's house from Nazareth into Dalmatia, from thence to Recanati, and thirdly to Loreto, and all the miracles achieved therein. I had never read a word of controversy on the subject, had never heard a 'Unitarian' preacher. My faith was as serene and orthodox as gross ignorance could make it. Until Canon Melville's sermon aroused and arrested my attention, I entered my usual place of worship in the same frame of mind as hundreds of my neighbours enter their parish church every Sunday. I repeated the 'Athanasian' Creed with the same intelligent and orthodox appreciation as the children in our parish church repeated the 'Nicene' on the Sunday following their 'confirmation' this summer. But alas for my 'orthodoxy'! The fervid and eloquent sermon of Henry Melville, B.D., roused the startling thought, If this dogma be '*fundamental*,' if upon it rest such tremendous consequences, that if 'without the doctrine of the Trinity there *is* no resting-place for guilty sinners,' how comes it that it is so seldom referred to in Holy Writ? how comes it that in this Book, which we have been taught to regard as a Revelation of God, from God Himself, the word Trinity is not to be found, or the doctrine anywhere distinctly and lucidly declared? Surely, thought I, I have overlooked large portions of its sacred pages. What could I do if asked to-morrow by anyone for Scripture proof of this solemn, this '*fundamental*' doctrine which alone secures a 'resting-place for guilty sinners'? St. Peter has commanded us to be ready to give an answer to 'everyone that asketh you a *reason of the hope that is in you*' (iii. 15); yet I could not supply even a solitary 'text.' But I felt there *must be many texts*, clear, bold, explicit, but hitherto overlooked. Some power bore in upon my soul the words

ἐρευνᾶτε τὰς γραφάς,

'Search the Scriptures.' Days and months and years I 'searched' prayerfully, searched solitarily, independently searched, with a *strong bias to sustain the idea* associated with all my early antecedents, yet with a stronger bias to accept simply what the Scriptures might teach thereon, be it what it may. The more I read the more was I astonished to find so little that sustained a doctrine of such overwhelming importance — a doctrine which both my pastor and the Church regarded as 'fundamental'; and again and again had I trembled lest my early bias should fade away for want of Scriptural support, lest I should lose that ' faith ' ' which except everyone do keep whole and undefiled, WITHOUT DOUBT he shall PERISH everlastingly!' No one around me seemed to have enough interest in the subject to discuss it at all. As you have now told me, only a very small sect (and of these I knew nothing) dissented from the doctrine. Noisy polemics, radical Ranters, Baptists, Independents, 'Methodists' —all acquiesced in the decree of the Church on this especial matter. And certainly if any *external authority* ought to decide in matters of faith, here was a case in point, *per urbem et orbem;* here, if anywhere, was ' *Catholicity* '; here Pius IX. and Mrs. Girling the Shakeress, Dr. Pusey and the youngest recruit of the 'Salvation Army,' Dr. Ryle (the Bishop of Liverpool) and the Rev. A. Heriot Mackonochie, Canon Liddon and the Rev. C. H. Spurgeon were in perfect accord, and it seemed for a *long, long time presumptuous* in me to pause, to hesitate, to doubt, where so many wise and good men were confident and believing, where even the 'Pharisees and Sadducees' were in accord, and the Jews (metaphorically) could have dealings with the Samaritans. Yes, my struggle was long and arduous; but 'light came at eventide,' and as Luther at Erfurt, after long prayers and meditations, was suddenly illumined and directed by the words the 'just shall live by faith,' even so has it been mine to know that if we 'ask we shall receive,' that if 'we seek we shall find.' Long did the blessed words sustain me : ' If any man of you lack wisdom, let him ask of God, that giveth to all liberally, and upbraideth not; and it shall be given him ' (James i. 5); long was I upheld by the assurance from Jesus that a great ' Comforter ' would come 'from the Father, even the Spirit of Truth, who shall *teach you all things* '; ardently did I pray God 'to send out His light and His truth' to lead me; and as to Luther there came like a voice from Heaven the words, 'The just shall live by faith,' even so came to me the words of Jesus to the young man seeking the way to eternal life, 'Why callest thou *me* good? there is *none good but God*,' and also His words to the adoring Mary after His Resurrection, ' Go to my *brethren* and say unto them, I ascend unto *my Father*, and to *your Father;* and to *my God,* and *your God*' (John xx. 17). *Thenceforth* all was calm, clear, and bright. Mists, doubts, and perplexities vanished. The 'Great Comforter' *had come* down upon my soul. The Spirit of Truth *had spoken*. The voice alike of Councils and mobs was silenced; they became to me as were the 'familiar spirits, and wizards that peep, and mutter' to Isaiah (viii. 19, 20); and if thousands, nay tens of thousands, clamoured out their dogmas my spirit would remain calm, because, with that great prophet, it could say, 'To the law and to the testimony: if they speak not according to this word, *it is because* there is no light in them.'

Vicar. I have listened with great patience to your long dissertation. I have done so because, however erroneous your conclusions, I plainly see that they have not been hastily and lightly arrived at, and, moreover, they have cost you some thought and research; and when you add that you have earnestly and continuously sought guidance from on High through prayers in private, my respect is enhanced; although it would have been better if, at first, when your conscience was unquiet on this subject, and you needed comfort or counsel, you had come to me, 'or to some other discreet and learned minister of God's Word, and opened your grief,' so that by 'ghostly counsel and advice' your 'scruples and doubtfulness' might have been dispersed. I trust, however, that even now you may be delivered from all false doctrine, heresy, and schism, because you have admitted that the great body of Christians and the most ancient of Churches, or rather, I ought to say, the 'one Catholick and Apostolick Church,' from the earliest ages has decreed the Trinitarian doctrine to be the 'true faith,' 'which faith except everyone do keep whole and undefiled, without doubt he shall perish everlastingly.' You have said that if ever there was 'Catholicity' it is found on this point, and if '*authority*' could determine a question, *here* was the unanimous authority not only of the Church, but of the numberless schismatics who had separated themselves from her pale; and this being so, I hope you will perceive that you must necessarily be wrong. It is absolutely imperative that individuals should be guided by authority; it is schism and a sinful thing to neglect to hear and obey the Church; and therefore, my dear friend, you are in the sad position of those of whom St. Paul spoke in writing to his beloved saints in Rome—'I beseech you, brethren, mark them which cause *divisions* and offences *contrary to the doctrine* which ye have learned, and *avoid* them' (Rom. xvi. 17); and our Divine Lord Himself has declared of such, 'If he neglect to hear the church, let him be unto thee as a heathen and a publican' (Matt. xviii. 17). It pains me deeply to have thus to speak, but I trust that you will be able to see that it is a wicked thing to be at variance with the Church; that it *is* not only unbecoming, but arrogant, in an individual to place himself in a matter of doctrine in opposition to an overwhelming majority. For I need not remind you that in all the momentous questions which spring up, even in matters of life and death, such as trials by jury, decisions of Parliament, and the like, the vote of the majority is final. It is so likewise in spiritual things. The Church at Jerusalem in the early days of Christianity was the final appeal, and St. Paul and St. Jude alike denounced those who despised dominion and who separate themselves. But I am unwilling to think that you have reached so sad a stage. I shudder to think that one whom I so much esteem should become ' a wandering star to whom is reserved the blackness of darkness for ever,' and as you still revere the Scriptures, and say 'to the law and the testimony,' I hope and pray that you may discard the pride of reason, and be 'led to hear the Word, and to receive it with pure affection,' and that it may please God, although you have erred and are deceived, to bring you back into the way of truth. And since, my dear friend, you still appeal 'to the law and the testimony,' let me *again* remind you of the words of St. John— ' There are three that bear record in heaven : the Father, the Son, and the Holy Ghost : and *these three are one.*'

THE DIVINE SPIRIT AS TEACHER. 43

Parishioner. I thank you for you tender sympathy, and I assure you that you do me no more than justice when you say that I have not adopted the opinions I have formed lightly or without much hesitation, and without appealing by prayer to the Great Source of all illumination. I have, indeed, prayed long and continuously. I have pondered most profoundly on the fact that my conclusions are at variance with the decrees of Councils, with the writings of the venerable Fathers, who in a dark age were the chief sources of light and truth to the people around them. I have felt, yea, keenly felt, who and what am I that I should presume to differ from the wise and holy men of the olden and the present time? Long, long have I kept silent under the fear that it was possible that I might be among those who cause 'divisions and offences'; for many weary and anxious months I said, 'I will take heed to my ways, that I sin not with my tongue: I will keep my mouth with a bridle . . . I was dumb with silence, I held my peace.' But there came a time when, like unto David, 'My heart was hot within me, while I *was musing* the fire burned; *then* spake I with my tongue' (Ps. xxxix.). Yes. 'Blessed be *God*, even the *Father* of our Lord Jesus Christ, the Father of mercies, and the *God of all comfort*' (2 Cor. i. 3); a moment came to me, yea, even to me, as it did to St. Paul, when 'I conferred not with flesh and blood, neither went I to them which were apostles before me' (Gal. 1). My prayers had been heard. Although 'I lacked wisdom, yet in this matter it was ultimately given.' Most assuredly 'the eyes of the blind were opened.' The path of truth was revealed; was made so plain and so smooth that 'the feeble knees' and 'the fearful heart' could march forward, 'and the wayfaring man, though a fool, could not err therein.' The subject became clear and visible as did the outer world to the blind man whose eyes the beneficent Jesus had anointed with clay and then bade him wash in the pool of Siloam. Like him, I could say: 'One thing I know, that, whereas I was blind, now I see' (John ix. 25), and to feel with Paul, 'Necessity is laid upon me, yea, woe is unto me,' if I preach not the Gospel.' 'Woe unto me' if I do not proclaim with all my feeble powers the sweet, the precious truth that GOD 'will have all men to be saved, and to come unto the KNOWLEDGE OF THE TRUTH. For there is ONE God, and one Mediator between GOD and men, the MAN Christ Jesus; who gave himself a ransom *for all*, to be testified in *due* time' (St. Paul to Timothy ii. 3, 4, 5, 6). That, dear sir, is a statement plain and clear as the sunlight, derived from no uncertain source of oral tradition, coming to us from no doubtful epistle or late gospel imbued with, if not interpolated by, the philosophy of the Schools of Alexandria; coming from a source more trustworthy even than the 'logia' or sayings of the synoptic gospels, for no historian has questioned the genuineness of the Pauline Epistles; they are the most certain, as they are the earliest, writings which have come down to us from the Apostolic Age, and therefore I abandon for ever, as erroneous and heretical, the statement that 'The *God*-head of the Father, of the Son, and of the Holy Ghost, is all *one;* the glory equal, the majesty co-eternal,' and accept the statement of Jesus (in one of His tender, prophetic addresses to His disciples): 'Let not your heart be troubled, neither let it be afraid. . . . If ye loved me ye would rejoice, because I said, I go unto the Father, for my Father is greater than I' (John xiv. 28).

Vicar. You are becoming somewhat too warm —too impassioned in your arguments, and in the confidence you place in the text you have last quoted, you have forgotten a cardinal principle in exegesis, namely, that you should not (as the Church instructs us in her Twentieth Article) so 'expound one piece of Scripture that it be repugnant to another.' But this subject of the Trinity is too profound to be dealt with summarily by a single text, and for its full elucidation requires a large survey, with the full aid of philosophy and the teachings of nature and of natural science. I must remind you of some of your favourite studies, and ask you to contemplate history, and even the habits of Pagan nations, for all these things contribute to elucidate this profound mystery. Historians and travellers have shown us that even among Pagans a triad of gods was recognized. The philosophic Cudworth, in his great work on *The Intellectual System of the Universe*, published in 1678, affirmed that in the esoteric religion of the Egyptians the Divine Nature was recognized as a Trinity in Unity. The writings of the great Egyptologists, Birch, Wilkinson, and Rawlinson, accompanied by special drawings and descriptions of the respective Gods which form the Trinity, go far to sustain the idea which we know to be prevalent in the mythologies of Egypt, Assyria, and India, and would seem to predicate the opinions, or rather the dogmatic beliefs, of the Fathers of the Church. It is impossible to read the writings of Herodotus, or even of Bunsen and Wilkinson, without being impressed deeply with the analogies which these ancient religions possess in reference to the Catholic doctrine, to the great Creed of St. Athanasius, which you have so ruthlessly denounced. At Philœ we have Osius, Isis, and Horus. Sir J. G. Wilkinson, in his great work on the Ancient Egyptians, tells us 'In these triads the third member proceeded from the other two, that is, from the first

THE DIVINE SPIRIT AS TEACHER. 47

and the second.' This idea being correspondent (if one dare thus to associate Pagan superstitions with the hallowed mysteries of the Catholic faith) with the decree of the Fathers who presided at the Council of Toledo in 1589, which determined for ever that 'the Holy Ghost proceeded from the Father and from the Son.' We have, furthermore, the evidence of a like idea in the great temples and palaces of Assyria, where colossal figures, with a human head and face, a bull's body and an eagle's wings, represent a Trinity of attributes, as Wisdom, Power, and Omnipresence. In India, again, we have Brahma, Vishnu, and Siva, typical of creative, preserving, and transforming powers. But, leaving these facts as subsidiary and altogether subordinate, and reverting to the most Holy Scriptures, I must remind you that when you quoted St. John, you altogether disregarded, or overlooked, the very decisive words of that Apostle which I recited to you as sustaining, nay *proving*, the ancient and catholic view of the blessed doctrine of the Trinity.

Parishioner. I have listened with great satisfaction to your remarks on the statements of the ancient historian, Herodotus, and the researches of the distinguished Egyptologists, Wilkinson, Birch, and Bunsen ; and more especially on those colossal figures from Assyria, which, thanks to the energy and skill of Layard, now adorn our British Museum. They are superb effigies and very expressive types of Wisdom, Power, and Swiftness of Presence. No one can look at these sculptures without admiration; but your remarks have gratified me inasmuch as they so fully confirm my conviction that the trinitarian idea is wholly Pagan in its origin, and comes from the time and place when and where there were 'gods many and lords many': when men assigned a god to every river and every wood, to every mountain and every cave; in fact, perceived a Deity in all the changes of seasons, and in every phenomenon of nature; saw a god 'in clouds and heard him in the winds.' Still, all you have said once impressed me most deeply, and never more than when my mind had recognized that there was *no scriptural basis* for the primitive faith, and conscience had begun to speak within on its sinfulness. As a drowning man snatches at a straw for help, so does a sensitive mind torn from its early convictions, grasp eagerly at any fact which may seem to give credibility to the fond associations of the past. Believe me, my dear Vicar, it *is* a most painful process, as I have already said, for the heart to give up those impressions which have been made upon it by kind parents and teachers in the plastic days of childhood. Yea, most painful to the loving and sensitive person whose memory clings to the past and associates the teachers and their teachings together. In such struggles, I repeat,

THE DIVINE SPIRIT AS TEACHER.

the mind clutches at any fact which would seem to give support to its early belief; and right well do I remember how I pondered on such circumstances as that the ancient Egyptians often decorated their temples with the three primary colours, 'red, blue, and yellow,' and that philosophic research had shown that these *three* colours may be so blended as to become *one;* that the 'Triangle' implied the 'Trinity,' that man himself, consisting of body, mind, and spirit, became a living representative of this august mystery! Oh! what semblance is there of any kind which a heart clinging to and loving a maternal creed will not seize upon for transient support? How long have I not dwelt upon such dreamy analogies as that the world was formed of 'earth, air, and water,' that the firmament was built up of 'sun, moon, and stars,' and that the earth as a unity was composed of 'minerals, vegetables, and animals'! And alas! when once the judgment yields to fancy, under the impulse of the strong emotions to which I have referred, how readily and universally do the senses and other circumstances minister to its delusion! As Tertullian could see the symbol of the cross in every buoyant bird, in every floating fish, in the trunk and branches of a tree, and in the outstretched arms of a man, and in endless other things, even so did I once perceive an 'argument' for the Trinity, not only in the things I have named, but even in such far-fetched facts as that in grammar 'a first, second, and third person,' were recognized; and also 'a positive, comparative, and superlative degree,' 'good, better, and best': and, more especially, in the 'length, breadth, and thickness' of the 'cube': and even in the leaf of the shamrock (the alleged illustration of St. Patrick) was I anxious to recognize and welcome illustrations of an impossibility! To come to the most important part of your argument, important because it affects a scriptural basis, I do not admit the words you give from St. John to be authentic, whereas the words of St. Paul to Timothy, 'There is *one* God, and one Mediator between God and men, the *Man* Christ Jesus,' belong to that higher 'law and the testimony' from which there is no appeal, and from which I dare not depart until a text as clear, as explicit, and as unquestionably authentic can be found to sustain the Athanasian Creed. Nay, it should be more clear and more authentic—if that were possible—for the first enumerates a fact, which is not opposed to all the instincts of common sense and to the conclusions of right reasoning; while the other can be accepted only by the prostration of reason before a blind faith —faith which finds its best, as it has been its most eulogized, commentary in the devotee who cried, '*Credo quia impossibile est*' (I believe because it is impossible).

Vicar. Your last words are not quite respectful to the Church from which you have not formally and officially seceded, and I am therefore compelled to remind you that the Thirty-fourth Article of the Church of England decrees that 'Whosoever, through his private judgment' [and it is on this you are acting], 'willingly and purposely doth openly break the *traditions*' [*traditions*, mark] 'and ceremonies of the Church, which be not repugnant to the Word of God, and be ordained and approved by common authority, ought to be rebuked openly (that others may fear to do the like) as he that offendeth against the common order of the Church.' Now, that which you have been considering is most certainly 'ordained and approved by common authority'; and you, in common honesty, have been compelled to admit that as a 'tradition' it is of the most hoary antiquity ; that it is all but universally accepted, practically, one might say (to use one of your quoted phrases) *per urbem et orbem;* that it is one of the most catholic doctrines. And yet, alas ! sad it is that against all these ancient, august, and sacred authorities, you are rash enough, I might say wicked enough, willingly to bring your 'private judgment' and 'purposely' and 'openly' break its traditions. It is a fearful path you are treading, and my interest in your welfare compels me to use strong language and to spare no effort for your recovery. By-the-bye, in your sceptical musings—to which you have made so sad a reference—did it never occur to you that the most spiritual of the Greek philosophers recognized and expressed a Trinity, in the compound character of Man, as 'Being, Reason, Soul'; and that, although in his writings the words νους and λογος are sometimes interchanged, yet that he recognized in each spiritual unit, or entity, the attributes of 'Being, Reason, and Soul'; and that, over and above the many striking analogies which you brought forward from the records of history and of science [only to refute, however, although they once appeared weighty], there remained many others? More especially the Scriptures themselves contain many incidental statements and facts which, although not immediately relating to the subject, do in truth sustain it, acting, as it were, like external buttresses to the citadel of Truth. I allude to the Jewish benediction, in which the solemn name of Jehovah was pronounced three times—to the three benedictions used by Jacob in blessing Joseph—and I will add, the marvellous vision of Isaiah described in the sixth chapter of his Prophecy—where the *six* wings of the Seraphim were used in a *triple* function, thus, 'with twain he covered his face' —'with twain he covered his feet,' and 'with twain did he fly'; but more especially that 'one cried unto another, and said, "Holy," "Holy," "Holy" is the Lord of Hosts.' This sublime utterance, when remembered in conjunction with the august words of the Most High [after the creation of the earth and its denizens], 'Let us make man in our own image,' and subsequently the expression, 'Behold, the man is become as one of us,' point to a plurality of persons and contributed to the induction of The Church, and which, at the Council of Nicæa, she formulated and promulgated as a tenet of faith, so solemn, that except a man 'keep' it 'whole' and undefiled without doubt he shall perish everlastingly.

Parishioner. Permit me to say, that as yet [for reasons which I have heretofore described to you] I have not 'openly' broken the 'traditions' of my baptismal Church; and there is a clause in the Article you have cited to my reproof which robs it of all its sting and its power—inasmuch as I am not desirous of breaking any tradition—which in the words of the said Article ' be not repugnant to the Word of God.' I dispute the tradition of the Athanasian Creed solely and exclusively, because I am sure it is 'repugnant to the Word of God.' You admit St. Paul to be an inspired Apostle, and you regard his writings as a most important portion of 'the Word of God'; and his words to the young minister he loved— 'unto Timothy my own son in the faith'— were those which I have cited to you as the justification of my contemplated secession, and the foundation of my present faith—words bearing directly on the question before us, surpassing in clearness the words of the Greek sage Plato, and drowning in the effulgence of their light such far-off figurative expressions as those you have quoted from Isaiah and from Genesis in support of your ecclesiastic dogma. The quotation of *such* texts proves the weak support to be obtained for it from the Scriptures; yet these very texts, and others like unto them, were accepted by myself, until research and reflection proved their futility for the purpose in question. Any student of rhetoric may perceive that these reiterations of Isaiah were used solely to make the expression more august and more emphatic, in the same manner as Jeremiah employs triple reiteration when, uttering the judgments of Coniah, he exclaims, 'O earth, earth, earth, hear the Word of the Lord' (Jeremiah xxii. 29); and the eloquent Ezekiel also, when censuring some 'profane wicked prince of Israel,' represents the Lord God as saying, 'I will overturn, overturn, overturn it' (Ezekiel xxi. 27). Nor am I able to accept the expressions you quote from Genesis, as throwing light upon, or giving support to, the Trinitarian hypothesis. It is not unusual for Hebrews to use a plural word in describing persons of great dignity, and even in our own country royal personages, or rather the Queen or the King in issuing a Proclamation, uses the word 'we' or 'our'; and further, it is an indefinite plural : '*our* image,' or 'as one of *us*,' may signify two, equally as well as three, or five, or six. Some honest expositors of Scripture, like unto Calvin, have set aside these texts from Genesis as futile and delusive. A very able theologian, Dr. Campbell of Aberdeen, in his lectures on Systematic Theology, assures us that ' Luther stood up for the Trinity from the word "Elohim," but Calvin refutes his argument, or quibble rather, at some length ' (p. 489); and even the orthodox German Oehler, in his work on *The Theology of the Old Testament*, tells us that 'the meaning of this plural is not numerical, neither in the sense in which some older theologians understand it, who seek the secret of the Trinity in the name.' 'At present,' he adds, 'this view requires no further refutation.' And Dr. Havernick, in his erudite work, *Historisch-critische Einleitung ins alte Testament*, while proposing the word 'Jahveh' for ' Jehovah,' as meaning 'the Existing *one*,' derives ' Elohim ' from an ancient Hebrew root, 'coluit,' and thinks the plural is used to signify the boundless richness contained in the Divine Being. Oehler and Hengstenberg's strong [I might almost say prejudiced] ' orthodoxy ' makes them reluctant to forego the text without wringing *something* out of it in favour of their darling ' doxy'; and, therefore, we are quietly assured by these writers 'that even this *erroneous* view has some truth at its foundation, since the plural form, indicating the inexhaustible fulness of the Divinity, serves to combat the most dangerous enemy of the doctrine of the Trinity, viz., abstract Monotheism' (p. 131). Such a powerful bias must dim perception and vitiate conclusions. Whenever an 'erroneous view' is welcomed, because '*it serves* to combat' the opponents of a pet doctrine, the honesty or the judicial capacity of the writers who welcome it must be of little value. I confess again that my passive acquiescence in an ecclesiastic dogma was first disturbed by a sermon made in its defence, and my present convictions are, if possible, strengthened daily by such inductions as those of Luther, and by statements like unto those of Oehler and Hengstenberg.

Vicar. Bias, strong, prejudiced, and blind, is seldom confined to one party in a dispute, and think you not that it is something akin to it which blinds you to the illustrative importance of all the facts which you yourself have enumerated? I need name two only of the many in which three separate entities have blended or combined to form a unity—as length, breadth, and thickness to form a cube; three distinctive colours blending into one, forming what we call light. Is it not something mentally akin to 'colour-blindness' which disables you from perceiving that the mythologies of Egypt and Assyria contained something of the germs of that development of Christian doctrine which culminated in the decrees of the Nicene Fathers, or that they might be the 'remains,' 'the relics,' the 'fossils,' if you will, of a purer and primæval religion which had been departed from? Does it not strike you as a most remarkable circumstance that a writer of so philosophic, learned, and intellectual calibre as Cudworth should assert that, according to the Egyptian idea, the Divine Nature was a Trinity in Unity? All these facts indicate that, however much the theory may transcend the capacities of the human reason, yet that it is not essentially contradictory or repugnant to it.

Parishioner. There is no limit to the allegorical fancy when once indulged, whether as regards the meanings of Scripture words and texts or the force of special illustrations like to those enumerated. The words 'let us' in Genesis sufficed, as we have seen, to establish the doctrine of the Trinity in many minds, and a Bishop of Antioch in the second century, the pious and zealous Theophilus, could even see the words ' εν ἀρχῇ,' ' in the beginning,' to mean ' by Christ,' while the three days preceding the creation of the sun and moon, 'τύποι εισιν τριάδος τοῦ θεοῦ,' were expressive of the Trinity of God and His Word and His wisdom; and here, according to the translators of Mosheim, in the edition edited by the learned Dr. Stubbs, we have the first use of the word Trinity by the Fathers; and a most worthy origin it is of such a baseless dream! And as to the analogies which have been cited, each analogy is a delusive analogy, a verbal *ignis fatuus* or 'will of the wisp,' and not a trustworthy light to guide us. Each and all of them by their respective combinations or separations produce a *tertium quid* different to themselves. Length, breadth, and thickness become in their combination a cube, and the prismatic decomposition of a ray of light produces colour, and *vice versâ*, and, therefore, in no manner represents the paradoxical statement, 'the Father is Lord, the Son is Lord, and the Holy Ghost is Lord, and yet not three Lords but one Lord.' Were it not irreverent I would say that such illustrations are as irrelevant to the purpose as the example I have somewhere heard or read of as having been given to Horne Tooke. This witty clerical philologist was speaking to a friend upon the self-contradictory character of the statement I have just given from the Athanasian Creed, when his friend replied that, 'It was not contradictory at all, it is only like the thing I have just witnessed in the streets, three men riding in one cart.' 'It would have been more to the purpose,' replied the philologist, 'if you had seen one man riding in three carts.' This is most true. Metaphor and analogy are often so imperfect as to obscure rather than enlighten a difficult subject. The logical sequence of such analogies is overlooked, and a perverse induction made, as by Mr. Horne Tooke's friend. In respect to Cudworth, Mosheim subsequently demonstrated how that philosopher had been misinformed and mistaken in respect to the esoteric opinions of the Egyptian priesthood, and that their mythology had never included a 'Trinity' in the strict sense of that term. That Pagan 'Triads' became transformed by priestly ingenuity into the paradox of a 'Trinity' I believe fully, for the entire idea is antagonistic to the grand idea of the Hebrew 'Jahveh'—the One Supreme—and wholly consonant with the alleged gods of Paganism, and the verbal, empty, profitless subtleties of Greek philosophy. It sprang up at a time when, to use the words of Macaulay, 'Christianity had conquered Paganism and Paganism had infected Christianity. The Church was now victorious and corrupt. The rites of the Pantheon had passed into her worship, the subtleties of the Academy into her creed. In an evil day, though with great pomp and solemnity—we quote the language of Bacon—was the ill-starred alliance stricken between the old philosophy and the new faith.' (*Macaulay's Essays*, p. 395.) Anterior to this *mésalliance* the creeds of the Church were comparatively clear and simple, although even in Paul's day there was a tendency to add to 'the truth as it was in Jesus,' so that he cautioned his young and able disciple not to 'give heed to *fables and endless genealogies*'; he pointed out to him some who, desiring to be teachers of the law,' 'have turned aside to *vain jangling, understanding neither* what they *say* nor *whereof* they *affirm*.' (How very like the teachers who debate and 'jangle' to the effect that 'there are not three incomprehensibles, nor three uncreated, but one uncreated and one incomprehensible!') To this 'dearly beloved son' he appealed, imploring him to 'hold fast the form of sound words' which he had heard from him, to avoid 'profane and vain babblings and oppositions of science falsely so called, and to commit that which he had heard from him' to faithful men who shall be able to teach others also.' In his dying moments, so to speak, when he was 'ready to be offered, and the time for his departure was at hand,' Paul, in the most impassioned manner, and dreading that the time would come when men 'would turn away their ears from *the truth* and shall be turned unto *fables*,' besought Timothy to 'preach the word,' and, inasmuch as he 'had fully known his doctrine,' 'to continue thou in the things which *thou hast learned* and *hast been assured of*, knowing of whom thou hast learned them'; and this 'doctrine' and this 'truth'—the cardinal spring, 'the *fundamental doctrine*'—was not the 'jangle' of 'there is one Father, not three Fathers; one

Son, not three Sons; one Holy Ghost, not three Holy Ghosts: in this Trinity none is afore or after other, none is greater or less than another, but the whole Three Persons are co-eternal together and co-equal. So that in all things, as is aforesaid, the Unity in Trinity and the Trinity in Unity is to be worshipped. He therefore that *will be saved : must thus* THINK *of the Trinity.*' No, Paul did not thus address his dearly beloved son in the faith, to whom he bequeathed his noble mission of carrying forward 'the faith once delivered to the saints'; he did not hand down to him the crude metaphysics of the Alexandrian School of Philosophy, 'the *babblings* of *science falsely* so called,' but he bequeathed to him these clear and noble words : ' There is *one God* and one *Mediator* between God and men, *the Man* Christ Jesus, who gave himself a *ransom for all*, to be testified in due time' (1 Timothy ii. 5, 6). This statement is so *definite*, so unmistakable, is written *so* 'plain upon tables, that he may run that readeth them' (Habakkuk ii. 5), and the revelation is complete.

Vicar. Some of the greatest saints, and Fathers of the Church, and I may add, also, that some of the greatest theologians and scholars, whom all Christendom honours, have accepted such like analogies, which I have given to you, as powerful subsidiaries to the Scriptures in explaining and sustaining the deep mystery of the Trinity, a full faith in which is so necessary to salvation. The principle which so many wise and good men have found useful is entitled to more respect than you have given it. Theophilus, Bishop of Antioch, in the second century; the holy Clement, Irenæus, Tertullian and Origen have employed analogy and allegory largely in inculcating the various truths of Christianity; and Justin Martyr, that exalted saint, and early martyr to the Christian faith, in chapter 55 of his first Apology to the Roman Emperors, employs the form or figure of the cross as a symbol and exposition of the Christian faith of the highest meaning and importance, and that the power and rule of Christ is proved by the things which fall under our observation. 'For the sea is not traversed except that trophy which is called a sail abide safe in the ship; and the earth is not ploughed without it; diggers and mechanics do not their work except with tools which have this shape. And the human form differs from that of the irrational animals in nothing else than in its being erect, and having his arms extended, and having on the face extending from the forehead what is called the nose, through which there is respiration for the living creature, and this shows no other form than that of the cross. And so it was said by the prophet: "The breath before our face is the Lord Christ,"' and he concludes the chapter with words which I would adopt and address respectfully to you: 'Since therefore we have urged you both by reason, and by an evident form, and to the utmost of our ability, we know that now we are blameless, even though you disbelieve.' (*Justin Martyr's Writings*, p. 55. Clark, Edinburgh.) The accumulated mass of symbolism which has been brought before you illustrative of the Trinitarian Mystery, confirmed as it has been by the long-continuous teachings of the Catholic Church, and by Holy Scripture, ought to suffice to disperse your doubts, and to bring you home to the flock of the Lord. All these things, as St. Paul assures us by a more recondite and distant history, even that of Agar and Sarah, the bondwoman and the free, and the symbolism of the two places Mount Sinai in Arabia—the Jerusalem which now is, and the Jerusalem which is above (Galatians iv.), are 'an allegory' of hidden mysteries, even, indeed, as were some of the parables of our blessed Lord. Coming from such high sources, they ought to be hand-posts and helps, as it were, to guide you unto the truth. But passing from these great collateral facts, I would remind you that Paul not only wrote to Timothy the words you have quoted so emphatically, and which seem to foster your erroneous belief, but that he also wrote an epistle to Titus, to which I draw your most earnest attention. It contains a statement which cannot fail, I think, to cause you to forego your present conclusions, and to re-adopt those of your earlier and better time. To embrace the true faith, the Catholic faith, which is acquiesced in, as I have again and again pointed out to you, by the vast crowds of Nonconformists, by the Councils of the past, and the great Oriental and Occidental Churches, or, as I ought to have said, by all the great branches of the supreme Church Catholic. St. Paul in giving instructions on pastoral duties to Titus, even addressing his Epistle thus, 'to Titus, my true child after a common faith'—bade him to be 'looking for that blessed hope and the glorious appearing of the great God and our Saviour Jesus Christ' (ii. 13). Here the attributes of God and the Son are distinctly blended—the words, 'the Father is God, the Son is God,' of the august Creed are reflected, and yet the Unity of the Godhead remains. In this text, quite irrespective of the powerful collateral reasonings which have been supplied to you from secular history, and from the strong ground of 'Analogy' [which, in passing, I may remind you was the basis on which was built up the great philosophic work, *Butler's Analogy*, for which you have always expressed admiration], you have a full authority for accepting the Athanasian Creed, or rather the 'Catholic Faith';—the Catholic faith into which you were baptized, in which you were 'confirmed,' in which you long lived, and which I hope henceforth you will 'keep whole and undefiled' to your everlasting peace.

Parishioner. It will serve no useful purpose to repeat and reiterate what I have already said respecting symbols and allegories. They served as feeble props to my faith for a time, but they have become as broken reeds. The text you have given from St. Paul's Epistle belongs to another, and far more weighty, order of arguments. Did it stand alone, with no other writings of St. Paul with which to compare it, no other expressions which could aid in unfolding its purport, it would certainly uphold your statements as to the equal Godhead of the Son, although it would still leave the paradoxical and unintelligible Creed of your Church practically textless. Your quotation varies somewhat from the revised version, which takes the adjective 'glorious' from the word 'appearing,' and the article from the words 'great God,' and causes the text to read—'and appearing of the glory of our great God and Saviour Jesus Christ.' Dean Alford also translates it—'the manifestation of the glory of our great God.' And again, the Rev. Sheldon Green, in a new text and translation published by Bagster, gives it—'appearing of the glory of the great God and our Saviour Jesus Christ.' De Wette gives a corresponding translation, which suggests two separate persons; but Canon Liddon, in his Bampton Lectures on the Divinity of our Lord, quotes it as 'the blessed hope and appearing of the glory of our great God and Saviour Jesus Christ.' This may have been expected in one with such a powerful bias and strong ecclesiastic feelings as the Canon, but, in thus translating it, he has the powerful support of the good Bishop Ellicott, of Gloucester, who, in his learned treatise on the Pastoral Epistles of St. Paul, gives a precisely similar version, but he tenders reasons for the same in a more frank spirit, although a distinguished *littérateur* has told us that 'Everyone remembers the Bishops of Winchester and Gloucester making in convocation their remarkable effort to do something for the honour of our Lord's Godhead.' Still, with this alleged bias, the good and conscientious divine gives scholarly reasons for his conclusions, and recognizes the fact that, viewed grammatically, the Greek words would admit of another arrangement; indeed, in reference to τοῦ μεγάλου κ.τ.λ. he writes, 'It must be candidly avowed that it is *very* doubtful whether, on the grammatical principle alluded to in the preceding note (the identity of reference of two substantives when under the vinculum of a common article), the interpretation of this passage can be fully settled' (p. 201). He properly states that the true rendering of the clause really turns more upon exegesis than upon grammar, and lays great stress

ST. PAUL'S LUCIDITY.

upon the circumstance that 'ἐπιφάνεια,' 'appearance,' 'manifestation,' is a term specially and peculiarly applied to the Son and never to the 'Father,' and states further that μεγάλου would seem uncalled for if applied to the 'Father,' and he comes to the conclusion that 'the text is a direct, definite, and even studied (which word he emphasizes) declaration of the divinity of the Eternal Son.' After his own ingenious reasonings and verbal criticisms to reach the precise meaning of the words, few judicious and impartial persons could assent to the statement that the text is 'a *definite*, and even *studied* declaration' of the fact, which the Bishop declares it to be; however little they may be inclined to dispute the fact itself. Had St. Paul, or his amanuensis, 'studied' in an especial sense to make it the 'direct' and '*definite*' declaration of the Divinity of our Lord, would he have left it in so obscure a form as to be wrangled over by Greek scholars of such high attainments as Ellicott, Winer, De Wette, Meyer, and others? Wiclif, in his translation of 1380, I find, translates the text with a comma; and otherwise gives a different wording to the Bishop. Thus, 'the blessid hope, and the comynge of the glorie of the grete God, and of oure sauyoure ihesus Crist.' Tyndale, in 1534, also gives a comma—'that blessed hope and glorious apperenze of the myghty God, and of our saviour Jesu Christ'—and our authorized version of 1611, as printed by Bagster, gives the comma also, although it is omitted in later copies issued by Her Majesty's Printers. Winer, perhaps the highest authority in the grammar of the New Testament, considers that 'σωτῆρος' is not a second predicate; but that the article is omitted because of the genitive ἡμῶν. He acknowledges, however, as does the learned Bishop, that the meaning of the passage can be definitely decided by exegesis only; but just as the Bishop makes 'ἐπιφάνεια' the guide of his inference, so, in like manner, does Winer use the word 'θεός'; and argues, that as St. Paul in no other of his writings applies this word to Christ, it is not likely that he should, in this Epistle, have applied the exalted term, 'the *great* God,' to him; and finds, in this fact, a justification for his exegesis and resultant interpretation. The Bishop in his notes on the phrase frankly informs the reader that 'it ought not to be suppressed, that some of the best versions, Vulgate, Syriac, Coptic, Armenian (not however Æthiopic), and some Fathers of unquestionable orthodoxy, adopted the other interpretation: in proof of which latter assertion Reuss refers to Ulrich, *Num Christus in Tit.* ii. 13 *Deus appellatur*, Tig. 1837; a treatise, however, which the present editor has not seen' (*Pastoral Epistles*, p. 201). But with all this, while feeling profound respect for his Lordship's sincerity, it becomes evident that he is under the powerful bias of a preconceived and cherished idea, and that the strictly judicial spirit is wanting. A judicial exegesis demanded that something else in addition to the word 'ἐπιφάνεια,' should have been remembered; and that St. Paul, whose epistle is being considered, never once, in all his writings, applies the term 'θεός' to Christ; and therefore it was not probable that he would use the term here, emphasized by the adjective 'great' as well as by the article 'του, του μεγάλου θεου.' All things considered, my own reflections, aided by the observations of Meyer, De Wette, and Winer, compel me to believe that, in the text you have quoted, *two* persons are referred to; and all the more do the observations of these learned men confirm my conviction, because the ancient Greek MSS. are without stops or punctuations, and hence, it is more than probable that by the arrangement of a single stop, and by this alone, the text you have quoted possesses the solemn weight which *à priori* appears to belong to it. At present, it stands in direct contradiction to scores of other texts, and to the whole tenour of the Scriptures. Especially is it at variance with the words of St. Paul, which I have given to you, from his epistle to Timothy, whom he addressed with the same affectionate terms as he did Titus, as 'my true child in faith.'

Indeed, the entire correspondence between Paul and these his children, 'after a common faith,' testifies that he regarded Timothy as more directly, of the two, his especial successor and representative. His letters to the latter are almost impassioned. What can be more touching than such appeals as these to his young disciple—'This charge I commit unto thee, my child Timothy'—'O Timothy, guard that which is committed unto thee'—'Thou therefore, my child, be strengthened in the grace that is in Christ Jesus'—'Do thy diligence to come shortly unto me: for Demas forsook me, having loved this present world, and went to Thessalonica, Crescens to Galatia, Titus to Dalmatia;' and the like. His epistles to Timothy are indeed the overflowings of a tender heart—conscious that the 'time of his departure was come,' and anxious to confide in one he so much loved, the prosecution of the great task which was dearer to him than life. I cling, therefore, to the knowledge and instructions he imparted to Timothy as being the brightest outpourings of his inspired spirit. I think this exceptional text (if it be exceptional in its obscurity) may find a solution in the circumstance that it relates wholly to the second coming of our Lord, when, as we learn from His own words, He will be accompanied by 'the Great God.' The text, therefore, may refer to two Persons; for St. Luke records (ix. 26)

Jesus as saying to the persons listening to Him, 'Whosoever shall be ashamed of me and my words, of him shall the Son of Man be ashamed when he cometh in his own glory, *and* the glory of the Father, and the holy angels'; and it is impossible to forget that the same Paul, when writing to the Corinthians, expressly informs them that when God said that He had put *all* things in subjection under the feet of Jesus, '*it is evident* that he is excepted who did subject all things unto him. And when all things have been subjected unto him, then shall the Son also himself be subject to him, that did subject all things unto him, that God may be all in all' (1 Cor. xv. 27, 28). These statements are so lucid, so emphatic, that, coupled with the clear language which I have already cited from Paul's Epistle to Timothy, leaves my conviction unshaken, and, as I think, unshakable. The more I ponder on all the facts, the more vivid does the real truth appear. I need not have said I think. To my mind and to my conscience the whole matter is clear. Demonstrated by Scripture and by reason alike, my soul accepts the testimony, accepts it absolutely; and henceforward, as I have already said, crowds, creeds, councils, and Churches, by whatever name they are called, have no 'authority' with me upon this topic. They are, as was the decree of Nebuchadnezzar to Shadrach, Meshach, and Abednego: 'the law and the testimony' outweigh the clamour of crowds. If priests or prelates proclaim dogmas which are not in accord therewith, I am compelled to say unto them as Peter and John said to 'Annas the High Priest, and Caiaphas, and John, and Alexander,' and other dignitaries, 'kindred of the High Priest,' who were gathered together at Jerusalem :—'Whether it be right in the *sight of God* to hearken *unto you* more than unto *God*, judge ye' (Acts iv. 19). No, my dear Vicar, from the above statement of Paul there can be no appeal, for it is in harmony with all the teachings of Holy Writ. 'Hear O Israel, the Lord thy God is *one* Lord' (Deut. vi. 4), was the old emphatic proclamation of the *Old* Dispensation, and 'There is *one* God and *one* mediator between God and men—the Man Christ Jesus' (1 Timothy ii. 5, 6), is the equally positive declaration of the New Testament. The words in each case are simple, clear, and definite. No language could by possibility be plainer. No person hearing them *in adult life* for the *first time could* mistake their meaning. It is astounding to the unsophisticated understanding how such a confused and mystic idea as the one embodied in the Athanasian Creed could have been concocted out of the book called the Bible. In truth, it never was derived from that source. It sprang out of the subtle disquisitions of so-called Greek philosophers. One of the 'inspired'

ST. PAUL'S LUCIDITY.

writers of the Bible has told us, 'Lo, this only have I found, that God hath made men upright; but they have sought out many inventions' (Eccles. vii. 29); and of all the 'inventions' and the staggering statements which the subtlety and the sophistry of speculative minds have spun from their 'inner consciousness,' none can possibly exceed in absurdity that paradox of words ' the *Son* is *co-eternal* with the *Father*.' How amazed would the learned Arabian Mohammedans of the seventh century (these philosophers who, even at that early date, had catalogued all the stars in their visible heaven, had determined the true length of the year, and other scientific matters) have been to have heard 'a Christian,' or as they would have called him, 'the infidel,' utter such a statement! How confirmed would they have been in their superiority, and the superiority of their creed over a race which chose to talk in such a paradoxical manner and elevate into 'a creed,' a 'shibboleth,' a statement which overturned the meaning of words and *subverted the order of nature and of things!* Indeed, daily experience shows this, although dogmatic zeal blinds the mind to the fact. An instance of such obfuscating power has just occurred. That enthusiastic Anglican, Canon Liddon, wrote the other day to *The Guardian*, complaining 'that the divisions of Christendom, to which a new impetus was contributed by Bishop Gobat's Episcopate, do more to hinder conversions to

Christ than anything else,' more even than the
'trinitarian theory.' This popular preacher told
the readers of *The Guardian* that 'a clever
Mohammedan, when meaning to pay a compli-
ment, said to me, " We look upon an English
Protestant as an imperfect kind of Moslem"; and,
as a gibe upon the efforts of Protestants under
' Bishop Gobat's Episcopate,' and as a sop to
Anglican bigots, the Canon added, ' If Protestant
missionaries tone down their teaching sufficiently
in an Arian or a still more purely deistic direction, they may gain the good opinion of Moslem
hearers.' This is gratifying testimony from such
a source, despite the frightful words 'deistic
direction,' which to many minds convey the very
opposite of its true meaning, and suggest a
progress Satan-wards. As a matter of practical
fact, *it is* the priestly invention of the trinitarian
dogma, and not the nature of the Christian doctrine in its purity, which has prevented its
progress among the myriads of the East. Mr.
Hugh Stannus, in a recent prize essay on the
'Origin of the Trinity,' tells that 'some years
ago, when there were disturbances in India as to
the Province of Oude, a proclamation was issued
by our Government in which the Christian
religion was referred to. This proclamation
called forth a counter-proclamation from the
Queen of Oude, to the effect, " In the Queen of
England's proclamation it is written that the
Christian religion is true, but that no other creed

will suffer oppression, and that the laws will be observed towards all. What has the administration of justice to do with the truth or falsehood of religion? That religion is true which acknowledges ONE God, and knows no other. Where there are three Gods in religion, neither Mussulmans nor Hindoos, nay, not even Jews, Sun Worshippers, or Fire Worshippers can believe it true."' Ovid tells us '*Fas est et ab hoste doceri*,' and this 'heathen' Queen teaches us a grand lesson. 'He that hath ears to hear, let him hear.' 'Not even Jews,' writes the disdainful Queen, 'can believe it true.' Most assuredly they cannot 'believe it true.' In the first century of the Christian era, hundreds of Jews became the believers in and followers of Jesus Christ; but since the fourth century it has been different. When the 'Church' promulgated the unscriptural doctrine, that the Father is God, the Son is God, and the Holy Ghost is God—'and in this Trinity none is afore or after the other; none is greater or less than another; but the whole three Persons are *co-eternal* together and co-equal,' the 'conversions' became very few indeed, and these of a suspicious character. Can it surprise any rational person that the Jews, who reverence their ancient Scriptures, who honour the wisdom of Moses and of Solomon, the piety of David, and the sublime utterances of Isaiah and Ezekiel, should for well-nigh two thousand years turn with disdain from a religion couched in such phrases? Is it to be wondered at that the gentle Hindoos and the thoughtful Buddhists in their myriad numbers remain 'unconverted' as a people, despite the hundreds of thousands of pounds and the many noble lives which Christian England and other nations have poured forth for their 'conversion'? Is it a marvel that in the nineteenth century of the 'Christian era' scepticism swarms in our cities and saturates our literature and our science; that wise and good and illustrious men like Sir Isaac Newton, the discoverer of the law of gravitation, the pious poet John Milton, and the moral and learned philosopher John Locke should consent to be branded as 'heterodox' and 'unsound' rather than accept the idea that *before all things* it was necessary *thus to think* of their Creator, or *without doubt* to '*perish everlastingly*'? The marvel of marvels is, that for this *fundamental doctrine* there is not *one* clear unequivocal verse to be found in the entire range of Scripture! The most painstaking reader will search the pages of the Bible in vain to find even the *word* which has been ingeniously fabricated to express the mystic and 'incomprehensible' idea. Nor was the word used in theological controversies, as far as I know, until the two-hundredth year of the Christian era. Tertullian used it; and, in the third volume of his immortal work, Gibbon writes, 'If Theophilus was the first to use it, then this abstract term which was familiar in the schools of philosophy must have been introduced into the theology of the Christians after the middle of the second century' (Cap. xxi.). Yet, 'most strange, passing strange,' though the doctrine be absolutely textless, though it was unknown in the pure and primitive periods of Christianity, yet such is the infatuated intolerance of the hour, that *not* to express your belief in the 'Trinity,' or rather to *disavow a belief in it*, will cause you to be branded by all the Christian Churches of the realm as a 'heretic' and a kind of social Pariah; and this notwithstanding that *from the first chapter of Genesis to the twenty-second and last chapter of Revelation this all-important word which embodies a 'fundamental doctrine' is nowhere to be found!*

Vicar. It is evasive and somewhat 'jesuitical,' as it is often called, that you should lay such emphasis on the absence of the Latin word 'Trinity,' which simply means 'three in one,' when you are aware that the same thing is distinctly stated in *English;* and that in the very early part of our interview I drew your attention to it, and have since repeated it, and had hoped, from the reverence you express for the Scriptures, that it would have reconciled you to the doctrine as being, in the words of the Eighth Article of our Church, 'proved by most certain warrants of Holy Scripture.' As you have so long ignored it, and have brought forward other texts with so much confidence, altogether forgetful of the great law of Exegesis, and of the 'Twentieth Article of Religion'—not 'so to expound one place of Scripture that it be repugnant to another'—I must remind you for the *third* time that St. John, in the fifth chapter of his first Epistle, distinctly states 'there are three that bear record in Heaven, the Father, the Word, and the Holy Ghost: and these three are one.' This verse refutes your very strong statements as to the entire absence of all Scriptural authority for the doctrine, and also your last assertion that the word 'Trinity' (for the words 'these three are one' are more than an equivalent for it) is not to be found from the first chapter of Genesis to the very last chapter of the book of Revelation.

Parishioner. I had by no means forgotten the quotation in question. When my mind was first directed to this question, under the circumstances I have detailed to you, this Epistle of John came as a great solace to my mind, and for many months sustained my primitive faith. I had heard the especial verse read year after year, on the first Sunday after Easter; read, too, from the very altar, as the most sacred spot in the church, and immediately following the collect in the communion service. It was read also in due course on the 29th of April in the service at Evening Prayer. The words are certainly most clear, most distinct, and they demonstrate the truth of the doctrine of the Trinity, so far as an inspired Scripture stating a fact must be accepted as a demonstration by all (and most certainly I *was then one of those*) who regard it as *the Word of God*. The enunciation 'and these three are one' leaves nothing to be desired as to explicitness. I bowed with reverence where I could not fully understand. I felt that great was 'the mystery,' but I no more questioned than Abraham questioned when he climbed the mountain of Moriah on his painful errand. God had spoken, and there was no sacrifice, whether the offspring of Reason or the offspring of the body, that could be withheld by one who had a due sense of his creatorship, his omnipotence, and his goodness. It was an unfathomable mystery, but so is the origin of God. Believing the words *to be* the words of God, through the immediate inspiration of His apostle John, my 'doubts' were annihilated, and I listened to the 'damnatory clauses' uttered by the priest on those who did not believe in the 'Catholic Faith' with the same kind of emotion I felt when reading of the curses of Ebal on those who 'setteth light by his father or his mother, who removeth his neighbour's landmark, or maketh the blind to wander out of his way.'

For, at that time I had not perceived the tremendous distinction between the two cases—one (Ebal) dealing with overt *acts*, with demonstrable *deeds;* while the other deals exclusively with the subtle and intangible speculations of the mind. One 'curses' wicked *acts;* the other 'curses' *ideas*. Each, however, *appeared to be* the declaration of the Almighty One, and to HIS command the response could only be as it was at Ebal—'Amen!' Imagine, then, my dear sir, if you possibly can, the awful revulsion of my feelings when the time came, as *come it did*, when the words you have recited to me turned out to be the *interpolations*, the forged utterances of some enthusiastic copyist of MSS. in the fourth century, who, seemingly, not finding any verses sufficiently distinct and clear to uphold the hypothesis of the 'Trinity,' deliberately invented and added the one you have quoted to me; but, whatever may have been its origin, it was wholly *unknown* to the followers of Jesus until some hundreds of years after the 'inspired' apostle had 'slept with his fathers'! Such a discovery overwhelmed at once all my reverence for the doctrine. It was the only spot of ground on which I could rest my faith; the one sole atom of Scripture which seemed to demand that reason should be prostrated to the requirements of 'faith'; the only verse which lifted the mystery from the dogmas of priestcraft into the requirements of the Gospel; and, lo and behold, it was worse than a broken reed on which I was leaning! It was no more the Word of God than were the words of 'Zedekiah, the son of Chenaanah,' when he made him horns of iron, and, standing before Ahab and Jehoshaphat in their royal robes, sitting on their respective thrones as the Kings of Israel and Judah, he said unto the King Ahab, '*Thus saith the Lord*, With these shalt thou push the Syrians until thou have consumed them' (1 Kings xxii. 11). In that case it is sad to know that the lying statement was repeated by all the prophets of Israel, and that honest Micah, who protested against the statement, was smitten on the mouth by the false Zedekiah, without a word of remonstrance raised either by kings or prophets; and yet it is sadder still to feel that for centuries in the Christian era words equally false, and alike imputed to the Most High, have been repeated and enforced by *Christian* priests; nor have many (if any) hesitated to smite on the mouth (nay, some have not hesitated to burn slowly to death at the stake, as Calvin did Servetus at Geneva) those who have gainsaid their statements. It is a most damaging fact against the Church in England that her priests and her prelates have *known* for years that verse to be a spurious introduction into the chapter; and yet to sustain a theory to uphold a Church dogma, they have read it to the

6

people, even to this very Easter, as 'the Word of God'! From the lowliest curate through all the ranks of the priesthood up to the loftiest archbishop, not one in the United Kingdom has had the simple honesty and fealty to the truth to pause in their public reading of the chapter, and to say of this verse, 'Here is something false and wrong; this verse does not occur in any of the earliest manuscripts.' No, not one of the entire Hierarchy! If anything were wanting to prove its spuriousness it would be found in the fact that it was never once quoted by the partisans of 'orthodoxy' in the great Arian controversy in the year of our Lord 325. It amazes me that this verse should be still read, in its turn, although its spuriousness is so well known to the priests who read it. Even 'orthodox' writers are, by the force of circumstances, compelled to admit that it is spurious. Neander tells us in his *Church History*, 'This doctrine [the Trinity] does not, it appears to me, belong strictly to the fundamental articles of the Christian faith [are you not ready to exclaim '*et tu, Brute*'? But listen], as appears from the fact that it is explicitly set forth in *no* particular passage of the New Testament, for the only one in which this is done, the passage relating to the three that bear record, is undoubtedly *spurious*.' (Bohn's edition, Vol. II., p. 286.) To me, this reticence—no, not reticence, but wilful acquiescence in a fraud—this public use of a falsehood (for 'Church' purposes) in the very 'House of God,' and in an act of adoration and worship, is revolting, and would of itself repel me from a creed in defence of which such nefarious practices were resorted to.

Vicar. I do not think that I am acting rightly in listening to such strong condemnation of the bishops and pastors of the Church, with whatever leniency I may be disposed to treat the censure which has been indirectly passed upon myself. I wish, however, to state that the grammatical construction of verses 7 and 8 in the chapter to which you refer would seem to *need* the presence of the disputed passage; for what can the article τὸ ἕν at the conclusion of verse 8 have reference to if not to the former 'ἕν' in the preceding verse? Moreover, the learned Erasmus prints the clause in the third edition of the Greek Testament, 1522; and our own learned Bishop Burgess, as also Horsley, and Bull, and Stillingfleet, and Pearson, are unwilling that the passage should be considered spurious. In a bishop or a priest to have done as you suggest, and to have proclaimed the passage *untrue*, would have been to shake the confidence of the common people altogether *in the whole* Bible; or probably have caused them to execrate the bishop in question for himself daring to doubt the truth of anything within the pages of that book, which from their childhood they had been taught to reverence, and which many, if not most of them, considered to be sacred, yea, as sacred as the consecrated elements of the Blessed Sacrament.

Parishioner. My dear Vicar, you astound me! What is this but doing evil under the delusive idea that it sustains a good object? Still, I ought to have remembered that in the past there were Apologists who endeavoured to explain the facts that this spurious text was not appealed to by the Fathers for analogous reasons to those with which you justify its detention, and the silence respecting its falsehood. Porson, in his erudite letters to Archdeacon Travis in 1790, tells us of one Kettner, who alleges that the reason why the Fathers refrained from appealing to the heavenly 'witnesses' was lest the text might seem to favour Sabellianism, and lest 'Constantine the Great being then a Catechumen should be scandalized.' Kettner, by enforcing this text thus prominently, thought he had done the Church a great service, and he burst into a wild rhapsody thereupon, which Porson has given at length. Canon Liddon himself could not be more exultant over a rhetorical triumph than is Kettner over this said spurious verse; he calls it Johannine theology in a nutshell. It is like to a star of the first magnitude in Scripture—a compendium of the Trinitarian faith, '*et flos Novi Testamenti pulcherrimus.*' It is almost laughable to read the recorded rhodomontade of Kettner over this spurious verse. He heaps eulogy upon eulogy through a long series of sentences, such as '*Latet inexhaustus scientiarum thesaurus in hoc excellentissimo dicto. Hic enim Theologi tres articulos fidei : Jurisconsulti tres advocatos cœlestes et testes summas. Medici tres animarum medicas inveniunt,*' and so forth. But all this hyperbolical praise has become of none effect. The Scripture star of first magnitude has waned and set, the flower of the New Testament has withered, and the compendium of the Trinitarian faith has been cast aside by great scholars as a large falsehood in a small space. But there remains the distressing thought that this spurious text was long used to confute honest inquirers, and to be the pretext for their persecution and imprisonment as 'blasphemers'! It was the 'scriptural text' used in argument against the pure-minded William Penn in the reign of the profligate King Charles II. Hepworth Dixon, in his graphic history of William Penn, tells us at page 60 : ' Alone in that vast crowd of men, the Quakers were obliged to yield, and let the wrangle take such form as Vincent pleased. Then Vincent rose and asked the two "blasphemers" whether they owned one Godhead, consisting in three distinct and separate forms? Whitehead and Penn asserted that the dogma so delivered by Vincent was not found in Holy Writ. Vincent answered by a syllogism. Quoting

St. John, he said : "There are three that bear record in heaven—the Father, the Word, and the Holy Spirit, and these three are one." ... Penn ultimately published a pamphlet to refute Vincent's statements and inferences entitled *The Sandy Foundation Shaken*. This led to his being placed in the Tower for a long period, where Bishop Henchman and Canon Stillingfleet were sent in vain to convert him.' 'In prison,' says his eloquent biographer, 'Penn was free. No gates could close upon his fancy; no restraints could chain his thoughts. The light of heaven was on his window-panes; the peace of God was in his soul. The strength with which he bore his trial brought him back his father's heart.' Penn possessed the true martyr-spirit. 'No cross, no crown,' was his theory and his experience. The very learned and very good Canon Stillingfleet tried in vain persuasion and entreaty and priestly authority to induce him to abandon his opinions. 'At the age of thirty-four,' says Dixon, 'the Canon was hailed as Stillingfleet the Great.' This eminent divine, so well prepared for argument with men like Penn, repaired to his apartments in the Tower. Of course, the prisoner was no match for him in learning, but his gentleness and fortitude impressed the Canon's heart. With nothing but an open Bible, Penn contested every inch of ground with one who had a perfect library of the Fathers and the Councils in his memory. He wanted Penn to yield so far that Charles could set him free as an act of grace. Penn wanted to confront his enemies in a court of justice. 'Tell the King,' he said to Stillingfleet, 'that the Tower is the worst argument in the world.' His visitor would not press that point. . . . The Canon spoke of the King's favour to his family, of the admiral's position in the service, of the prospects of advancement he was casting to the winds. Penn heard his plea in silence, for he held him, as all good and intellectual people held him, in the highest honour; but the words he uttered in the Tower were empty sounds. It was a case of conscience, not of policy, and Penn was only one of many who had been arrested for opinion's sake. His private ease was nothing while so great a principle was at stake. Penn could not own a fault when he was not in fault, and by his weakness put his persecutor in the right. 'Whoever is in the wrong,' urged Penn, 'those who use force in religion can never be in the right.' The Canon carried these words to his royal 'master' (p. 85). Many, many times the good Stillingfleet visited the Tower to hold discourse with Penn, but the pious prisoner had obtained his convictions from a source purer and higher than Church Councils and Fathers, and he has left on permanent record that the Trinitarian doctrine 'is not from the Scriptures nor reason, since so expressly repugnant; although all broachers of their own inventions strongly endeavour to reconcile them with that holy record. Know then, my friend, it was born three hundred years after the ancient Gospel was declared; it was *conceived in ignorance*, brought forth and maintained by cruelty.' These words of Penn are being received as (they are) the truth; and for you, at this time of day, to retain the spurious text as useful and expedient is very wrong. It astounds me, for practically considered, what is this conduct but the embodiment of the great sin which Protestants allege continually against the Church of Rome? What is it but carrying out to the full the daring maxim of the fourth century—' that it is an act of virtue to deceive and lie when it could promote the interest of the Church'? It is the upholding of the very spirit of forgery. You have often spoken with indignation of the shameful *Decretals of Isidore*—documents said to be written by the early pontiffs, containing grants to the Holy See from Constantine, upholding the supremacy of the Pope, and the like—which were proved by the clearest evidence to have been forged. In what does it differ from the degrading tricks of the olden time, such as the showing of a coloured fluid for many, many years at Hales in this county of Gloucester as the very Blood of Christ brought from Jerusalem? except, indeed, that it was worse, inasmuch as the *Decretals* were only alleged to be the productions of *men*, whereas the blood *was* something *visible* to the senses which *could* have been tested and determined by experiments, but here, here, *horresco referens*, was the daring impiety of giving the words of *men* as the utterances of the *Almighty and Eternal God;* and you, sir, indirectly justify it as being useful in sustaining the faith of the people in a dogma and in a book! Oh, this is pitiful— most pitiful!

Vicar. I did not admit that this important verse was forged; on the contrary, I gave grammatical reasons to show that it might not have been, and then pointed out the mischief which might arise from the utterances of a contrary opinion. Moreover, I told you that the passage is to be found in an edition of the Greek Testament issued by the learned Erasmus in 1522, and also that good and learned divines like unto Bishop Burgess, and Horsley and Bull, and Stillingfleet supported its authenticity.

Parishioner. Pardon me when I say that it amazes me to observe how education, a special profession and training, and party zeal can blind even a man of good intentions and a pure purpose. It saddens me to find what very shallow arguments will satisfy a mind full of preconceived notions and anxious to uphold a system to which it is attached. On any other subject apart from your priestly office and its relations, you, my dear Vicar, would smile at the simplicity of the person who quoted as an authority for a disputed statement that the statement was contained in a book published, as was Erasmus' Greek Testament, one thousand years or more after the alleged forgery had taken place! Moreover, Erasmus himself prevaricated much and varied his words from time to time. As to your other remarks, in a matter of Greek scholarship can Bishop Burgess be compared for a moment with Porson, who maintained the spuriousness of the verse in question? The other names given by you appear very weak on such a subject, when the learned Michaelis and the great investigators of Greek MSS. Griesbach, Scholz, Lachmann, Tischendorff, Tregelles, Alford, and Jowett have shown that it is spurious, and opposed to the authority of all authentic Greek MSS., of all ancient MSS., of the Latin Vulgate, and of the Greek, Latin, and Oriental Fathers. But what is perhaps of more weight to the ordinary English mind is the fact that an assembly of the most learned Greek scholars and devout divines of the *nineteenth* century have unanimously agreed that it *is* spurious and ought no longer to appear in the pages of our Bibles.

Vicar. I did not at all expect that our interview would end in this manner, nor was I in the slightest degree prepared to enter into so elaborate a discussion as you have opened up. Moreover, you have used expressions which I hope, upon reflection, you will feel to be unjust towards myself personally, for I should scorn to use a forged document for the purpose of argument if I had known it to be so. After your statement to the effect that it *is* excluded from the Revised New Testament by such ripe scholars and pious men as Bishop Ellicott and Bishop Lightfoot—or, as I ought rather to say, by the Bishops of Gloucester and Durham—and others possessing profound Greek learning, I must admit it to be spurious, and consequently not of the transcendent value in support of the Athanasian Creed as I had supposed. However, the doctrine does not rest exclusively on the passage in question; although I know of no other that directly refers to and declares it in the lucid, positive, and explicit manner as does St. John in that Epistle.

Parishioner. I should be sorry indeed to hurt your feelings, for I have great esteem, nay affection, for you, and will at once withdraw the implication of folly in reference to your quotation of Erasmus as an authority on this subject, and will consider it an inadvertence, drawn forth by the exigencies of your position at the moment. You have certainly been unfortunate in your scriptural quotation in defence of the Trinitarian Creed, nor less so for the one given to justify the *damnatory* clauses of the Athanasian Creed, for

SPURIOUS TEXTS.

I am sure that I have only to mention it and you will remember that the passage you quoted from Mark xvi. 16, to the effect, 'he that believeth not shall be damned,' is *also an interpolation*, and was *not* written by St. Mark. It was appended as early as the time of Irenæus, but was still absent from the majority of codices so late as Jerome's day.

Vicar. I have been conversing far too long, and urgent duties call me away. I was reading that chapter in Valpy's Greek Testament this morning, and he gives the passage in full, and makes no reference in his copious notes to any doubt of the kind you refer to. Moreover, it is certain, as you say, that Irenæus, who was acquainted with Polycarp, and is thus, through Polycarp's knowledge of St. John, linked with apostolic times, quotes from this portion of Mark without hesitation; and I am not, therefore, willing at this moment to admit that the verses are an unauthorized addition to the writings of the Evangelist.

Parishioner. I myself appealed to Valpy on this point, but obtained no information; and also to Wilkinson and Webster in their more recent edition of the Greek Testament, with no satisfactory result; but Griesbach, Tregelles, Tischendorff, and even Alford, declare that the verses from the ninth are *not* written *by Mark;* and I think that this would be conclusive to any mind, unbiassed by antecedents and thoroughly *judicial* in its nature, who would carefully read the verses from the 9th to the 20th in that chapter, and compare them with the preceding verses; for he would find in those twelve verses at least *sixteen* words which are *not* to be found in the other parts of this Gospel.

Vicar. Let me remind you that Dean Burgon has written learnedly on this very subject, and he is a better Greek scholar than even Alford, and he strenuously maintains that St. Mark did write those verses. They are contained in a vast mass of ancient manuscripts, and the conclusion of the narrative at verse eight seems to be abrupt: indeed, powerful writers like unto Michaelis and Hug, infer that the addition was made at a later period of the Evangelist's life, as St. John is said to have done in the 21st chapter of his Gospel. A writer in *The Quarterly Review* (who I believe to be Dean Burgon) alleges that Eusebius quotes these verses as genuine, and that Victor of Antioch vouches for their genuineness. Moreover, Canon Cook, the learned editor of the *Speaker's Commentary on the New Testament*, does not hesitate to affirm that the evidence of the immense majority of the MSS. of ancient versions of early Fathers, and of internal structure, is all in their favour. And even if it were admitted that the verses in dispute were not written by St. Mark, it does not destroy their authenticity. Professor Roberts, of St. Andrew's University, one of the Revisers of the New Testament, although he concludes that the passage was not the immediate production of St. Mark, regards it as possessed of full canonical authority: and to refer to the critic you have quoted—Dean Alford—he, I am sure, considers the verses in question as an authentic fragment, placed as a completion of the Gospel in very early times, and that it has strong claims on our reception and reverence. Moreover, everyone receives the Epistle to the Hebrews as authentic and part of the Inspired Word; although most, if not all, biblical scholars agree in stating that it was not written by St. Paul.

Parishioner. The scholarship of Dean Burgon no one would question; but his ecclesiastic bigotry is so profound as to vitiate his conclusions. I could accept the opinion of Cardinal Newman on the 'Immaculate Conception of the Virgin' as readily as I could accept the evidence of Dean Burgon on the concluding verses of the Gospel of St. Mark. The fact is there are some minds incapable of receiving evidence which clashes with the impressions received in earlier life: they resemble certain plastic materials upon which an effigy has been imprinted, and subsequently baked or burnt in, so as to remain changeless for ever. Like the Bourbons, who are said to have remained unchanged in opinion and conduct whatever may have been the new facts, discoveries, or circumstances. Such men are often genial, social, witty, and brave ; but are blind guides under new conditions. A very illustrative example of this was seen in the career of the great Lord Eldon. Profoundly learned, and in private life courteous and fascinating, yet were certain impressions as stereotyped on his mind as any figure or sign on a Babylonian brick. It now astounds a human mind to learn that both Houses of our Parliament could defend and preserve a law which inflicted a death penalty on any person who stole five shillings from a shop, and yet such a law was in existence during my childhood. It was earnestly and warmly upheld by Lord Eldon, and he prophesied fearful evils from its repeal. Such minds powerfully influence corporate bodies, and infuse in them a stolidity of thought and feeling which renders it difficult, nay, sometimes impossible for ages, to change a creed like the Athanasian, or to remove an injustice like to that of hanging a man for stealing five shillings. Such an one was Eldon. Brougham tells us, in his able and generous biography of the great lawyer, 'such as he was when he left Oxford, such he continued above sixty years after, to the close of his long and prosperous life ; the enemy of all reform, the champion of the throne and the altar, and confounding every abuse that surrounded the one or grew up within the precincts of the other with the institutions themselves; alike the determined enemy of all who would either invade the institution or extirpate the abuse.'* Corresponding and well-defined types of this order of mind are familiar to all of us—in the late Mr. Newdigate of Warwickshire, Archdeacon Denison of Taunton, and Dean Burgon of Chichester, from whom, and the immediate subject before us, I have too long rambled. But to return to our subject. Apart from the mental character which I have described —a mental condition which baffles all arguments, and is proof against demonstration itself, he would be a bold man who should declare that the Dean's critical scholarship, great as it is, surpasses the combined attainments of Scrivener, Hort, Kennedy, and the other great scholars who formed the Revision Committee of the New Testament; for it must not be forgotten that no alteration, no change in the text was adopted finally except with the consent of two-thirds of the Revisers present. This is a most weighty consideration. As respects the number of MSS. in which the verses are found, this is not of great consideration, when it is absent from the oldest, and the best, not that age, *per se*, can decide the question, for Dr. Sankey, in his Gospel of the second century, and Scrivener also in his writings, have abundantly shown that the inter-

* Brougham, *Statesmen of George III.*, 2nd series, p. 61.

polations, and 'the worst corruptions to which the New Testament has ever been subjected, originated within a hundred years after it was composed.' The passage is absent from two MSS. which are universally admitted to be most trustworthy, and other MSS. have the addition in varying forms. Westcott and Hort, two most orthodox divines, pronounce that the difference in style produces an impression unfavourable to the authorship; and this must be felt by all who, with unbiassed minds, compare the words of which the 'Appendix' is composed with those used in the body of the Gospel; and as to the 'internal' evidence to which Canon Cook refers, few would think it favourable. The discontinuity and abruptness of the ninth verse are obvious; and especially if Matthew's narrative of the same incidents be read and compared with the alleged verses of St. Mark. Dean Alford is in harmony with several of the Revisers in regarding the verses as 'authentic' and as having strong claims on our reverence; but, with all respect to these distinguished divines, I cannot accept their conclusions; for inasmuch as the external and internal evidence is against the *authorship* of St. Mark [which they themselves admit], and as the real author is unknown, then do I most strenuously maintain that it ceases to be evidence. I hold and affirm that when the author of a statement is *not* known, and when the date or first appearance of the statement is also *uncertain*, or *unknown*, although it may be accepted *provisionally* as to *unimportant* matters, yet, when 'INSPIRATION' is claimed for it, and it contains solemn, nay awful statements, involving the damnation of souls, and is quoted in *defence* of the damnatory clauses in *other* works and treatises, *then* I could not accept it as an *authority*, or admit that on *such* a *point* 'it has strong claims on our reception and reverence.' In fact, strict justice demands that it should *not* be accepted as *evidence*. It would *not be* accepted as evidence in any of our courts of law. If a witness should say of any statement, 'I do not know *by whom* it was said, or *when* it was said,' he would be requested to withdraw, and the statement in question would be set aside, unless supported by some other direct, positive, and personal testimony. These facts compel me to repeat what I have already said : that it is a moral delinquency on the part of the bishops, priests, and deacons of the 'Catholic Church' (and I say 'Catholic' to include all who read the 'Bible' in public places of worship) that they practically hand on a falsehood from generation to generation, and salve their consciences under the idea that it is better for the Church to do so lest 'the people' should have their 'faiths' disturbed. I hold that every man who in God's House reads the entire sixteenth chapter we have been discussing as 'the sixteenth chapter of the Gospel *according to St. Mark*,' *believing* at the same time that more than half of it was written by *someone else*, is guilty of a falsehood, has committed a wilful sin; for St. Paul himself declares, whatsoever 'is not of faith is of sin.' As Jeremiah said of Judæa, so may it be said of England in our day—'A wonderful and horrible thing is committed in the land; the prophets prophesy falsely, and the priests bear rule by their means, and my people love to have it so: and what will ye do in the end thereof? (v. 30, 31). It is a painful thought, and a fact dishonourable to the clerical profession, that from the time of Edward VI.—to go no further back—the priests and prelates of the Church of England, and nearly all the Nonconformist ministers, have been preaching *as the words of St. John* that 'there are three that bear record in heaven—the Father, the Son, and the Holy Ghost: and these three are one'; and further, have also been preaching *as the words of St. Mark*, 'He that believeth and *is baptized* shall *be saved*, but he that believeth not shall be damned'; *knowing all the time that neither St. John nor St. Mark wrote or spoke the words!* This they have done, deeming it politic or 'expedient' to give the sentences as they had received them, *because* there were no other words in the Bible which gave such immediate, direct, and lucid support to the doctrine of the Trinity in the one case, and to the teachings of the Church in respect to baptism in the other! This broad historic fact is in itself damnatory of the theory, and justifies scepticism on other seeming corroborative testimony given by the clergy as the testimony of Holy Writ.

Vicar. Neither the one nor the other doctrine is dependent on the texts quoted. They rest on the authority of the Church, on the decrees of Councils, on the universal acceptance of the great majority of Christians, and on the words of our blessed Lord, His Evangelists, and His Apostles. Moreover, as you have yourself admitted, we have the majority of professing Christians of nearly all sects with us, besides the ancient Fathers, and therefore THE DOCTRINES MUST BE TRUE.

Parishioner. I have very long and very painfully felt all the facts and circumstances you state. Your appeal touches me deeply; but only as a sentiment and a past memory—it no longer possesses an intellectual and moral force, because I now know that its premises are fallacious and misleading. The primitive Church—the Church of the Apostles and their immediate followers—is in accord with me; all recent discoveries of very ancient MSS. testify to this; and more especially the priceless treasure discovered by Bryennius, in the Jerusalem Monastery at Stamboul, and called, *Didache; or, The Teach-*

ing of the Twelve Apostles. Many of the Fathers, as I have shown from so biassed a source as Cardinal Newman, were as heterodox on many points as you deem me to be. Of all the Fathers, none were more holy, learned, and zealous than was Origen, and in the twelfth and thirteenth chapters of his reply to Celsus, who had taunted the Christians as worshipping others than the one God, this great Father writes: 'To this we reply, that if Celsus had known this saying—"I and my Father are one," and the words used in prayer by the Son of God, "As Thou and I are one," he would not have supposed that we worship any other besides Him who is the supreme God. . . . And if any should from these words be afraid of our going over to the side of those who deny that the Father and the Son are two persons, let him weigh that passage, "and the multitude of them that believed were of one heart and of one soul," that he may understand the meaning of the saying, "I and my Father are one." Grant that there may be some individuals among the multitudes of believers, who are not in entire agreement with us, and who incautiously assert that the Saviour is the Most High God; however, we do not hold with them, but rather believe Him when He says: "The Father who sent me is greater than I."' * The Scriptures wholly sustain

* The Writings of Origen. Vol. II., p. 105.

my opinion and my statements. Paul, Peter, James, John, and Jude, and, above all, Christ Himself, testify to the Unity and the Supremacy of God, and the entire *distinctiveness* between Jesus and the Most High. This is proved to an absolute demonstration on the memorable occasion when, in the course of an address, He had said: 'I and the Father are one'; whereupon the irate, vindictive, and bigoted Jews at once took up stones to stone Him, although a moment before He had told them 'My Father which gave them (His disciples), he is greater than all.' When Jesus inquired 'for which of the many good works he had shown them from the Father they stoned him'? they answered Him, 'for a good work we stone thee not, but for blasphemy, and because thou, being man, makest thyself God.' On such a supreme occasion as this, if ever, a man would speak the truth, and of all men Jesus was most truthful; and, therefore, He at once disclaimed having done anything of the kind. So far from calling Himself 'God,' or, 'making himself God,' he had not even called Himself by so high a title as their forefathers and themselves had voluntarily bestowed upon many before Him. With that wisdom and Godlike forbearance which ever characterized Him, Jesus calmly placed before them the words of their own law and the practice of their forefathers. Although they had so furiously assailed Him and declared 'he had a devil and was mad,' He gently replied—

'If he called them *Gods* unto whom the word of God came, and the scripture cannot be broken, say ye of him whom the Father hath *sanctified* and *sent* into the world, Thou blasphemest because I said (not that I am God—not even God the Son), "I am the Son of God."' This entire history shows that there is not the slightest attempt to claim Godhead. In fact, the entire opposite to such a claim is everywhere implied. Through the entire scene He shows Himself to be the *Recipient* of the Father's bounty; the *Delegate* of His Father's will. His emphatic words are, 'My Father which *gave* them is greater than all.' He said, 'many good works have I showed you from my Father; for which of these works do ye stone me?' *Here* is *seething irony*, but no arrogant claim. Further, he added, 'Say ye of him whom *the Father* hath sanctified' (that is, the sanctity had been imparted and had not been claimed as inherent) 'Thou blasphemest because I said I am the Son of God'? In your ancient histories, as in the twenty-second chapter of Exodus, even your judges were called 'gods,' and your psalmist, even David himself, speaking as the representative of God, of those who should die like men: 'I have said ye are gods and all of you are CHILDREN of the Most High.' In this very practical manner did Jesus show that He could not possibly be guilty of blasphemy in thus speaking of Himself. All the old

Scriptures and the New Testament give clear and decisive testimony that the appellation of 'Son of God' was no arrogant assumption on the part of Jesus, but simply a name which had been applied to others, and, as we know, was applied to many afterwards; but to which appellation He Himself was pre-eminently entitled. Angels and men are so called, frequently, in Holy Writ. In the early history of the world we are informed 'That the sons of God saw the daughters of men, that they were fair, and they took them wives of which they chose' (Genesis vi. 2). The book of Job tells us—'Now there was a day when the sons of God' came to present themselves before the Lord, and Satan came also among them' (Job i. 6). The Scriptures teem with illustrative proof that in calling Himself 'the Son of God,' Jesus did not arrogate to Himself any title which gave the Jews a right, or even an excuse, for saying that, 'thou, being a man, makest thyself equal with God.' It was the mere pretext for the gratification of preconceived envy and hate. Their Prophets had enunciated the title as among the privileges of the faithful and obedient. Even Adam has been so described, for the lineage of Enos informs us that he was the son of Seth, the son of Adam, the son of God.' The Prophet Hosea conveyed the glad intelligence, that 'in the place where it was said unto them, Ye are not my people, there it shall be said unto them, Ye are the sons of the living God.' The priests and Pharisees knew the full meaning of the words sons of God, and they might have known that Jesus was especially 'the beloved' Son of God, to whom the great task of revealing God to the world was intrusted, for verily 'God was in Christ reconciling the world unto himself, not reckoning unto them their trespasses (2 Cor. v. 19); but envy and hate can and do distort words and draw wicked inferences. In his poem of *Paradise Regained*, Milton gives fully, by the mouth of Satan, the effect this appellation 'Son of God' had upon him:

> Till the ford of Jordan, whither all
> Flock to the Baptist, I among the rest
> (Though not to be baptized), by voice from Heaven,
> Heard thee pronounced 'the Son of God belovèd,'
> Thenceforth, I thought thee worth my nearer view
> And narrower scrutiny, that I might learn
> In what degree, or meaning, thou art call'd
> The Son of God; which bears no single sense.
> The Son of God I also am, or was;
> And if I was I am; relation stands;
> All men are sons of God; yet thee I thought
> In some respect far higher, so declared:
> Therefore I watch'd thy footsteps from that hour,
> And follow'd thee still on this waste wild.'

The title 'bears no single sense,' and to us, under the New Dispensation, it has (or ought to have) no tendency to suggest the idea of supreme Divinity, as the Jews pretended to assert, but it is full of the deepest consolation to all faithful Christians; it is indeed 'a Gospel,' 'a message of gladtiding,' to learn, as St. Paul told the Galatians—'Ye are all the children of God by faith in Jesus Christ,' and to be assured by Jesus Himself 'that blessed are the peacemakers, for they shall be called the children of God.' Under the fearful charge of blasphemy, with the vindictive Jews piling up stones to stone him, Jesus was calm and truthful, even if their dastardly and cruel conduct did prompt Him, ironically, to inquire for which of the good works He had done they wished to stone him? No truth is so fully and clearly established by the Scriptures as that Jesus always testified His power to be a delegated power. His grateful heart was ever ready to exclaim, 'It is my Father that glorifieth me'; and at the close of His earthly career he comforted His followers by the assurance, 'I go to my Father, *and to your Father, to my God*, and to your God.' As if by prophetic vision, Jesus foresaw that a time would come when the natural tendency of the human mind 'to make Gods' and to cherish the idea that 'there are Gods many and Lords many' would reassert itself, and therefore He was frequent in such assertions as these—'I can of mine own self do nothing' (John v. 30). 'The word which ye hear is not mine, but the

Father's which sent me' (John xiv. 24). He seemed to feel that a time would come when the pure and simple faith (described years afterwards by Paul to the Corinthian Church) 'to us—there is one *God*, the Father of whom are all things, and we unto him ; and one *Lord*, Jesus Christ, through whom are all things, and we through him' (1 Cor. viii. 6)—would for a time be abandoned. Hence, never once did Jesus claim for Himself the creative power of Deity, but seemed ever desirous to give God the glory for all things. He always impressed His disciples with the solemn truth, 'My Father that dwelleth in me *he* doeth the works'; He always taught them to look to God as the supreme Arbiter of all things. 'To sit on my right hand, and on my left, is *not mine to give*' (Matthew xx. 23). No Omniscience, or other attribute of the supreme God, did He avouch as inherently belonging to Him; as He told His disciples, even the Judgment hour itself was unknown to Him. 'Of that day and hour knoweth no one, not even the angels of Heaven, neither the Son, but the Father only' (Matthew xxiv. 36). So frequent and so distinct and plain were these statements of our Lord, that not even this powerful and oft-quoted text, 'I and my Father are one,' is equal to the support of so paradoxical a creed as the one you espouse ; even if the above words had not been explained by Jesus, as they were in His last touching prayer for His disciples—'Make *them one*, even as I *and Thou art one*'; even, I say, if it stood in naked isolation, unopposed, as it now is, by a series of other scriptural statements, it would fail to build up the Pagan theory of the Trinity. If the text demonstrated the identity and equality of the Christ with God, yet it would even then serve only to prove a '*Duality*,' and the *Quicunque vult* would be anti-scriptural and, therefore, heterodox: all these are incontrovertible facts and statements, but with a perversity which will one day cause her ruin, the Church turns a deaf ear, or rather, administers a scornful rebuke, on anyone, however learned, or however pious, who may respectfully suggest a reconsideration of any of her tenets. She does not claim infallibility, as does her Mother Church of Rome, yet she always acts as if she wished and believed that her people did so regard her, and feared that any change of view may impress them with the idea that she was not infallible. She disdains reform and will, at no distant day, reap revolution. Fourteen years have elapsed since some of the wisest and purest of her dignitaries suggested a very modified arrangement in the wording of the Athanasian Creed, but their mild suggestions were crushed and passed over 'by Convocation,' and even the prayer that the 'damnatory clauses' may be omitted in the public reading of the 'Creed' was disregarded. The old leaven of Priesthood, with its arrogant claims to implicit submission, triumphed. As in an older Sanhedrim Caiaphas was obeyed, and the majority held fast the Athanasian Creed as the true test of orthodoxy. The counsel of the Bishop of St. David, the wise, learned, and judicious Connop Thirlwall, regarded everywhere (except in Convocation) as the Nestor of the Episcopal Bench, was disregarded. The pious Bishop of Ripon, Dr. Bickersteth, and the sagacious and large-hearted Bishop of Manchester, Dr. Fraser, pleaded in vain for its modification; and the Deans of Durham and of Westminster (Lake and Stanley), with the Christian courage which has characterized them, testified also in vain to its falsehood; the Dean of Durham declaring that.'when the Clergy read the Creed, they read what they themselves did not believe'; the Dean of Westminster declaring 'the damnatory clauses are not true, and are known to be untrue by every clergyman; by them are condemned many eminent Anglican writers, and the whole of the Greek Church.' But ecclesiastic stolidity triumphed, and the Church went on in her changeless mood to that inevitable death which is the heritage of insincerity and falsehood. The Petition of seven thousand of the Laity, obtained hurriedly, and of three thousand ordained Clergymen, was set aside, and the so-called National Church of England, fourteen times in a year declares that, '*without doubt*, he shall perish everlastingly' who does not keep 'whole and undefiled' a creed wholly unknown to the first two centuries of Christianity (according to some historians not before the eighth century)—a creed composed by no one knows whom, sanctioned by no general Council, not understood [except in its damnatory sentences] by five-sixths of the Laity who listen to it; disclaimed by the Eastern Church; and discarded also from all the usual public services of the thousands of Christian places of worship in the United Kingdom! Is not such conduct as unwise as it is ungenerous? Nay, is it not unwisdom? Is it not an infatuation which compels the thought, '*Quos Deus vult perdere, dementat prius*'?

Vicar. Your zeal is prompting you to use hard words, and you quote a line from ancient tragic poetry to illustrate a condition and to pourtray a doom. Is this right? A steadfast adherence to an established faith, and resistance to change when asked for by a few pious, able persons, and sustained by popular clamour, you indirectly represent as a demented condition, to be followed by a judicial death. You altogether overlook the fact that such yielding may be a weakness and a sin. Steadfastness has ever been regarded as a virtue, and not as a demented condition. You quote from the Latin a fragmentary piece of Greek poetry. Permit me to remind you of the classic ode of Horace in which he eulogizes the virtue and extols the man who is regardless of clamour : '*Civium ardor prava jubentium*,' and assures us that steadfastness is a high quality:

> Hac arte Pollux et vagus Hercules
> Enisus, arces attigit igneas ;
> Quos inter Augustus recumbens,
> Purpureo bibit ore nectar.

But above all the dreams of Heathendom and its poetry, we have the language of inspiration to guide us. Solomon tells us—'meddle not with them that are given to change.' David, in the seventy-eighth Psalm, gives us a graphic sketch of the miseries of the Israelites in consequence of their vacillation. 'For their heart was not right with (God), neither were they *steadfast* in his covenant.' St. Peter, after relating in prophetic vision the Judgment day and the physical doom of the earth, besought the disciples in Pontus, Galatia, Cappadocia, Asia, and Bithynia, 'seeing ye know these things before, beware lest ye also, being lead away with the errors of the wicked, fall from your own steadfastness '; and the ever-vigilant, loving, and anxious Paul implores his followers in Colosse to 'continue in the faith grounded and settled,' and tells them of the joy he felt in 'beholding your order, and the steadfastness of your faith in Christ.' And to the Corinthians, after giving them a glowing description of the resurrection, he writes: 'Therefore, my beloved brethren, be ye *steadfast, unmovable*, always abounding in the work of the Lord.' The Church, therefore, in Convocation would have done well in resisting the alteration and spoliation of an ancient creed, even if they had been unsupported ; but you forget that thousands of other clergymen took an opposite view to that of the three thousand you have named ; and under the guidance of Canon Liddon and Lord Salisbury determined that no change should take place in the public use of the Creed. Indeed, it was generally understood that had there been any alteration by any authorized official body, such as by Her Majesty in Privy Council, the Church would have suffered loss by the secession of two such distinguished divines as Dr. Pusey and Archdeacon Denison. A great loss this would have been, although you think so much otherwise. Minds vary as much as faces. Both Horace and Tacitus, although in different words, inform us—'*Quot homines, tot sententiæ.*' I reverence the fervour and learning of Dr. Pusey, and do not dislike the tenacity and courage of Denison. The Athanasian Creed was dear to these men, as it was and is to Cardinal Newman; but perhaps it is not surprising that the man who can feel ecstasy in the Mass, who can write that 'to me nothing is so consoling, so piercing, so thrilling as the Mass, said as it is among us; I could attend masses for ever and not feel tired,' should say also of the Athanasian Creed that 'it is the most simple and sublime, the most devotional formulary to which Christianity has given birth.' I myself regard the words 'the most simple' as exaggerated language when applied to this Creed; but the language itself proves how sweet, how dear, how precious is the venerable *Quicunque vult* to some and what a loss its removal from the service of the Church would be to many pious minds. The saintly author of the *Christian Year* reverenced it much, and even called it 'the Anthem of the Blest'; and this reminds me, that when speaking of the many symbols instructive and illustrative of the holy mystery of the Trinity, I might have quoted some verses of this charming poet's Ode or hymn for 'Trinity Sunday.'

> From each carv'd nook and fretted bend,
> Cornice and gallery seem to send
> Tones that with seraph hymns might blend.
>
> Three solemn parts together twine
> In harmony's mysterious line;
> Three solemn aisles approach the shrine:
>
> Yet all are One—together all,
> In thoughts that awe but not appal,
> Teach the adoring heart to fall.

These experiences of good and pious men, like unto Newman and Keble, ought to show you how rich in solace and sweetness is the mystery which, through some mistaken bias, appals you. Keble could find in it a

> Calm breathed warning of the kindliest love
> That ever heaved a wakeful mother's breast.

And a learned and eloquent archdeacon of our county, Archdeacon Hayward, has declared it to be, when 'grammatically understood,' a beautiful hymn of praise, which simple-minded Christians may join in singing, as they now do the *Te Deum*, or any other of our hymns. It is thus obvious that to scholarly minds, and to minds illumined by the spirit of poesy, and dowered with that receptivity which the teachings of the Church are designed to impart, the Athanasian Creed is full of comfort and instruction; and I even yet hope that, as a candid and honest man, you will perceive that its alteration, and especially its removal, would be a painful loss to many. Let me again ask you to pause and ponder on your conclusions. The solemn decision of the ancient Apostolic Church ought to be the source and guide of your convictions, and not your weak, erring, individual reason. She is the depository and exponent of God's Word, and on this solemn subject she speaks clearly, positively, and authoritatively. Her council and her conduct ought to be your guide in all the difficult problems of life and conduct. It moves me deeply, my dear friend, to have again to remind you that the Church which received you into her fold of

Baptism, which consecrated your vow by the 'laying on of hands' in Confirmation, which has so many times welcomed you at the Sacrament of the Supper of the Lord, and has so often and so fervently prayed that the Body and the Blood of our Lord Jesus Christ, which was given for thee and shed for thee, may preserve thy body and soul unto everlasting life, should have now to use the language of rebuke. Think of the sainted dead who now sleep the sleep of the just within her sanctuaries, at whose knees you first lisped a prayer, who brought you to her baptismal font, there to be 'received into the congregation of Christ's flock,' and 'to be grafted into the Body of Christ's Church,' and prayed that their child 'may lead the rest of his life according to this beginning.' Think what would now be the feelings of those honoured parents who taught you to love the rites of the Church, who, through their long and consistent lives, enjoyed those rites and ceremonies, and died within her fold, 'under the sure and certain hope of a joyful resurrection.' Oh! think of those respecting whom you heard the white-robed priest 'give hearty thanks to Almighty God, with whom do live the spirits of them that depart hence in the Lord,' and with whom the souls of the faithful 'are in joy and felicity,' that it had pleased HIM to deliver them out of the miseries of this sinful world. Would they not mourn over your decadence? Sure am I that it would grieve them to know that you were standing in the position condemned by the Thirty-fourth Article of their beloved Church: 'Whosoever, through his private judgment willingly and purposely doth openly break the traditions and ceremonies of the Church which be not repugnant to the Word of God, and be ordained and approved by common authority, ought to be rebuked openly.' In that sad position, as I have already said, you now are. I am compelled to repeat, that not only has your own Church—the Church of your forefathers—spoken emphatically on this cardinal Christian doctrine, but also the great Church of Rome; and not only these, but the Eastern Church also [to which you seem somewhat favourably disposed]; and even the Schismatics also, in their tens of thousands, are confident of the truth of that mystery, which you so pertinaciously refuse to accept! You thus, I repeat, incur a most fearful responsibility, at which I tremble, and all the more, because through this rash assumption you abstain from the holiest of rites, the origin and importance of which you do not deny. I cannot divest myself, moreover, of the solemn responsibility which rests upon me also, as your pastor, in respect to the views you avow; they are so contrary to the teachings of the Universal Church, that I must, to free my own soul, again implore you to abandon your dangerous error. Believe me, dear sir, it is no matter of form that I am anxious about. It is a vital question, for on it hinges your eternal salvation. The words of St. John, or rather of Jesus, as reported by St. John, are absolute, and they are so lucidly given that there is no escape from their meaning. The Jews were, as you now are, doubtful and disputatious, saying, 'Can this Man give us his flesh to eat?' Jesus therefore said unto them, 'Verily, verily, *except* ye eat the flesh of the Son of Man, and drink his blood, ye have not life in yourselves. He that eateth my flesh, and drinketh my blood, hath eternal life; and I will raise him up at the last day' (John vi. 54). This being so, I bid you in the name of God, I call you in Christ's behalf, I exhort you, as you love your own salvation, to abandon your erroneous ideas, and come and be a partaker of the most Holy Communion.

Parishioner. I agree cordially with all you have said respecting steadfastness. You could not accept more frankly than I do all that you have quoted from Horace, Solomon, David, Peter, and Paul in its praise. It is nearly four thousand years ago since Jacob said of his first-born, Reuben, 'unstable as water, thou shalt not excel,' and, from that hour to this, mankind has ever regarded the unstable man as fickle and untrustworthy. As I have already observed, even a courageous obstinacy has its admirers, as shown in the lives of Newdigate, Burgon, or Denison. Nevertheless, the quality borrows its excellence from the cause or opinion with which it is associated. It is no virtue to continue in wrong-doing, or obstinately to cling to an opinion which has been fairly proved to be false. No one now blames Paúl because he abandoned the opinions of his fathers and his teachers, and his own once zealous feelings and opinions and acts, with which he 'persecuted the Church of God.' It often requires higher courage and a more *steadfast spirit* to change opinion and conduct than to adhere to them. Martyrdom more frequently awaits the Pauls than the Sauls of mankind. Christ was crucified, and Stephen was stoned, not because they 'profited in the Jew's religion' above many of their own nation, but because they were 'steadfast' and 'immovable' to a higher and purer revelation. As the priest of a 'Reformed' Church, you would admit, probably, that Luther exhibited a higher 'steadfastness' when he burnt the Pope's Bull at Wirtemburgh than when, years before, he crawled on the ground 'bathed with the blood of martyrs' at the Convent of his Order near the gate Del Popolo. We are in perfect accord as to the supreme duty of remaining steadfast and immovable to a true faith, and 'always abounding in the work of the Lord,' but we are wholly at variance as to the trinitarian theory being a fundamental condition of the saving faith. On this principle I hold that the Convocation acted unwisely in disdaining and rejecting the councils of such wise and good men as Bishop Thirlwall and Dean Stanley, sustained, as these were, by the petition of three thousand clergymen and seven thousand of highly intelligent laymen, including judges and others of the learned professions. The threatened secession of the Church dignitary, Dr. Pusey, who had been suspended for preaching the doctrine of 'Transubstantiation,' and who wrote to the public papers, declaring 'that he cannot and will not subscribe to the Articles of the Church in the sense in which they were propounded by those who wrote them'; and of Archdeacon Denison, who protested against the proceedings of the Convocation of Oxford in respect to Mr. George Ward, who advocated subscription to the said Articles 'in a non-natural sense.' You are quite right, my dear Vicar, in supposing that I have no profound reverence for such men. What private or individual opinion or feeling the Roman Catholic Cardinal Newman, the Anglican poet Keble, or the rhetorical Archdeacon of Cirencester may indulge respecting the simplicity, the sweetness, and the devotional character of the Athanasian Creed concerns no one but themselves. There is no explaining the mental idiosyncrasy of individuals. The Creed must be judged by its literal meaning as 'understanded by the common people'; by such people as those to whom our Divine Lord preached the Beatitudes on the Mount of Olivet. The records of fanaticism show that the continuous utterance of certain cabalistic words has excited devotional ecstasy akin to that so eloquently described by Cardinal Newman, as has also the counting of a string of beads, or the steadfast contemplation of a special part of the human body (ὀμφαλος). Travellers inform us that in Thibet, to the devout Buddhist, the repetition, for many hundreds of times in succession, of the four words, 'Om-Mani Padme Hrum,' brings a sweet and sacred joy, and that to have uttered them three hundred thousand times secures to the worshipper a high place in the favour of Buddha. Such idiosyncrasies as these belong to the eccentric phenomena of psychology rather than to the practical domain of sober religion. Therefore, your plea that the mystical 'Athanasian Creed' should be retained in the public religious service of the realm because it has been pleasing and profitable to certain poetic pietists, is as futile as would be the argument that the blatant buffoonery of 'General Booth' ought forthwith to be introduced into our National Churches because it has brought 'salvation' and hysteric raptures to some foolish fanatics in the back slums and alleys of our large towns. Your appeal to the authority of the Church as the depository and exponent of the truth and of Christian conduct is full of weight, but that she has erred and errs has been abundantly testified in the annals of our history. How many good and learned men like unto Richard Baxter and Bishop Frampton, of Gloucester, have had to refuse her conditions; and the sermons of good Bishop Latimer tell how deeply she has erred in theory and practice. I cannot myself forget that she resisted all change in our unjust 'criminal' laws; that she was the upholder of the infernal Slave Trade, and other iniquitous practices which have been set aside by a humane and intelligent public. All that you have so tenderly said respecting parental love and its teachings; all that you have graphically recited respecting Baptism, Confirmation, the Holy Communion, and the Burial of the Dead have, as you well know, touched me deeply in the past, and have been, and are, the severest trials and throes of my heart in its new birth to a better faith. What you have said on all these tender matters dim my eyes with tears, as the last sight of his birth-cottage may swell the soul of an emigrant with a throb of woe, but its acuteness passes away (however long its shadow may remain) under the certainty that a brighter home and happier circumstances await him in another land. As respects the Thirty-fourth Article of the Church of England, I know that I reject no tradition 'which is not repugnant to Scripture,' and claim for myself the same freedom of interpretation on this point as did Latimer and Ridley against the

'Church' of their day, and as Gorham and Colenso in modern times against the decrees of Bishops or Convocations. As to the overwhelming numbers from whose opinions I dissent, it is a most grave and solemn matter, and has weighed with me heavily, as I have more than once stated. No one but myself can realize how presumptuous it seemed in me to stand apart from all others. For a long time I painfully felt all this, but when a strong conviction takes possession of the soul it becomes incontrollable. Observation soon revealed to me that the majority of men are gregarious in their opinions, and disposed to follow a leader and be the slaves of a custom. Thought and studious reflection are distasteful to the many, they like others to think and to determine for them, and hence they become the echoes, the 'items' of the leader in whom they trust, and their 'paper' or their 'parson' becomes their sole authority and their guide in religion and politics alike. This being so, a preponderance of numbers, *per se*, has long ceased to affect me. The minority is often right : Jesus had not many to sustain and carry forward His doctrines when in the Garden of Gethsemane, 'All His disciples forsook Him and fled.' The Christians were not in the 'majority' when they returned from Olivet, and sought an 'upper chamber' for counsel and prayer. Paul, as he stood before the crowd of Greeks, philosophers, and others on Mars Hill, would not have obtained a show of hands in his favour. Necessarily, in the history of truth, there is a period when its supporters are in a minority. Therefore, *mere numbers do not influence me.* Christianity itself is in a minority yet among the religions of the world. The 'Bible' has not displaced the 'Koran,' the 'Vedas' of the East, or the writings of Confucius. *Facts,* and the conclusions derived from them by the reason honestly and logically applied, are of greater weight with me than the opinion of the multitude. *Vox populi* is NOT *Vox Dei.* Barabbas was preferred to Jesus. Ecclesiastic authority has often, as I have said, condemned that which was true and just. Witness the Protestant Reformation, witness the condemnation of Galileo, the abolition of slavery, and the improvements in our 'Criminal Code.' But in respect to my absence from the Lord's Table, I am most truly sorry to have caused you so much anxiety, and grateful indeed do I feel towards you for your friendly interest in my welfare. After this warm and solemn appeal to me you will be able to say, with a clear conscience, '*Liberavi animam meam.*' You have done your duty as a 'watchman,' you have 'blown the trumpet,' you 'have warned the people,' you can comfort yourself with the words recorded by Ezekiel xxxiii : 'If thou warn the wicked of his way to turn from it, if he do not turn from his way, he shall die in his iniquity; but thou hast delivered thy soul.' I repeat that *all* the solemn responsibility rests upon my own head. If 'eternal life' *depends* exclusively upon partaking of this holy rite in the manner, and method, and with the preliminaries enjoined by the Church of England, I am in a most perilous position. As I have already told you, these things have weighed heavily upon my soul; it was with no light heart that I ceased from the practice of many years, from that 'communion' which once brought peace and consolation, and which recently I have been invited to share with one who was dearer to me than life itself. But a more imperious voice has spoken; and, as Christ said, 'He that loveth father or mother, brother or sister, more than me is not worthy of me,' and remembering that whatsoever 'is not of *faith* is of *sin*,' and, as St. Paul said respecting a far inferior matter, namely, that of partaking of a special kind of food, under special circumstances, 'He that *doubteth is damned* if he eat, because he eateth not of faith,' it is not possible that I should partake of so solemn a feast as that to which you invite me.

Vicar. But *why* should you doubt?

Parishioner. Because, as I told you, I could not repeat the words, 'God of God, Light of Light, very God of very God, begotten not made, being of one substance with the Father,' and I *might* have added that I could not 'acknowledge one baptism for the remission of sins.'

Vicar. Your state of mind grieves me much. I had hoped that reflection upon the statements I made earlier in our interview had dispelled your doubts; that 'increase of grace' had been imparted to you, and that you were now prepared 'to hear meekly the Word, and to receive it with pure affection,' and that it would have been my joy to learn that my prayer had been in some measure answered; and that, if not '*all* such as have erred and are deceived had been brought into the way of truth,' yet that *one* I esteemed *had* been brought into that happy condition.

Parishioner. I assure you, Mr. Hierous, that, although my views of inspiration are wholly changed, and I am no longer a Bibliolater, yet am I still disposed to hear meekly the Word, and to receive it with pure affection,' for, as I have said, my convictions as to the nature and character of Christ have been derived wholly from the Bible; and at the time when my faith in the Trinity began to be unsettled I was as complete a believer in the verbal inspiration of the Scriptures as you are at this moment; but I have described this so fully that I need not, and hope not to enter upon this phase of the subject again. *It was the Bible, and the Bible alone that shattered my early opinions*, and even now I repeat, 'to the law and the testimony'; and if you can show me that the *balance* of scriptural evidence in favour of the Athanasian belief is such as to outweigh its logical and intellectual difficulties I shall at once succumb. Most gratefully then should I accept your invitation, and in your own 'Communion Service' partake of 'bread and wine' in remembrance of Him 'who grew in favour both with God and man,' of whom it was said, 'never man spake like this man,' 'who went about doing good,' and who was 'obedient unto death, yea, the death of the cross.'

Vicar. I am gratified to hear you thus speak, and especially as, I must now admit, you have shown the untrustworthiness of the powerful passages that I placed before you in the former part of our conversation from 1 John v. 7, and from the concluding portions of St. Mark's gospel. Happily, as I said before, this essential doctrine does not hinge on these strong texts, nor yet wholly on the authority of the Church and of the early Fathers, but upon clear and indisputable statements of Holy Writ; in truth, upon the very words of Jesus Himself, for I will again, irrespective of all that you have said, impress upon you the solemn import of the words, 'He that hath seen me, hath seen the Father,' and not less, 'I and my Father are one.'

Parishioner. The subject we are considering is so solemn, has for so many ages occupied the thoughts of good and wise men, that almost any amount of repetition is justifiable in order to

HOLY COMMUNION. 127

impress the facts indelibly upon the mind. Therefore, I repeat that Christ and God were one—but in no 'Athanasian' sense. They were 'one' even as in the later period of His history Jesus prayed that *all* His disciples may be *one*. In that tender prayer, when 'he knew that his hour was come,' Jesus revealed His whole nature to His disciples, and the words of the prayer throw a flood of light on the words which you have quoted, and *settle for ever their meaning*. There is nothing more lucidly stated in the whole range of Holy Writ than is the nature of that unity, that *oneness*, to which you have referred. To me the exposition is complete—so complete that loyalty, fealty to Jesus would compel me to disregard all other statements, come from whom they may. Popes, Councils, Doctors, Athanasius or Augustine, Church Articles, Prayer Books, and 'creeds' clamour in vain. *The Master has spoken*, and His words are a 'lamp unto my feet and a light unto my path' (Ps. cxix. 125). All so-called 'authorities' who speak at variance with these words are to me 'as sounding brass or a tinkling cymbal.' To repeat what I said at a former part of our interview, Christ has spoken, and all other voices are futile. I feel as Paul felt (without using the maledictory phrase) when, writing to the Churches of Galatia, he said, 'Though we, or an angel from heaven, preach any other gospel unto you than that which we have preached unto you, let him be accursed. ... For I neither received it of man, neither was I taught it, but by the revelation of Christ' (Galatians i. 8-12). Christ has been to me the Expositor of the words you have quoted, and *therefore* all else becomes, as I have said, 'as sounding brass or a tinkling cymbal.'

Vicar. Some words have, indeed, impressed you strongly, but you have not given them; and really, at this moment, I cannot recall anything —that is, any words of Jesus—which so clearly define and explain the nature of the unity existing between Himself and the Father, as could in any degree divest it of that mystery which appertains to the Nicene or Athanasian Creed. Indeed, as St. Paul said to Timothy, 'without controversy great is the *mystery* of godliness; God was manifest in the flesh, justified in the spirit, seen of angels, preached unto the Gentiles, believed on in the world, received up into glory.'

Parishioner. I said they explained the *meaning* of your text quoted. They unfold the nature of the unity which existed between Him and the Father, and they do this so completely that not a single word needs to be added to or taken from them to enhance their lucidity. They occur in the impassioned prayer which, towards the close of His ministry, He offered up for His disciples, and they are these : ' *Sanctify* them through thy truth : thy word is truth. As *thou hast sent me* into the world, even so have *I* also sent THEM into the world. Neither pray I for these alone, but for them also which shall believe on me through their word; THAT THEY ALL MAY BE ONE; as *thou, Father, art in me,* and I in thee, *that they also may be one in us;* that the world may believe that thou *hast sent me.* And *the glory* which *thou gavest me* I *have given them;* THAT THEY MAY BE ONE, EVEN AS WE ARE ONE: I in them, and thou in me, that *they* may be made *perfect in one;* and that the world may know that *thou hast sent me,* and hast *loved them,* AS thou hast loved me' (John xvii. 17-23). Such are the words, my dear Mr. Hierous. They require no ingenious explanations, no verbal sophistry, to elucidate their meaning; they stand out plain, clear, luminous, yea, as incisive and distinct as the command of the Decalogue, 'Thou shalt not kill.' These words are not plainer or more clear to the simple mind than are the words, 'that *they* may be *one, even as we are one.*' It is a moral unity, a spiritual affinity, to be understood by everyone, and having no relation to the 'substances,' 'the co-equalities,' and 'co-eternities' of a mystical creed. It is a 'unity' of thought, feeling, and purpose such as the disciples might possess in relation to each other as fully and as completely as Jesus with the Father —'THEY MAY BE ONE, EVEN AS WE ARE ONE.' Moreover, that nothing should be wanting in Christ's revelation to men as to His true relationship with the Father, and the dignity and power which respectively belonged to them, in this tender address to His disciples (which possesses all the pathos of a final farewell) Jesus said to them: 'If ye *loved* me, ye would rejoice, because I said, I go unto the Father: FOR MY FATHER IS GREATER THAN I.' I base my faith on these clear, strong words of Jesus Himself. As Luther said on a great occasion, 'Here I stand.' Henceforth it matters not to me what Paul, or Apollos, or Cephas, or 'even an angel from heaven' may say. All the Athanasiuses the world has ever known, and all the priests of Baal, of Rome, of Russia, of England—Pagan, Papal, Eastern, and Anglican—may shout until they are hoarse, 'Heretic!' and may say of me *because of this*, 'Without doubt he shall perish everlastingly.' I should remain fearless and calm. Jesus has spoken. His words are graven on my soul deeper and more indelibly than 'with an iron pen.' Wherever from high altars and priestly lips the words go forth—'In this Trinity none is afore or after another; none *is greater* or less than another; but the whole three Persons are co-eternal together, and co-equal: so that in all things, as is aforesaid, the Unity in Trinity and the Trinity in Unity is to be worshipped. *He, therefore, that will be saved must thus think of the Trinity'*—'a voice from heaven' seems simultaneously to say, 'My Father is greater than I,' and, as a sweet antidote to the anathema, there come the comforting words, 'These things I have spoken unto you, that in *me* ye *might have peace.* In the world *ye shall have tribulation :* but be of good cheer; I have overcome the world.'

Vicar. I am almost embarrassed by your earnestness, by the zeal and confidence with which you express yourself. And indeed the words you quote are emphatic and lucid; but you forget that when Jesus said, 'my Father is greater than I,' He meant in reference to His manhood—in the words of our Creed 'inferior to the Father as touching His manhood'; that, in fact, a *double* nature appertains to Christ as declared at the Council of Chalcedon, A.D. 451. The words, therefore, as quoted by you, were spoken in respect to His human nature—His *man*hood. You should remember that Jesus was the Son of Mary, as well as 'very God of very God,' and that, therefore, during His mission, He spoke sometimes as man, as in the instance you have given—where Christ asserts the Father to be 'greater' than Himself, that is, as the Creed expresses it, 'inferior to the Father as touching His manhood.'

Parishioner. I have often heard clergymen say this, but I have never met with one who could give the slightest *scriptural* authority for the statement that Christ was in the habit of speaking *in two characters*. I have heard it said of one who claimed to be His viceregent on earth—the infamous Pope Alexander VI.—that, when he was swearing and cursing in a passionate rage, and was reminded by a pious attendant of the 'holiness' of his office, he exclaimed, 'I am not swearing as Pope, but as Rodrigo Borgia,' to which came the natural inquiry, 'When Rodrigo Borgia is in Purgatory, where will the Pope be?' No, sir, this 'double nature' is the subtle invention of a later time, a sophistry to mystify, an expedient to explain the 'inexplicable'; and yet this assertion of a 'double nature,' if viewed philosophically, is a weak expedient, for its inventors seem to forget that if Christ was, as they allege, 'a perfect man,' He must have been endowed like other men with an *immortal soul;* and this being so, what became of this immortal soul when, after His resurrection, Christ assumed his Godhead? This 'double nature,' ingenious and explanatory as it may appear to unreflecting minds, practically leaves us with a mystery as profound and as paradoxical as the one it was invented on purpose to remove. Like all falsehoods, it fails to effect the object for which it was issued! It is sad to find in ecclesiastic history that enthusiasts have not seldom invented plausible stories to uphold what they deemed a holy cause, and have afterwards appeased their consciences with the delusive idea that their object or purpose justified and sanctified the means! Under this delusive belief zealots and creed-makers and creed-believers have not only spoken falsehoods, but, with greater daring, have even introduced words and sentences into the MSS. of the Gospels to sustain their aims. Whole verses, even, as I have shown, have been thus interpolated to serve 'a pious purpose': and not only have these things been done, but subtle ecclesiastics at Chalcedon availed themselves of the fanciful speculations and scholastic crudities of the platonic philosophers of Alexandria and Egypt, and invented for the 'Church' a 'double nature,' and a 'God-Man' or a 'Man-God' to sustain and explain their schemes and theosophies. Popes, like unto Alexander VI., may find it convenient to have a 'double nature,' but not so Jesus. He could say, 'Which of you convinceth me of sin? And if I say the truth, why do ye not believe me?' (John viii. 46). Of Him it could be said, in the words of the prophet Malachi, 'Saith the Lord of Hosts. My covenant was with him of life and peace; and I *gave them* to him *for the fear wherewith he feared me*, and was afraid before my name. *The law of truth was in his mouth*, and *iniquity* was not found *in his lips:* he walked with me in peace and equity, and did turn many away from iniquity' (ii. 5, 6). No, sir; sophistry and subterfuge did not belong to Jesus. At all times, and on all occasions, He uttered the simple truth; He never once claimed to *be God*, and even when simply called 'good' by a young man earnestly seeking guidance and information as to eternal life, Jesus at once exclaimed, 'Why callest thou me good? *there is none good but God.*' On another occasion, when the Jews, furious and vindictive on the subject of their descent from Abraham, were ready and anxious to destroy Him, He calmly said, 'Now ye seek to kill me, a MAN *that hath told you the truth*, which I *have heard of God: this* did not Abraham' (John viii. 40).

Vicar. As I have said before, so must I repeat now, that all these words were spoken by Jesus in His character as a man, and not as God: He had not at that time revealed Himself as God.

Parishioner. Most true, He had not at *that time* revealed Himself as *God*, nor at *any other time did He do so.* Being no impostor, but an honest man, 'a teacher sent from God,' as Nicodemus called Him, He told the people 'the truth, which he had heard from God.' He was no dissembler, but the fearless Truth-bearer and great Revealer, and in that capacity He said, 'I can of *mine own self* do nothing: as I hear, I judge: and my judgment *is just, because* I seek not *mine own will*, but the *will of the Father which hath sent me*' (John v. 30). If Christ had been the Almighty God would He have thus spoken?

Could He have so dissembled as to say '*I can of mine own self do nothing*'? Lactantius, one of the orthodox Fathers who wrote in the early part of the fourth century, states 'Christ never calls himself God.' Had He been the supreme God —'very God of very God'—had He claimed to be co-eternal and co-equal with the Highest— would He, on this occasion, have veiled His Deity —nay more, *falsified* and denied His real character by uttering the words, 'Ye seek to kill me, a *Man* that *hath told you the truth*, which I have heard of God? Could HE have thus designedly misled the Jews to their moral ruin? It is a clear impossibility! Such a wild idea as that of a 'double nature' would never occur to any educated European of this century who read the New Testament for the first time in his adult age, and whose mind in its early and plastic stage had not been saturated and moulded by the scholastic inventions of pedants and divines.

Vicar. If Christ had not been God how could He have possibly said 'That all men should honour the Son, even as they honour the Father'? (John v. 20).

Parishioner. Surely the mystic dogma of a Trinity cannot be based upon so slender a foundation as this? It is impossible that the very plain statements which I have just given from the speeches of Jesus can be nullified by the phrase which you have just quoted. Why, a corresponding incident occurs every day in the political actions of all European nations. Has not our own beloved Sovereign on more than one occasion during the current year requested that the nobility and gentry attending the Court *levées* should honour the Prince of Wales *even as* they honour her by attendance on the said ceremonials? and has she not affirmed that introductions to the Prince should *in all respects convey the same honours* and *privileges* as if they had been made to herself personally? Are not the myriads of her subjects in Hindustan and the empire of India requested 'to honour the Viceroy "*even as*" they honour the Queen?' Are not all those who attend the *levées* at Dublin Castle requested to honour the Lord Lieutenant 'even as' they honour the Queen? This is done, but the homage given and received do not make the Lord Lieutenant the King of Ireland, or the Viceroy the Emperor of Hindustan. It has according to the Epistle to the Hebrews pleased God to elevate and dignify Jesus above 'all his fellows.' The writer of that book, whether Paul or Apollos, or whoever the 'inspired' author might have been, records the fact thus: 'Thou hast loved righteousness, and hated iniquity; *therefore* GOD, even THY GOD, hath anointed thee with the oil of gladness above thy *fellows*' (Heb. i. 9). It was thus, you see, a *delegated honour*, precisely as were those honours of the Viceroy, and of the Lord Lieutenant to which I have referred, and the verse I have quoted (if there were no other in the whole range of the inspired writings) is sufficient to confute your statements and to justify me in asserting the sole and supreme Godhead of the Father, and reiterating emphatically the clear, unclouded statement of our Divine Lord: 'This is life eternal, to know thee THE ONLY TRUE GOD, and Jesus Christ, whom thou hast sent' (John xvii. 3).

Vicar. Let me remind you further that Jesus claimed to be able to forgive sins, as when He cured the sick man of the palsy; as recorded by St. Matthew, ix. 2, He said, 'Son, be of good cheer; thy sins are forgiven thee.' Surely, this is arrogating a power surpassing all mere human capacities.

Parishioner. Mr. Hierous, you astound me. 'To forgive sins!' Was not this a power possessed even by His disciples? Did He not say to them, 'Whose soever sins ye remit, they are remitted; and whose soever sins ye retain, they are retained'? (John xx. 23). Why, upon this principle, and if I am to take these words as a demonstrative proof that the person speaking them is God, is the Almighty, I should have to prostrate myself in reverence before you; for not a week since, in the cottage of Job Thresher, when visiting him in his sickness, I distinctly heard you say to him, 'I absolve thee from all thy sins.'

Vicar. But you omit the very important words that I used preceding these. I told him that 'our Lord Jesus Christ had *left power to His Church* to absolve all sinners who truly repent,' and by His authority committed to me I absolved him from all his sins.

Parishioner. Precisely so; the cases are exactly parallel; as I have already said, the power was a DELEGATED POWER; the honour claimed in the words 'even as' was a delegated honour: and as the Lord Lieutenant of Ireland and the Viceroy of India could by the authority committed to them absolve from certain political penal sins, so could Jesus 'forgive sins.' He *has Himself declared this*—declared it so emphatically that it cannot be gainsaid. It is among the marvels, it is among the stupendous facts which amaze the unsophisticated and philosophic mind, that any other idea should have been formed respecting it; and it never could have been formed by the tens of thousands who have acquiesced in it had it not been enforced by powerful authority in the ages of barbarism and ignorance by potentates in State and Church to serve their own purposes. Children were trained up to accept these inventions as truths, and this system having been carried on for generations, Error has usurped the place of Truth, and the minds of many are become so enfeebled and timid, speaking generally, that they are no more capable of investigating facts and drawing correct and logical conclusions in *matters of religion* than are domestic geese capable of flying in high air and for long distances as their ancestors did. Just as man has so modified the organizations of these creatures that they can now only waddle on the surface, instead of winging their way through the clouds, as did their remote forefathers, so has he, by early training carried on through a long series of years, so moulded the plastic minds of his children that they are now receptive of any absurdity in one special direction. Their minds have become as incapable of healthy and vigorous action in theological matters as the domestic goose in the matter of flying to high altitudes. This training and its hereditary influence carried on for ages have dwarfed the intelligence and its perceptive power, so that it can now acquiesce in the wildest phraseology and the most absurd paradox. It cannot soar into the high and clear regions of ratiocination. It 'waddles' and paddles in the muddy paradoxes of 'logomachy'; can accept the proposition that one is three, and three are one, and that Jehovah is God, Christ is God, the Holy Ghost is God, and yet that there are not three Gods, but one God! This is a curious phenomenon in psychology, more especially when there is no statement in history, there is no fact in science, placed more clearly on record than is the true nature of Jesus in the following words of His biography by His disciple John: 'But Jesus answered them, My Father worketh hitherto, and.I work. Therefore, the Jews sought the more to kill him, because he had not only broken the sabbath, but said also that God was his *Father*, making himself equal with God. *Then answered Jesus* and said unto them, VERILY, VERILY, I SAY UNTO YOU, THE SON CAN DO NOTHING OF HIMSELF, but what he seeth the Father do: for what things soever he doeth, these also doeth the Son likewise. *For the Father* loveth the Son, and *showeth him* all things that himself doeth: and *He will show him* greater works than these, that ye may marvel' (John v. 18-20). Nothing can be more plain than these words, and yet there are tens of thousands of persons who do not accept them in their integrity. To repeat a former illustration, they are become like the ducks described by Darwin, which by special environments and hereditary transmission of habits have lost the capacity of ducks, dread the water, and cannot swim. In like manner and from like causes many Christians seem incapable of accepting plain words in their plain meaning, and in 'matters of faith' have the same dread of honest research and truthful investigation (which to a natural and healthful mind are genial and pleasant) as the aforesaid ducks have of water. This fact seems to have been recognized by the Greeks long ago, for Archbishop Whately, in his first essay on the love of truth, informs us that 'the illustrious Greek historian expresses it in language which will hardly admit of an adequate translation. 'The generality of mankind are so averse to the labour of investigating truth, that they are willing rather to *adopt any statement* that is ready prepared for their acceptance.'*

Vicar. I am distressed to observe how deeply you have fallen into heresy through abandoning the authority of the Church. Not content with bringing scriptural texts in support of your opinions, you now daringly bring in the material conditions to explain personal characteristics, and give to 'circumstances' or, as you call them, 'environments,' a potentiality which is startling to listen to. I never in my life heard so bold—I may say so rash—a statement as that the reason why the mass of Christians accept the doctrine of the Blessed Trinity is that the doctrine having been handed down through many generations, and inculcated by authority on the plastic minds of children, it has become a kind of *instinct* to acquiesce in it ; and that were it not so the mind would be staggered by its incongruity, and,

---

* ''Αταλαίπωρος τοῖς πολλοῖς ἡ ζήτησις τῆς ἀληθείας, καὶ ἐπὶ τὰ ἕτοιμα μᾶλλον τρέπονται,' *p.* 34.

aided by the facts you have quoted, would expel it from the Christian Creed.

Parishioner. It may be all that you call it, but it *is nevertheless* TRUE. It is observable in other 'religions.' How otherwise can be explained the fact that for many *centuries* tens of thousands in China and elsewhere, when too poor to have a special *wheel* to themselves, make fatiguing journeys to temples where wheels are kept—'*praying wheels*'—whose every revolution is considered as a prayer, and where man's favour with Buddha or God is in exact proportion to the number of prayers he can wheel off—the prayers consisting of a shibboleth of these words, 'Aum-mi-to fuh'?* If reason had not been perverted into an 'instinct,' how could such things go on for centuries among people otherwise intelligent? I did not obtain the

* Sometimes given as O-mi-to fu. In Thibet travellers affirm that the words ' Om-Mani Padme Hrum ' are regarded as a holy mystic charm of special sacredness, and are to be found roughly carved on slabs of stones piled on high mountain-passes, or the faces of rocks, and on pillars and terraces of stones built especially for their accommodation; as also, of course, in temples and monasteries. To utter these words three hundred thousand times gives the devout Buddhist a high place in the favour of Buddha. ' Om ' is the equivalent of the Hebrew Jah; ' Mani,' the Jewel; ' Padme,' Lotus; ' Hrum,' Amen, or, So be it. The Japanese cry, ' Namu Amida Butzu,' ' Save us, O Buddha '; the Chinese as given above. Millions of Foists cry hourly, ' O-mi-to-fu.' The rosary is common to the worshippers of East and West, to the Foists and to

notion of hereditary *instinctive* ideas from the illustrious Darwin, but I was glad to have the support of so accurate and acute an observer of *facts*, who has written, 'It is worthy of remark that a belief constantly inculcated during the *early years of life, whilst the brain is impressible,* appears *to acquire almost the nature of an instinct;* and *the very essence of an instinct is that it is followed independently of reason*' ('*The Descent of Man*,' p. 100).

Vicar. It is a wicked and dreadful idea.

Parishioner. It is quite easy to apply the words 'wicked and dreadful' to anything. The entire Christian world applied them to Galileo in the seventeenth century (1634), when he said that the earth moved round the sun. He 'recanted' to save his life, but in private he was heard to mutter in his own Italian language,

the Papists; and Gordon Cumming alleges that four hundred and fifty millions of Buddhists find solace in counting such beads. Mohammedans use it also. After the funeral of a friend they cry, ' Allah el Allah!' three thousand times, and check the number by beads. Hindoos follow the example of the Buddhists, and the different sects have varying rosaries; among the very wealthy the beads are formed of various precious stones.

The *wheel* had a mystic meaning from early times. In the sixth century before Christ it formed a very prominent item in the Visions of Ezekiel, such as, 'The wheels were full of eyes round about, even the wheels that they four had. As for the wheels, it was cried in my hearing, O wheel' (Ezekiel x. 12, 13).

'*e pur si muove*' (the earth does move). They were applied to Latimer, and he was burned to death because he could not recognize and would not acknowledge that 'bread and wine' had been transformed by the utterances of a priest into the body and blood of his Redeemer. Your favourite theory of numbers of the vast majority of mankind as a test of truth was fallacious in these and countless other instances. Five names of dissentients occur to me which would counterbalance some fifty of many others. Weight is a force as well as are numbers. William Whiston, M.A., in 1728, published a series of 'Records,' in one of which he informs us that 'Sir Isaac Newton had early discovered that the old Christian faith had been changed; that what has been called Arianism is no other than old uncorrupt Christianity; and that Athanasius was the grand and very wicked instrument of that change.' The five Dissentients, then, are Sir Isaac Newton, John Milton and John Locke, Samuel Clarke, and the pious Dr. Watts, these five renowned Englishmen, renowned alike for intellectual power and moral worth, no more accepted the Nicene Creed than I do. And as a matter of 'AUTHORITY,' I would rather bow to them than to five thousand of the ordinary people who throng church and chapel, and utter phrases no more intelligible to themselves or to others than the mystic words, 'Aum-mi-to fuh,'

FALLACY OF NUMBERS.

babbled by the Buddhists of Asia, or whirled as a printed prayer by rapid gyrations of the 'praying wheels.'

Vicar. The test of numbers may not be always infallible, but, as I have already said, it is the only possible practical way of deciding disputed matters.

Parishioner. And, as I have also shown, has, on the most important occasions, *decided* them *wrongfully.* It was a very decided majority that shouted on a solemn occasion, 'Not this man, but Barabbas!' 'Now Barabbas was a robber.'

Vicar. That was certainly an unjust decision, but it was necessary to the scheme of salvation.

Parishioner. I will not believe it—you must pardon my being thus abrupt. My whole nature revolts against the supposition that, in the councils of the Eternal, it was a *necessity* that *injustice* should be perpetrated in order that God 'might be just, and the Justifier of him that believeth in Jesus' (Rom. iii. 28).

Vicar. That unfortunate axiom of the 'right of private judgment,' so much insisted on at what has been unfortunately called the 'Reformation,' is leading you into sad errors, and is imbuing you with a spirit most unfavourable to true piety. But, as your spiritual pastor, as the priest appointed to this parish, I must wrestle with your errors; and I must call back your mind from the new and *dangerous* speculations of hereditary influence.

Parishioner. Pardon me for interrupting you, but I must protest at once against the appellation 'new,' for they are not 'new,' and against their being called 'speculations,' for they are not '*speculations*,' but *facts*. As to the word 'dangerous,' it is the old cry of selfishness and ignorance when any truth new to them is brought forward which apparently clashes with their interest. It was old when, eighteen hundred years ago, Demetrius shouted as against Paul in the streets of Ephesus, 'Not only this our craft *is in danger* to be set at naught; but also that the temple of the great goddess Diana should be despised, and her magnificence should be destroyed, whom all Asia and the world worshippeth' (Acts xix. 27). It has been repeated ever since by the timid, the superstitious, and those who adhere to old habits and custom instinctively (that is, as Darwin says), 'independently of reason'; and it is especially clamoured forth when any humble individual like myself presumes to inquire into the truthfulness of any mystic 'double nature,' or Trinitarian God, or goddess, 'whom *all Asia* and the *world* worshippeth.'

Vicar. Your interruption is embarrassing, and I hope that you will give me the same patient hearing as I have always given to you, even under circumstances of considerable provocation. My thread of thought has been broken, but show me in what sense your theory is not '*new*,' and that it is not a '*speculation*,' but a fact.

Parishioner. Yes, from a source more acceptable to you than from Tyndall, or Huxley, or

Spencer, or the great and truth-loving Darwin; from no less a person than your charming Horace, whose Odes are so dear to you, that you will be surprised that the striking lines have not leaped into your memory during this discussion.

> *Fortes creantur fortibus et bonis:*
> Est in juvencis, est in equis patrum
> Virtus: neque imbellem feroces
> Progenerant aquilæ columbam.
> (*Carminum*, Lib. IV. iv.)

That statement is at least nineteen hundred years old. That young ducks, newly hatched ducks, descended from ducks of natural habits, rush into the water and swim merrily on its surface from an *inherited* impulse, even if hatched by *a hen*, who calls them in maternal terror from the dangerous element; that the said ducks do not attempt to fly, although the wild-duck, their remote ancestor, does; that young pointers who have never seen their parents 'point,' do themselves point—are *facts, and not speculations.* And that posthumous children often repeat in their own lives the *habits* of their parents whom they have never seen are also *facts*, and *not speculations;* and although the first-stated 'facts' are taken from the 'lower animals,' and not from the habits of mankind, they are not the less germane to the subject; for, as Pope has said, and it bears repeating—

> The first almighty cause
> Acts not by *partial*, but by *general* laws.

Vicar. We have dwelt too long on those 'general laws' in your desire to find a physiological explanation for what you conceive an anomaly, viz., that tens of thousands believe in a faith which has been handed down to them for ages, but from which you, in your intellectual pride, recoil. *Reason*, remember, was the 'goddess' raised to honour when France, mad with crime and blood, deserted all that was holy, and appalled the nations by her demoniac frenzy. You must place 'reason' in the secondary place, and approach the 'mystery of godliness' in the spirit of faith if you desire to profit by it. 'Verily, I say unto you, Whosoever shall not receive the kingdom of God *as a little child*, he shall not enter therein.'

Parishioner. The French Revolution of 1789, most horrible as it was, has long ceased to be a bugbear to religious inquirers, because its true origin is now well known. It has been the policy of priestly powers to descry 'Reason,' and they do so with an intensity corresponding to the unworthiness and rottenness of the system they espouse. The system MUST be a bad one that requires the prostration of the highest attribute of Man. I am glad to know of some divines, however, who take wiser and higher views of this function. Warburtom, the Bishop of this diocese in 1659—certainly one of the most able prelates the Church of England has produced—

tells us 'that the image of God in which Man was first created lay in the faculty of reason only.' Archbishop Tillotson, in one of his Sermons (Vol. III.), has said, 'he who sincerely desires to do the will of God is not apt to be imposed upon by vain pretences of Divine Revelation; but if any doctrine be proposed to him which is professed to come from God, he measures it by those sure and steady notions which he has of the divine nature and perfection.' I may add, also, that a great philosopher and defender of the Christian faith, Samuel Taylor Coleridge, in the sixteenth of his Introductory Aphorisms, writes: ' The word rational has been strangely abused of late times. This must not, however, disincline us to the weighty consideration that thoughtfulness, and a desire to bottom all our convictions on grounds of right reason are inseparable from the character of a Christian,' and in the twenty-fifth of his Religious Aphorisms, he tells us, 'He who begins by loving Christianity better than truth, will proceed by loving his own sect or Church better than Christianity, and end in loving himself better than all.' The learned Chillingworth has said: ' For my part I am certain that God has given us reason to discern between truth and falsehood: and he that makes not this use of it, but believes things he knows not why, I say that it is by chance that he believes the truth, and not by choice; and that I cannot but fear that God will not accept the homage of fools.' Moreover, on this topic, I can quote the words of one whom you reverence, and whose orthodoxy you, at least, will not question. William Ewart Gladstone, in his controversy with the Vatican, said: 'Authority can only be defended by *reason*; it is a part of what reason sanctions and recommends. But there is no escape from this; it must be *tried by reason*, as even the being of God—with reverence be it spoken—must be tried by reason, tried by reason under a great responsibility, but under no coercion, either physical or moral.' Moreover, the great Bishop Butler has told us: 'By reason is revealed the relation which God the Father stands in to us'; again, 'Reason is the only faculty whereby we have to judge of anything, even revelation itself.' And in his essay on the *Importance of Christianity*, p. 177, he writes: 'Indeed, if in revelation there be found any passages the seeming meaning of which is contrary to natural religion, we may most certainly conclude such seeming meaning not to be the real one.'

Vicar. I revere Coleridge, Gladstone, and Butler; but a greater than Coleridge or Gladstone or Butler in a divine sense, even St. Paul himself, has said, 'The world by *wisdom* knew not God.'

Parishioner. And St. Paul enunciated an historical truth in that statement. The 'σοφος,' the wisdom, or the philosophy of the Greek schools; the quibbles of the Jewish Rabbis; the disputers of the age ('σαξητητης'), the Stoics, Epicureans, and other disciples of special schools of philosophy had failed to reach the knowledge of God: yet, nevertheless, is the Reason the ultimate test of what is, and what is not spiritual; and to this faculty St. Paul appealed to the lovers of disputation, 'the disputers of the age,' in the Areopagus and elsewhere, and for the exercise of this special faculty he praised the Bereans. The Prophets of the older time censured the priests for their ignorance. The mournful words of censure uttered by Hosea occur to me. 'My people are destroyed for lack of knowledge; because thou hast rejected knowledge, I will also reject thee, that thou shalt be no priest to me' (iv. 6). And Solomon, who 'was wiser than all men,' has written: 'Fools despise wisdom'; but a greater than Paul, and a wiser than Solomon, even Christ Himself, has commanded—'Be ye wise as serpents' (Matthew x. 16). Still, without stopping to determine whether 'wisdom' and 'reason' mean the same, I repeat that reason, illumined by the Spirit of God, is man's sole guiding star amid the perplexities of the Churches and Creeds of Christendom.

Vicar. I hold, on the contrary, that God has

appointed His Church to be the interpreter of His Word, and that it becomes you and me to bow to her authority.

Parishioner. Ah, me! That, I am sorry to say, is a dogma most pleasing to the mass of mankind: for, strange as it may seem, the reason-endowed man is reluctant to exercise habitually this his highest and special faculty, and willingly accepts the dogmas of others of seeming authority. So much is this so, that Coleridge, in his day, wrote: 'The indisposition, nay the angry aversion, *to think* .... is the phenomenon that forces itself on my notice afresh every time I enter into the society of persons in the highest ranks' (*Aids to Reflection*, p. 3). And this is especially so, as I have already said, in religious matters. Even John Milton has told us, 'A man may be a heretic in the truth; and if he believe things only because his pastor says so, or the assembly so determines, without knowing other reasons, though his belief be true, yet the very truth he holds becomes his heresy. There is not any burden that some would gladlier post off to another than the charge and care of their religion. There be (who knows not that there be?) of Protestants and professors who live and die in as errant and implicit faith as any lay Papist of Loretto."* Moreover, had there been but one Church and, therefore, one authority, what you

* *Areopagitica*, p. 85, Milton's Works, Vol. II. Bohn's Edition.

have said may have carried weight; but as there are two Churches on the Continent and one in this island, that is, the Western, the Eastern, and the Anglican, issuing conflicting decrees, the honest man has still to call in his individual reason to decide between their respective claims.

Vicar. We have made a considerable *excursus* from your last-quoted text, in which you endeavoured to prove the humanity of Christ, to the loss of His Godhead; but that Christ was superhuman was proved by the fact that He had no human father, and by the circumstance that this miracle was distinctly and unequivocally foretold by Isaiah some seven hundred years before, viz., 'A virgin should conceive, and bring forth a son, and that his name should be called Immanuel.'

Parishioner. I have not, as yet, stated that Jesus was not 'superhuman,' and was simply 'co-equal' with all men; on the contrary, I have quoted a text to show 'that *God*, even his *own God*,' had 'anointed him with gladness *above* his fellows'; but this is at an ineffable distance from showing that He was 'co-equal' and 'co-eternal' and 'co-almighty' with God.

Vicar. It shows Him to be the Son of God, with whom, we are assured, 'God was well pleased.'

Parishioner. This has never been in dispute between us : what I maintain is, that there is no fact and no statement in the whole range of well-authenticated Scripture which would justify you in calling Him 'God the Son.'

Vicar. Yes; the text quoted by me from Isaiah, to the effect that the Child of the Virgin should be called 'Immanuel,' 'which being interpreted is God with us.'

Parishioner. I am not concerned at this moment to discuss the facts in relation to the miraculous incidents which, according to St. Matthew, preceded and accompanied the birth of Jesus. All that I desire to say now is that the circumstance of the Child being called 'Emmanuel' as a *name* is by no means equivalent to the declaration that he was *God;* for among the Jews it was not an uncommon thing to give their children names which should associate them with the God of Abraham, of Isaac, and of Jacob. Thus we have 'Elizabeth,' 'which being interpreted' is 'the oath of God'; 'Elijah,' 'which being interpreted' is 'my God is Jehovah'; 'Elidad,' 'which being interpreted' is 'whom God loves,' and so on, with a number of names like unto Elisha, Elkanah, Elihu, and others. In connection with what you have said, it appears to me a most astonishing circumstance that in neither of the *synoptic* gospels is the name 'Emmanuel' applied to Christ, and equally astonishing is the fact that the angel which appeared to Joseph, and the angel also who came to Mary, directed that He should be called by a very different name than 'Emmanuel,' Jesus; and more extraordinary still that Matthew himself, leaving the prophetic record, and becoming the historian of the circumstances, writes of Joseph, that when his first-born Son was brought forth 'he called his name' (not Emmanuel, but) 'Jesus.'

Vicar. You pass by the stupendous fact, the holy mystery of the incarnation. You omitted the circumstance which preceded and gave all significance to the request that the Child should be called 'Emmanuel'—namely, that the Prophet said, 'A virgin should conceive and bear a Son.'

Parishioner. I intentionally avoided it, as I did not wish to introduce matters affecting the credibility of St. Matthew's gospel. It is well known that the word 'Virgin' in the Hebrew language, and as used by Isaiah, does not convey the same meaning as it does to us. Moreover, good Hebrew scholars have maintained that the article 'the,' and not 'a,' should have been prefixed to 'virgin'; and instead of the future, the present tense should have been used, and the sentence translated into English thus—'A virgin is with child and beareth a Son.' The context proves that the Prophet had no far-distant events in his mind, and that his 'prophecies' had a direct and immediate relation to Ahaz, to the kings of Samaria and Syria, and to the formidable King of Assyria. In many so-called 'Messianic' prophecies, there is traceable in the interpreters a disposition so to manipulate the Hebrew text as to make it conformable to after-events. To specify one instance: in our version of the second Psalm the words are 'Kiss the Son,' whereas in the Septuagint, received as the authority by the Greek Church, the words are 'Δράξασθε παιδείας'— 'Lay hold of instruction'; and even in our New Testament translation, we find the same tendency to exaggerate in this direction, for most assuredly the Greek words, ' " Πνεῦμα ἅγιον επελεύσεται ἐπὶ σὲ," καὶ δύναμις ὑψίστου επισκιασει σοι,' do not critically admit of the words, 'The Holy Ghost shall come upon thee.' There is no article prefixed to 'Πνεῦμα,' and nothing more can *honestly* be made of the five first words than 'a holy breath shall come to you.' It cannot be regarded otherwise than as a singular fact that none of Christ's disciples appear to have been aware of the 'miraculous conception.' St. John, referring to the early mission of Jesus, writes: 'Philip findeth Nathaniel, and saith unto him, We have found him of whom Moses in the law and the prophets did write, Jesus of Nazareth, the son of Joseph.' It is equally surprising that St. Paul never once in all his energetic epistles to Rome, Corinth, Ephesus, Galatia, and Thessalonica, refers to the miracle, although it would have been useful to him, probably at Mars Hill in Athens, as being in harmony with much of Greek mythology ; and the Jews might have welcomed it as an analogous incident to that which raised the name of 'Sarai' to 'Sarah.' Moreover, His 'brethren' and the townsmen of Nazareth appear unconscious of the stupendous miracle. There are several curious anomalies in relation to it, for even St. Matthew, who with Luke records the incident, writes thus naïvely on another occasion, respecting Jesus, 'When he was come *into his own country*, he taught them in their synagogue, insomuch that they were astonished, and said, Whence hath *this man* this wisdom, and these mighty works? Is not this the carpenter's son? is not his mother called Mary? and his brethren, James, and Joses, and Simon, and Judas? And his sisters, are they not all with us? Where, then, hath this man all these things? And they were offended in him. But Jesus said unto them, A prophet is not without honour save in his own country, AND IN HIS OWN HOUSE' (Matthew xiii. 54-57). In this narrative there is not the slightest indication that the writer was conscious of the supernatural circumstances attending the birth of Him whose wisdom and mighty works 'filled the minds of his townsmen and neighbours with wonder and astonishment. Is it not, moreover, remarkable that in no instance, when taunted by the Jews of His humble birth, did Jesus assert His celestial origin? On a memorable occasion, when the Jews inquired, 'Is not this the son of Joseph, whose father and mother we know? how is it, then, that he saith, I came down from heaven'? Jesus vouchsafed no information to them of the alleged historic fact of His supernatural birth, but told them, 'Murmur not among yourselves' (John vi. 42-43), and spoke to them metaphorically respecting His mission, His relationship to the Father and to mankind as their Teacher and their Saviour. Still more embarrassing, in an historical sense, is the fact that Luke, who alone of the Evangelists gives the details of this miraculous event, when describing their first visit to the Temple, says, when 'the parents,' and again, 'his parents,' 'γονεῖς' (Luke ii. 21), went to Jerusalem every year.' *Both* parents, Joseph and *His mother marvelled* at these things, which Simeon, in prophetic vision, spoke of 'the child Jesus'; again, when they had found Him after His sojourn in the Temple, His mother said unto Him 'Son, why hast thou thus dealt with us? behold *thy father* and I have sought thee sorrowing,' and when the young Christ said, 'Wist ye not that I must be about my father's business?' 'they' (neither father nor mother) 'understood not the saying which He spake unto them' (Luke ii. 50); and, still further on in His ministry, when large numbers had joined Him, and He had chosen His twelve disciples, the Evangelist Mark tells us that 'when his friends heard of it, they went out to lay hold on him, for they said "He is beside himself,"' and John informs us 'neither did his brethren believe in him' (vii. 5), so that it is evident that the Angel's announcement of the 'Miraculous Conception' had been kept a secret, and was wholly unknown to 'James, and Joses, and Simon, and Judas' (Matt. xiii. 55). No one reading the description of St. Matthew by itself in reference to the Prophet in his own country, and in his own house, could believe that the historian was himself aware 'whence' and wherefore the power and the wisdom came. St. Matthew gives no indication that he himself knew 'Where, then, hath this man all these things'? He does not seem conscious that the Teacher was *not* 'the carpenter's Son'; moreover, the incident is not in harmony with the historic genealogy which Matthew gives of Jesus, who traces His descent from David, through *Joseph*, and not through the lineage of Mary. The annunciation resembles those angelic communications in the Old Testament which related to extraordinary births in this, that the angel commanded that the child be called Jesus, as the respective angels who visited Hagar and Sarai commanded special names to be given to the children who were promised; and as the angel who appeared to the barren wife of Manoah declared that the child to be born should 'deliver Israel out of the hand of the Philistines,' so was Jesus to 'save his people from their sins.'

Vicar. There is a dangerous tone in all that you have just said to me. It certainly implies that St. Matthew is not trustworthy so far as the supernatural facts are concerned, and that you are inclined to regard St. Mark and St. John as the more historic, and that the narrative of the first Gospel has been tampered with or added to by the legendary fancies of a later time. I do hope that this is not so. I have been particularly struck—nay, I might truly say that I have been pained—by your implying that Matthew had strained the facts to accommodate them to *prophecy;* that in doing so he had mistaken the meaning of the word 'virgin'; and that all in connection therewith may be regarded as a myth.

Parishioner. I will not disguise from you, my dear Vicar, that such thoughts *have* crossed my mind (although I purposely withheld them from our discussion), for I cannot forget that what we call the 'Inspired Word' has, in the progress of time, been wickedly tampered with; while errors innumerable have crept in undesignedly, in the process of copying one MS. from another, mistakes from marginal notes, from imperfect writing, from defects of hearing when writing from dictation, and many other well-known causes. Hundreds of such errors have been too slight practically to affect historic truth, or influence dogma, as have these which appear to have been inserted wickedly, with a 'pious purpose,' such as the statement which you, reluctantly, have admitted to be an interpolation, namely, the words imputed to St. John, 'There are three that bear record in heaven, the Father, the Son, and the Holy Ghost, and these three are one.' It is universally admitted (I believe) by scholars, that these words were not written in the original Epistle, and I am convinced that they were fraudulently inserted, at a late date, to support the Church's dogmatic theory of the Trinity. This being so, I frankly admit that I am sometimes disposed to think with Sir Isaac Newton, that 'the time will come when the doctrine of the Incarnation, as commonly received, shall be exploded as an absurdity equal to transubstantiation.'*

Vicar. How is it possible that such an irreverent, such a wicked doubt could have been suffered to dwell in your mind? I say *dwell*, because transient doubts, possibly suggested by the powers of darkness, will occasionally intrude upon our souls; but, unfortunately, you now say, 'I *am* suspicious.'

Parishioner. I say so because the narrative partakes so largely of the character of the legendary myths of the widespread 'religions' which you and I regard as false. I will mention only a few. In the vast empire of China it is universally

* A *Cordial for Low Spirits.* Being a collection of curious Tracts. London, 1763. P. xxiii.

alleged and universally believed of the birth of Fohi, or Fow, that three nymphs descended from heaven to bathe, that a lotus-plant adhered to one, and that thus she became pregnant and gave birth to a son, who became the founder of a religion, and a law-giver. The birth of one person is said to be the result of a *virgin* having haunted a forest expecting the advent of a god long predicted, and that she became pregnant by the sunbeams; and the great, almost unpronounceable, Huitzilipoehtle in Mexico was born of a woman who caught in her bosom a featherball which descended from heaven; and Ellis, in his *Polynesian Researches* (good missionary as he was), published in 1829, gives one or two most beautiful legends of a like kind. One is especially striking, namely, that Taaroa, the creator of the earth, sent forth *Oro* to be *the medium between celestial and terrestrial things.* Now, the birth of Oro was in this wise: the *shadow* of a bread-fruit leaf, shaken by the power of the arm of Taaroa, passed over Hina (as we read in St. Luke of Mary—' the power of the Highest shall *overshadow* thee '), and she afterwards became the mother of Oro. Hina, it is said, abode in Opoa at the time of his birth; hence Opoa was honoured as the place of his nativity, and became celebrated for his worship (p. 194, vol. ii.). The parallel is so striking that Hina certainly suggests Mary, and the village of Opoa brings to mind the village of Bethlehem, which the angel called the City of David.

Vicar. Is it not more than probable that these islanders have confused a true narration which centuries ago may have reached them through some travellers; and that this historical truth became converted into legend, and subsequently, by continuous tradition and fancy, became a 'myth'; imagination or poetry substituting the beautiful bread-fruit tree with which they are so familiar, and the shadow of its leaf shaken by the arm of Taaroa, for the sober facts of the Gospel narrative?

Parishioner. I do not think it probable that those beautiful islands of the Southern Seas were ever visited by Europeans until the discovery of Captain Cook in 1778; and even admitting the possibility of such a visit, I think it still more impossible that such visitors knew the language of the Sandwich Islanders, or that the Sandwich Islanders knew theirs. That the marvellous story of St. Matthew should have been treasured up by these simple idolaters through the rolling centuries passes belief. But that the facts of sober history *do* get transformed, magnified, and blended into the mystic legends of fancy, has been abundantly proved. Uncultured people, and these constitute the vast majority of mankind, love 'myths,' and upon them have based their 'religions.' 'Immaculate Conception,' or its equivalent, humanity springing directly from Divinity, was a tenet of Paganism thousands of years before it was enunciated as a dogma of Catholic faith. Some Egyptian legends give the birth history of Epaphus or Apis, who is said to have been born of a Virgin Mother by the breathing of Dyans. Indeed, the 'air,' the 'wind,' 'the breath' are closely associated with the genesis of all things in ancient or pagan religions. Virgil, in the third book of his Georgics, tells us that sometimes mares became impregnated by the gales of Spring—

> Et sæpe sine ullis
> Conjugiis, vento gravidæ (mirabile dictu).
> (*Line* 275.)

Parthenogenesis was imagined by poets, and engrafted in mythology, long before it became recognized in the teachings of botanical or biological science; and it was a popular belief among classic pagans that extraordinary men had a Divine origin. Even one of the great Fathers of the very early Church, Justin Martyr, in the twenty-second chapter of his first Apology to the Roman Emperor, in respect to this matter writes, 'If we even affirm that he was born of a Virgin, accept this in common with what you accept of Perseus.' And a later Father, Jerome, could write of Plato thus, '*Sapientiæ principem non aliter arbitrandum, nisi de partû virginis editum.** This birth of Plato from a virgin, according to the legend, resembles much the narrative of St. Matthew. His father on his marriage was warned by Apollo, in a dream, that his wife Perictonia was with child, but that the babe was of Divine conception, and that he must live apart from her until the child had been born. All these facts show that the world, through 'wisdom,' knew not God. The 'philosophy' of Zeno, and of Epicurus, alike failed to teach that 'God is a Spirit,' with all its ennobling consequences, as Christ taught us, and until illumined by the inspiration of God, men built, and build, their 'religion' upon myths and fables as baseless as the story of Venus springing from the spray of the sea or of Saturn devouring his children. There have been writers who have endeavoured to explain all the mysteries of the Gospel histories by 'myths,' and their transformations. The German writer, David Strauss, has written ably with this object, and followed as he has been, on somewhat similar lines, by the brilliant writer and learned Oriental scholar, E. Renan, their writings combined have done more injury to the popular Christian Creed on the Continent than have the writings of the 'scientists' and 'biologists' to the popular biblical

* *Apologia des L. I.*, s. 92.

story of the Creation, in this country. But neither the critical German, nor the French *savant*, nor the English 'scientists,' nor all combined, have done so much to disturb men's faith, and to create distrust, as the extravagant statements of the Church herself, and the audacity with which her most zealous servants have declared that those who cannot accept her statements 'shall *without doubt* perish everlastingly.'

Vicar. I am ignorant of the writings of the persons to whom you refer. I have heard of them from time to time, but, knowing from the writings of Jude that there 'should be mockers in the last time,' I have most scrupulously and conscientiously avoided them. I wish that you had been equally prudent, for I fear greatly that you have read them, and that they have influenced your opinions. Let me beg of you to read the Epistle of Jude at your earliest possible opportunity. Ponder on its solemn prophecy, and the doom which will befall the unbelievers, on these unhappy beings who deny 'the only Lord God, and our Lord Jesus Christ.' I will see you again shortly, but I cannot parley longer. Important duties call me hence; moreover, the sun is going down, and a storm seems impending.

Parishioner. Farewell, and many thanks for your time and attention. Still, let me ask you to remember that I did not open the discussion, but have been all along on the defensive, giving my humble reasons *why* I have hitherto been unable to accept your pastoral invitation to the most Holy Communion. Please accept my little flower; it is very rare in this neighbourhood. I shall look forward for your promised visit most anxiously. Good-bye.

PAROCHIAL PARLEYS.

INTERVIEW THE SECOND.

Rev. H. Hierous. Good morning. I hope that I am not calling at an inconvenient time. I perceive you are surrounded with books and engravings; you are always busy, and seem to enjoy life quite as much as many young men. My neighbour Thompson tells me that you were quite enthusiastic last night, at the Anniversary Meeting of the Mechanics' Institute, positively fervid in your speech, not as [according to Horace] one might have anticipated,

" Laudator temporis acti
Se puero, censor castigatorque minorum ";

but in praise of the present time in contrast with the past, and sketching a still brighter future for the rising generation. I was very glad to hear it, because, as you were so hopeful, I trust that, since I saw you, you may have discovered some mitigating circumstances in the present scepticism which both of us were deploring, and which had been prophesied in such dark colours by the Apostle Jude, to whose Epistle I drew your most serious attention.

Mr. Truman. I thank you very much for your kindly wish. 'The lines have indeed fallen unto me in pleasant places,' and, thanks to a merciful Providence, I can also say with Adam, the old servant, whom Shakespeare has so well drawn in his play *As You Like It*—

> In my youth I never did apply
> Hot and rebellious liquors in my blood;
> Nor did not with unbashful forehead woo
> The means of weakness and debility;
> Therefore my age is as a lusty winter,
> Frosty but kindly.

As to my enthusiasm of yesternight, it was perhaps too jubilant through the joy the retrospect furnished, and the contagiousness of the happiness around me. There *is*, however, one solemn, solid fact which weighs upon my mind, otherwise the material prosperity and progress of the productive and middle classes would be exhilarating in the extreme. That fact is a ballast to buoyancy of feeling. There is among the aristocracy, or rather, I ought to have said in the wealthy or 'plutocratic' classes of the country, a moral hebetude, a flabby faith either in good or evil, a 'want of heart,' a cultured passivity, a stoic apathy to holy or spiritual things in their essence [although conforming conventionally to æsthetic or sensuous forms of worship] from which I fear much, as being the 'little rift' leading to great mischief. Were it not for this stoic selfishness, so general in what is called 'Society,' the beneficial changes which have taken place in England within my remembrance, would prompt me to believe in the realization of the golden age which has been sung by poets from the days of Isaiah to those of Browning and Tennyson. Even with this deep shadow resting upon the surface, the advancing years are ever filling me with wonder. The discoveries and inventions of science, and of mechanical skill, and the economic results which have followed in their train, are simply astounding. Distance has been practically diminished fifty-fold. Verbal communication is so quickly obtained from shore to shore of the widest sea, that the fiction which Shakespeare had assigned to Puck in the *Midsummer Night's Dream*—

> I'll put a girdle round about the earth
> In forty minutes—

has become a reality, and this rapid transit of thought and wish accompanied, as it has been, by a corresponding development in the speed and carrying power of vessels and carriages by sea and land ; by a better knowledge of geography and navigation, and by the repeal of unwise fiscal laws, has effected marvels in the physical development and external surroundings of all the working classes. The 'penny postage' for letters has in itself effected marvels in the education of the people, in strengthening domestic moral ties, and adding to the wealth and convenience of Society. The younger recipients of these advantages accept as a matter of course the things which fill the mind of the septuagenarian with wonder. Utility and beauty have gone hand in hand, progress pervades all things, and the aged man is impressed accordingly; whether he recalls the clumsy flint and steel and tinder box of his earlier time, as he takes up a box of Bryant and May's 'safety matches,' or makes a comparison of the good things which one penny can now secure in all directions, and contrasts it with the little it could obtain some fifty years ago. The contrast is great and wide-spreading, from a box of lucifer matches, up to a high-class newspaper bringing authentic intelligence daily from all the capitals of Europe, as does *The Daily Telegraph*. And nowhere does such a mind behold a greater change than in the homes, in the dress, in the food, and in the manners of the people in agricultural towns and villages, 'agricultural depression' notwithstanding. Whether it be that a class by necessity accustomed to extreme thrift and prudence, was the earliest to avail itself of the results of cheap production and ready transit, I cannot determine, but most certainly the change for the better has surpassed the expectations of the most sanguine, not only at the close of the French War in 1815, but even at the passing of the Reform Act in 1832. Many cottages, I might almost have said most cottages, possess a flower in the window, or a picture on the wall; and a large number of these cottages, once with walls quite bare, or glaring with the cold glare of whitewash, are now bright and cheery with coloured papering; and, as I have said, the dress of the agricultural labouring classes at holiday time represent a corresponding increase in taste and comfort. It makes the closing days of my life bright as a summer sunset, to know and observe these things. Miracles will never cease to those who have eyes to see or ears to hear. Science has a 'wonderland' as rich, and far more useful, than was ever conjured up by the wand of a fairy. It might be said, almost without metaphor, that the lightning and the sunshine are practically made to illumine our rooms, and then to adorn our walls and our portfolios with pictures. What will not a few shillings now procure in the way of art production? Look at the beautiful prints now before me, which have given me such pleasure as to call up my retrospect. Look at this fine autotype of the graceful 'Madonna del Sisto,' by Rafaelle; at this accurate transcript in form and texture of the 'Doge Leonardo

Landreno,' by Bellini; and of this sweet and touching 'Pieta,' by Francia. Would not the great masters and teachers of taste in the past generation, men like Archibald Alison, Payne Knight, or Samuel Rogers have been astonished to see such exquisite productions gracing the homes of country surgeons and ill-paid curates? In all the facts I have narrated I seem to see not only one of the factors of the changes which have crept, and are creeping into the Ritualism of our churches; and of the love of the rising generation for graceful robes, the 'pealing organ,' rich flowers, light and colour, even while it possesses no clear vivid realization of what the service is intended to signify, or has but a very dim sense of that which the æsthetic symbolism professes to unfold. I feel assured also, that the perplexing creeds and the coarse and revolting theology which have in the past caused so many to abandon religion, even to the fearful extent of denying the existence of God, will be blotted out, or rather will be absorbed, as darkness by sunshine, in the prosperity and culture which are springing up around us. The 'sweetness and light' which have for a time obscured the sense of reverence and of faith in the soul by causing it to recoil from the horrors of a vindictive God, and of a material burning hell of everlasting torment, will, in its secondary and more continuous action, reveal to the soul the permanent presence of One, of whom all purity, and all sweetness, and all light are but emanations. These, and such like thoughts, as I have stated in our former interview, sustain one's faith during the transient mists of darkness, and give a 'silver lining' even to the prophecy of Jude, which I had quoted at our former interview, but have re-read under your counsel. The contents of the Epistle are impressed on my memory, and in common with the statements of Paul and Peter, and James and John, have tended to overthrow and dissipate my early faith in that awful creed upon which we conversed so long last week.

Vicar. How is that possible? I had relied on its startling statements to check you in your downward way and to bring you back into the paths of truth.

Parishioner. I am glad, my dear Pastor, that the reserve of mere courtesy has been set aside between us. The subject we are discussing is too solemn, too momentous, for etiquette. You have from time to time spoken with warmth, and I must plead guilty of having overlooked in some moments our respective positions. My path may —nay *must*—appear to you *downward*, and your solemn oaths and your naturally kind disposition would alike make you desirous to bring one 'who had erred and was deceived' back again 'into the path of truth.' But I *feel* that my progress is not 'downward,' but *upward*, and that I *am* 'in the path of truth.' Still more am I confident that I am further removed even than yourself from the condition of those whom Jude has described with such graphic power; inasmuch as those upon whom he poured forth his indignation were those who were 'denying the ONLY Lord *God*' AND 'our *Lord* Jesus Christ'; and all my feeble efforts are devoted to affirming instead of denying 'the ONLY Lord GOD,' and to recalling the solemn asseverations of Jehovah (as recorded by Isaiah)—'there is *no God* else beside me; a just God,' and 'there is none beside me. Look unto *me*, and be ye saved, all the ends of the earth: for I am *God*, and there is *none else*' (Isaiah xlv. 21, 22).

Vicar. These words were spoken under the Old Dispensation, before 'the fulness of time' had come, *i.e.*, before the 'appearing of our Saviour Jesus Christ, who hath abolished death, and hath brought life and immortality to light through the Gospel' (2 Timothy i. 10). And you seem to forget that, while the Creed states that Christ is God, yet it states also that there is 'not three Gods, but one God'; and that Christ *was* God, is distinctly proved by two great facts: He raised the dead, and He was distinctly seen to 'ascend into heaven.' Surely you do not mean to assert that a *man* could raise the dead, and be seen bodily to ascend into heaven?

Parishioner. Personally, I should not dare to assert anything so contrary to all modern experience. But, most certainly, the Scriptures, which you hold to be verbally and in their entirety the inspired and infallible Word of God, tell us of *men* who have raised others from the grave, and also of a man who, with great pomp, visibly ascended into the heavens. Moreover, as regards the power of raising the dead, they tell us that even the *dead bones* of a man sufficed to do this; for we read: 'they were burying a man . . . they cast the man into the sepulchre of Elisha: and when the man was let down, and *touched the bones* of Elisha, he revived, and stood up on his feet' (2 Kings xiii. 21). One is not surprised that the holy prophet, whose dead bones effected such a miracle, had previously raised to life again the dead child of a Shunammite woman (2 Kings iv. 34, 35). As to the ascension into heaven, Marks tells us of our Lord that after He had spoken unto His disciples 'he was *received* up into heaven.' Luke tells us that 'he was parted from them, and carried up into heaven.' Now, in neither of these accounts— and they are *all* we possess from the Evangelists themselves—is there that distinctiveness, that absolute freedom from all possible optical illusion, that explicit clearness of detail, which marked the ascension of One whom, I think, you will not claim to have been God. Mark tells that Jesus was received up into heaven. May that not be said of any true Christian dying in the faith? St. Luke tells us 'that he was carried up to heaven.' This is a more striking statement than that of Mark, but it has not the detail or the splendour of description which has been given us of the ascension of Elijah, of whom we read : 'And it came to pass, as they still went on and talked, that, behold, there appeared a *chariot of fire*, and *horses of fire*, and parted them both asunder, and Elijah went up by a whirlwind into heaven' (2 Kings ii. 11). So that we have in these records instances of the dead being raised by men. Moreover, in your eager desire to establish the Divinity of Jesus, you have not only overlooked these remarkable incidents in the history of Elijah, but have also forgotten for a time the fact that Peter raised Tabitha from the dead ; that Paul performed a like act on the person of the young man Eutychus at Macedonia, who went into a deep sleep while Paul was 'long preaching,' and 'fell down from the third loft, and was taken up dead.' Thus, neither the circumstance of the ascension nor the raising of the dead to life again suffices so to mark off Jesus from all other prophets and saints of God as to justify us in addressing Him as 'very God of very God.' And, moreover, even apart from this circumstance, we have, as I have again and again shown, the distinct and unmistakable words of Jesus Himself—'the Son *can do nothing* of *himself*, for, as the *Father hath life in himself*, so *hath he given to the Son to have life in himself*'; and St. Paul is emphatic in his testimony to the Romans, to the effect that, 'if thou shalt confess with thy mouth *the Lord Jesus*, and shalt *believe in thine heart that God hath raised him* from the dead, thou shalt be saved.' How consolatory is such a clear apostolical statement as this to one who, like myself, has been awed by the maledictions of 'the Church'; who, for long, distrusted his 'private judgment' because of the thousands who *appeared* to acquiesce in the creed which, in that 'judgment,' appeared contrary to the Scriptures and to common sense! Before I *knew* that the said thousands were apathetic, passive, and uninquiring as to religious theories and dogmas, such a clear, lucid text was a consolation and support. To *all* the Churches St. Paul has spoken with equal plainness.

To the Romans

he writes, '*I thank my God*, through Jesus Christ, for you all' (Rom. i. 8).

'To God only wise, be glory through Jesus Christ for ever' (Rom. xvi. 27).

'Much more did the *grace of God*, and the gift by the *grace of the one man* Jesus Christ abound unto the many' (Rom. v. 15).

To the Church at Corinth.

'But I would have you know, that the head of every man is Christ; and the head of the woman is the man, and *the head of Christ is God*' (1 Cor. xi. 3).

'All are yours ; and ye are Christ's, and Christ is God's' (1 Cor. iii. 22, 23).

'And when all things shall be subdued unto him, then shall the Son also himself be subject *unto him* that put *all things under him, that God may be all in all*' (1 Cor. xv. 28).

To the Church in Galatia.

'Paul an apostle (not from men, neither through man, but through Jesus Christ, and *God the Father* who raised him from the dead' (Gal. i. 1).

To the Church at Ephesus.

'Blessed be *the God*, and Father of our Lord Jesus Christ, who hath blessed us with every spiritual blessing' (Eph. i. 3).

'One Lord, one faith, one baptism, *One God* and Father of all, who *is above all*, and through all, and in you all' (Eph. iv. 5, 6).

To the Philippians.

'And *my God* shall fufill every need of yours according to his riches in glory in Christ Jesus. Now unto *our God and Father* be the glory for ever and ever. Amen' (Phil. iv. 20).

To the Colossians.

'Grace to you, and peace *from God* our Father, we give thanks to God the Father of our Lord Jesus Christ, praying always for you, having heard of your faith in Christ Jesus' (Col. i. 2, 3).

'And he is the head of the body, the church: who is the beginning, the firstborn from the dead; that in all things he might have pre-eminence. For it *was the good pleasure of the Father*, that *in him* should all fulness dwell' (Col. i. 18, 19).

To the Thessalonians.

'Unto the church of the Thessalonians which is in *God* the Father, and in the *Lord* Jesus Christ. Grace be unto you, and peace from *God* our Father, *and the Lord* Jesus Christ' (1 Thess. i. 1).

'For *God* appointed us not unto wrath, but unto the obtaining of salvation through *our Lord* Jesus Christ, who died for us,

RAISING THE DEAD. 181

that whether we wake or sleep, we should live together with him' (1 Thess. v. 9).

' So then, brethren, stand fast, and hold the traditions which ye were taught, whether by word, or by epistle of ours. Now, our *Lord* Jesus Christ himself, and *God our Father* which loved us, and gave us eternal comfort and good hope through grace, comfort your hearts and stablish them in every good work and word' (1 Thess. ii. 15, 16).

' And we have confidence in the Lord touching you, that ye both do and will do the things which we command. And the *Lord* direct your hearts *into the love of God*, and into the patience of Christ' (2 Thess. iii. 5, 6).

To Timothy.

' Paul an apostle of Christ Jesus, according to the commandment of *God our Saviour, and* Christ Jesus our hope ; unto Timothy my true child in faith : Grace, mercy, peace *from God the Father and Christ Jesus our Lord*' (1 Tim. i. 1).

' For there is *one God*, one mediator also between God and men, himself man, Christ Jesus, who gave himself a ransom for all' (1 Tim. ii. 5).

' Now unto the King, eternal, incorruptible, invisible, *the only God*, be honour and glory for ever and ever. Amen' (1 Tim. i. 17).

' I charge thee in the *sight of God, and Christ Jesus, and* the elect angels, that thou observe these things without prejudice, doing nothing by partiality' (1 Tim. v. 21).

To Titus and to Philemon he makes salutations, as in my last quotation from the Epistle to Timothy. Paul preserves the individualities of 'God, Christ Jesus, and the elect Angels'; so, to Titus and to Philemon does he distinctly mark off the respective distinctions of ' *God* the Father, and the *Lord* Jesus Christ ' : and, the unknown author of the Epistle to the Hebrews, received by the Church as ' canonical,' or divinely inspired, keeps visibly before the Hebrews the supremacy of the 'first Person,' and writes, 'Now the *God* of peace who brought again from the dead our *Lord* Jesus, that great shepherd of the sheep, through the blood of the everlasting covenant, make you perfect in every good work to do his will, working in you that which is wellpleasing in his sight, through Jesus Christ ; to whom be glory for ever and ever. Amen' (xiii. 20, 21). The stately and steadfast Apostle James, also defines himself as a 'servant of *God*, and of the Lord Jesus Christ,' and writes, 'Thou believest that *God is one;* thou doest well'; he implores the twelve tribes' not to hold 'the faith of our Lord Jesus Christ in respect of persons,' and describes clearly the religion which is pure and undefiled 'before our God and Father,' and that every 'good gift and every perfect boon' cometh from 'the Father of lights, with whom can be no variation, neither shadow that is cast by turning' (i. 17). Peter in his epistles, equally with Paul, observes the same principle, and all whom he addresses are reminded of 'the foreknowledge of *God the Father*, in sanctification of the Spirit, unto obedience and sprinkling of the blood of Jesus Christ' : as Jesus Himself assured Mary in the garden, that He was about to ascend 'unto my Father and your Father, and to *my God* and *your God*,' so does Peter keep vividly before the recipients of his Epistle, that

'Blessed be the God and Father of our Lord Jesus Christ, who, according to his great mercy, begat us again unto a living hope by the resurrection of Jesus Christ,' and calls upon them, that 'like as he which called you is holy, be ye yourselves also holy in all manner of living,' reminding them that they 'were redeemed not with corruptible things, with silver or gold, from your vain manner of life handed down from your fathers; but with precious blood, as of a lamb without blemish and without spot, even the blood of Christ . . . who through him are believers *in God*, which *raised him from the dead, and gave him glory;* so that your faith and hope might be in God' (1 Peter i. 21); always urging them so to act and speak, 'that in all things *God may be glorified* through Jesus Christ, whose is the glory and the dominion for ever and ever. Amen' (1 Peter iv. 11). And again, and perhaps more instructive and decisive than all, in the glow and fervour of recent events; and all the startling phenomena of the day of Pentecost, when 'they were all filled with the Holy Ghost,' Peter exclaimed, 'Ye men of Israel, hear these words; Jesus of Nazareth, *a man approved of God* among you by miracles and wonders and signs, *which God did by him* in the midst of you, as ye yourselves also know. . . . Whom *God hath raised up*, having loosed the pangs of death, because it was not possible that he should be holden of it.' Can words be more plain and explicit? And when he, and John 'at the gate of the Temple which is called Beautiful,' had healed a 'certain man lame from his mother's womb,' and the people all marvelled, and were disposed to pay divine homage to Him, and to John, He disclaimed it all, and showed that it was through the fact that ' *God had glorified* his son Jesus' this healing had taken place, and added, ' for Moses truly said unto the fathers, A prophet shall *the Lord your God* raise up unto you *of your brethren like unto me ;* him shall ye hear in all things whatsoever he shall say unto you' (Acts iii. 22). Is it possible to have more demonstrative proof of any fact than is to be seen in these words? Of all the Evangelists and Apostles, St. John seems to me to be preeminently the exponent of the supremacy of God, and of the relationship between HIM and the beloved Son, whom *He* sent to be the propitiation for 'the sins of the world!' Again and again have I reiterated his grand statement in the Gospel, which is the foundation of my faith and my hopes, namely, the prayer of Jesus that all His disciples may be *one*—' That they all may be one; as thou, Father, art in me, and I in thee, that they also may *be one* in us ; that the world may believe that *Thou* hast sent me'— because this plain statement elucidates and clears up the paradoxical sophistries of the

'Athanasian Creed.' I have reiterated it again and again, and shall continue to reiterate it, because the dogmatic assertions of individuals, and the decrees of Councils, melt away before this enunciation, and all doubt of the future life is expelled by St. John's record of other words of Christ, namely, 'And this is *life eternal*, that they might *know thee, the only true God*, and Jesus Christ, *whom thou hast sent*' (John xviii. 4). As in this Gospel so necessarily in his epistles is the same note sounded, and the same doctrine enforced, and my soul clings with joy to the emphatic statements, 'Herein is love, not that we loved God, but that he loved us, and *sent* his Son to be the propitiation for our sins.' 'And we have beheld and *bear witness* that *the Father hath sent* the Son to be the Saviour of the world' (1 John iv. 10-14). In the sole Epistle of St. Jude we have like ringing words, like clear and succinct statements of what is expected of man in doctrine and practice. 'But ye, beloved, building up yourselves on your *most holy faith*, praying in the Holy Spirit, keep yourselves in *the love of God*, looking for the mercy of our *Lord* Jesus Christ unto eternal life.' 'Now unto him that is able to guard you from stumbling; and to set you before the presence of his glory without blemish in exceeding joy *to the only God our Saviour*, through Jesus Christ *our Lord*, be glory, majesty, dominion and power, before all time, and now, and for evermore. Amen.' Jude's Epistle, and [as if nothing whatever should be wanting to make the testimony complete] even the mysterious and mystical writer of the Apocalypse calls his book 'The Revelation of Jesus Christ, which *God gave unto him*, to show unto his servants things which must shortly come to pass,' and he sends grace and peace to the seven Churches which are in Asia, 'from him which is, and which was, and which is to come ; and from the seven spirits which are before his throne ; and from Jesus Christ, who *is* the faithful witness, and the first begotten of the dead, and the prince of the kings of the earth. Unto him that loved us and washed us from our sins in his own blood, and hath made us kings and priests *unto God* and his Father'; and further informs us that when in the spirit of prophecy he saw the future as the present, and the kingdoms of the world had become the kingdom of Christ, and the time had arrived sketched by Paul in his Epistle to the Corinthians, when 'God should be all in all'; then he saw that 'the four-and-twenty elders which sit before God on their thrones, fell upon their faces and worshipped God, saying, We give thee thanks, O Lord God, the Almighty, which art and which wast, because thou hast taken to thee thy great power, and hast reigned' (Rev. xi. 16, 17). Thus do I show to you the supremacy of God the Father, and the delegated power and authority of the Son; not from an isolated, incongruous, individual text snatched at random from the miscellaneous writings of the Bible, but by the unanimous testimony of the speakers and writers of the entire New Testament; a full 'consensus' of statement, and in systematic order as the writers themselves are arranged in the Holy Scriptures. Not *one only, but all testify* to the same historic truth. On this rock, 'a Rock of Ages,' I take my stand, and smile with compassionate pity at all the anathemas of the Athanasian Creed. Whenever priest, or whenever layman says of me in respect to *this* matter, 'without doubt he shall perish everlastingly,' he, by a necessary inference, says the same thing and assigns the same doom to Peter and Paul, to James and John, and Jude, yea, more (with all awe and reverence be it spoken), to Jesus also, for the whole of my 'creed' is tabulated in His words, ' And this is life eternal, that they should know *thee, the only true God*, and Him whom *thou didst send* (even) Jesus Christ' (John xvii. 3). I have, therefore, now no awe from the censures, or even the maledictions, of the 'Church' External, sustained as I am by the Church Invisible, whose head is Jesus Christ; and the fact of thousands *acquiescing* in the 'creed' Athanasian gives me no more personal spiritual anxiety than that thousands and tens of thousands of 'Christians' acquiesce in the doctrine of the 'Immaculate Conception of the Blessed Virgin,' and in the absolute 'Infallibility of the Pope'!

Vicar. Your familiarity with the Scriptures shows me that you have sought earnestly their counsel. From the tones of your voice, from the expression of your countenance, and from my knowledge of your life, I am assured that this is no mere polemic wrestle on your part. Never having had a transient doubt myself, and never having in the whole course of my ministry been consulted upon it before, I have not given the subject the minute attention which you appear to have done, and am therefore somewhat surprised at the number of quotations from the Scriptures you have produced in relation thereto. It is in my power, however, through the advice of a learned brother in the Church, to name to you a most orthodox work which fully sustains the Nicene and Athanasian Creeds in all their integrity. Pray read it. It is the Bampton Lecture by Canon Liddon 'On the Divinity of our Lord.' I am assured on the highest authority that it is wholly unanswerable. I *hope* and *believe* that it will bring you the intellectual satisfaction you need, and that we shall soon have you in spirit, as in body, within the pale of the Church, among the true believers, and thus removed far, far away from the consequences of those anathemas which you condemn so strongly as unscriptural and unjust.

Parishioner. I thank you very, very much for your kind words and good wishes; but, alas! your hope cannot be realized. The remedy you prescribe has *long since been tried*, and found *impotent.* I saw that a dignitary of the Church had called the Canon a great champion of the truth, and his book an invulnerable bulwark against the encroachments of infidelity. I hastened with joy to obtain it. My 'views' at that time were 'nebulous,' or rather like the first stage of a transformation scene in a magic-lantern; the old convictions were become hazy and dim, and no definite ones had taken their place. I longed for light and guidance. I yearned for some support to the cherished beliefs of my earlier life. General report as to the power and brilliancy of the lecturer made me hope that in Canon Liddon I should find a Joshua to conduct me from the wilderness of doubt into a bright land of certainty and repose. In a sense, he did this, for he convinced me that the *subject* 'doubted' *was* a mirage, an illusion, a baseless vision. He helped me to reach a region of light and peace, but he did this by unintentionally revealing to me that, stript of all subtlety, and read in a simple sense, with the aid of fit scholarship, the Scriptures negative the Athanasian theory, and lucidly proclaim ' *One God* and

Father of all, who is *above all*, and through all, and in you all' (Ephes. iv. 6).

Vicar. What can you mean? Surely you do not dare to gainsay the scholarship or the sincerity of the eloquent Canon?

Parishioner. Neither. The first thing that disheartened me was, in cutting open the book, to find no less than five hundred very closely printed pages, together with some thirty or forty others in the form of notes, and an appendix of texts. Five hundred pages [equivalent in the number of words to a thousand pages of some books] to prove what Melville, another eloquent Canon, called a *fundamental doctrine* of the Christian faith, were, *à priori*, a very suspicious circumstance. However, the fascination of the style, the dogmatic assurance of the lecturer, and the thrilling importance of the question discussed made me read on with avidity, although with lessening ardour at every page, until at length I closed the book, my mind and my conscience uttering, ' Unproven and unprovable.'

Vicar. As you are the first person I have heard speak of the work except in praise, and certainly the first that has intimated that the Canon has not demonstrated to every candid mind the Divinity of our Lord, I will ask you in what particular you were disappointed?

Parishioner. If brilliant diction: if eloquent, poetic, and impassioned appeals to the sentiments and preconceived notions and feelings of his hearers: if subtle scholarship and bold assumptions : if the concealment of negative evidence, the skilful marshalling of facts, and the dazzling display of forced inferences: if extravagant eulogy of the Church and the Fathers as exponents of and authorities in determining doctrine : if the consummate skill of a forensic advocate (with such scanty materials as the Scriptures supply) *could* have proved the Godhead of our Lord, *then* would Canon Liddon have proved it. He reminds me of a very distinguished special pleader—the late Serjeant Scarlett. It requires the calm and the coolness of a judicial mind, 'the clear cold light' of the intellect, and a firm grasp of the *evidence* of *all* the witnesses, to withstand his personal fascination and his wealth of words : but, possessing these, the verdict of every honest mind will be, 'Not proven.'

Vicar. Give me some instance or instances of what you call special pleading, the concealment of negative evidence, or the 'subtlety' of a forensic advocate.

Parishioner. A very conspicuous example occurs at page 250, where the Canon writes, 'Accordingly, Jesus *never* calls the Father *our* Father, as if he *shared his Sonship with his followers.* He always speaks of "my Father."' Can you suppose that this master of dialectics had *forgotten* the instruction given by Jesus to Mary Magdalene after His Resurrection—'go to my brethren, and say unto them, I ascend unto my Father, and *your* Father; and unto *my God*, and *your* God' (John xx. 17)? *Ex uno disce omnes.* Further, the Canon heads a page with the words 'Our Lord *reveals his Godhead explicitly*'; and then, after the mind of his reader has been dazzled and dazed by a series of brilliant interrogatories, he is informed that 'although the solemn sentences in which he (Jesus) makes that *supreme* relationship' [that of this 'Godhead' and that *explicitly*] '*are* comparatively *few*, it *is clear* that the truth is *latent in the entire moral and intellectual posture* which we have been considering'; then follow the marshalling of the confessions of Nathaniel, of Peter, and the words of Nicodemus; and at length comes (to me) the long-wished-for fact or utterance by or in which 'our Lord *reveals* his Godhead *explicitly*'; and lo! behold the circumstance! 'Philip preferred to our Lord the peremptory' [*sic*] 'request, "Lord, show us the Father, and it sufficeth us."' Well might the answer have thrilled those who heard it. 'Have I been so long a time with you, and yet hast thou not known me, Philip? he that hath seen me hath seen the Father, and how sayest thou then, Show us the Father. Believest thou not that I am in the Father, and the Father in me?' (p. 178). Thus it stands, with all the enforcement which capital letters to the pronouns can give, although the capital letters are not given in the received text of the Gospel. The concealment of negative evidence and the subtlety of the advocate are shown in the fact that the Canon *closes* the speech of Jesus at this especial point. Had he prolonged it, its metaphorical character would have been *intimated* by the words 'the words that I speak unto you I *speak not* of *myself*, but the Father that dwelleth in me, *he doeth* the works'; had the speech of Jesus been continued to its end, it would have '*explicitly*' demonstrated that He had been speaking *metaphorically*, by the statement, 'At that day *ye shall know* that I am in my Father, *and ye in me*, and *I in you.*' In these words are the proof that the truthful historian had been converted into a subtle advocate of a special theory. This shallow elucidation that our Lord had '*explicitly* revealed his Godhead' disappointed me much, after the bold and promising prologue. Despite the sacredness of the theme, the pungent lines of Phædrus obtruded themselves on my mind, and I could not refrain from uttering

> Mons parturibat gemitus immanes ciens,
> Eratque in terris maxima expectatio;
>   At ille murem peperit.

The final result left upon me after the study of this book was admiration of the Canon's scholarship, his diction, and his ingenuity as an 'advocate.' I felt that all that *could be said had been said;* but that facts were too stubborn to be welded into *such* a theory, even by his titanic energies. The truth emerges and shines forth when the Canon writes, 'Certainly, our Lord insists very carefully *upon the truth that* the *power which he wielded* was *derived originally from the Father*' (p. 181). Surely no rhetoric can enable the mind of a sane thinker to conceive of a supreme God 'wielding a power' *derived originally* from a power apart from Himself.

Vicar. I deeply regret that you have remained unconvinced even by Canon Liddon's eloquence and fervid arguments; but never shall I forget you in my prayers, and when, in our daily service in the sanctuary, our sublime Litany is read, I shall have you especially in my mind and heart as I utter the words, 'That it may please thee to bring into the way of truth all such as have erred and are deceived.'

Parishioner. No words of mine can sufficiently thank you for your pure and kind motives; and believe me, my dear Vicar, when I say that I too shall breathe out that prayer with equal ardour, and that my response, 'We beseech thee to hear us, good Lord,' will be in every way as earnest and as loving as your own prayer.

Vicar. Then your case is not so hopeless as I feared. So long as you feel the need of guidance, so long as your conscience whispers that *all is not well*, there is hope; and, remember that our blessed Lord Himself has said, 'If ye *do* my will, ye shall know of the doctrine.'

Parishioner. My responsive prayer will be for others rather than for myself. My troublous doubts on this especial subject are quite gone. I no longer 'sit in darkness'; the 'true light now shineth.' In *this* particular matter, as I have already said, I resemble the blind man whose eyes Jesus had opened, and who, when catechized and upbraided by the Pharisees for his convictions respecting Jesus, answered, '*One thing* I know; that, whereas I was blind, *now* I see' (John ix. 25).

Vicar. Although I do not know any theologian who could guide you into the truth more surely that Canon Liddon, yet would I wish to suggest that you read *Pearson on the Creed.*

Parishioner. Happily, I know a far more illuminating guide than either Liddon or Pearson. But that you may know that I have not neglected any source of information within my reach, I will tell you, that before I ventured to speak in the positive manner I am now compelled to do, I had diligently sought counsel from the pages of Pearson, Ellicott, Neander, Jeremy Taylor, Yonge, Hannah, Chalmers, Paley, Farrar, Bengel, Delitzsch, Davidson, Alford, Melville, Newman, Milman, Pressensé, Robertson, Lange,

Schleiermacher, Thompson, Westcott, Plumptre, Edersheim, and last, though not least, Geikie, whose *Life of Christ*, on the orthodox side, is worthy of comparison with any of the others which I have named.

Vicar. It is a goodly array for a layman to have studied; but I fear that along with these, and perhaps preferred before them, were many of a heterodox character.

Parishioner. I have read some of the writings, which are so-called, of such as Matthew Arnold, Baur, Strauss, Renan, Channing, and Martineau ; but never with so strong a bias as I read the writings of those you deem 'orthodox.' Not *one* of these writers *originated* in my mind a *conviction previously unheld*. My lapse into 'heresy,' as you call it, is wholly due, as I have already said, to Mr. Melville's sermon enforcing a belief in the Trinity, or rather the impulse which that sermon gave me to 'search the Scriptures daily' in order to ascertain 'whether those things were so' (Acts xvii. 11), and before that incident I had never read a page of any Socinian writer whatever.

Vicar. Your last words painfully remind me of a sentence in St. Paul's Epistle to the Corinthians, which asserts that there is a 'godly sorrow which worketh repentance,' and also a 'sorrow of the world which worketh death ' (2 Cor. vii. 10) ; and so I perceive that there may be *a* reading of the Scriptures themselves which leads to heresy and all its fearful consequences. Had these holy Writings been read in a proper spirit you could not have failed to learn that *the doctrine* you dispute ought (in the words of the Eighth Article of Religion of our Church) thoroughly to be received and believed; for they may be proved by *most certain warrants* of Holy Scripture.

Parishioner. Your esteemed champion of the faith, Canon Liddon, in his third sermon, speaks of the Rev. John Keble as 'the boast and glory of his university, great as a poet, greater still, it may be, as a scholar and *theologian*, greatest of all as a Christian saint'; and yet, if my memory does not greatly deceive me, he in his sermon on tradition implies that this doctrine is *not* anywhere distinctly and clearly enunciated in Holy Writ, but that it has been handed down to the Church *by tradition ;* and in the writings of his friend and admirer Cardinal Newman the same fact is enunciated. If this be so—and I feel assured that it is so—I cannot be blamed for *not finding* it there; and as to 'tradition,' I regard it as a most unsafe guide, and, as Jesus said to the 'Scribes and Pharisees which were at Jerusalem,' so am I—with reverence be it spoken—inclined to say of the Councils and 'Fathers' and dignitaries of the Church—' Thus have ye made the commandment of God of none effect by your tradition' (Matt. xv. 6).

Vicar. You have descended deeper into the

depths of doubt and of heresy than even I had feared! You have abandoned not only the Creed—which had given (I must now admit) some perplexity and pain to more than one bishop and archbishop of our Church, and which perplexity, therefore, was in some measure to be excused in a layman—but you disregard the Church's authority, and even dare to place 'private judgment' on an equality with her decrees! This is a sinful act of schism, which calls for my reproof. The Thirty-fourth Article of the Church directs and declares that 'Whosoever, through his *private judgment, willingly* and *purposely* doth openly break the *traditions* of the Church, which be not repugnant to the Word of God, and be ordained and approved by common authority, *ought to be rebuked openly*, for he thus offendeth against the common order of the Church, hurteth the authority of the magistrate, and woundeth the consciences of the weaker brethren.' Moreover, to reject the 'traditions' of the Church is in itself a sin. Had the early Christians done so we should not have possessed the Gospels themselves, inasmuch as for several decades they were *traditions only*, handed down orally by faithful men of one age to those who followed them, until they became embodied in manuscript, and have since reached us as the Gospels of SS. Matthew, Mark, and Luke.

Parishioner. And having been so embodied,

the authority of 'tradition' has ceased, as far as *Protestants* are concerned. I am aware that this term 'Protestant' is *now* disdained by 'Anglicans'; but it is the most explicit term still to describe the countless Christians who are without the pale of the Catholic, or perhaps I ought to say the Roman Catholic, Church. But in respect to your observation of my being guilty of 'the sinful act of schism' calling for your reproof, I must demur to it. Some words of John Milton, in his noble defence for the liberty of unlicensed printing, occur to me, and I hope you will not deem me offensive if I repeat them, as I wish to do, in support of a *general* principle. I do not quote them to you personally, for it would be unjust as well as arrogant towards you, but I recite them in justification of myself, and argumentatively in defence of a tolerant individualism as to what may, or may not, constitute 'the sinful act of schism.' The great Puritan wrote, 'there be who perpetually claim of schism, and make it such a calamity that any man dissents from their maxims. It is their own pride and ignorance which causes the disturbing, who neither will hear with meekness, nor can convince, yet all must be suppressed which is not found in their Syntagma. They are the troublers, they are the *dividers of unity*, who neglect and permit not others to unite those dissevered pieces which are yet wanting to the body of truth'

(p. 90). Such persons fail, as Milton writes, to 'see that while we still affect by all means a rigid external formality, we may as soon fall again into a gross conforming stupidity, a stark and dead congealment of "wood, and hay, and stubble," forced and frozen together, which is more to the sudden degenerating of a church than many subdictotomies of petty schisms' (p. 97).* Moreover, the Sixth Article of your Church has another aspect, for the said Sixth Article of your Church affirms distinctly that 'Holy Scripture containeth *all things* necessary to salvation; so that whatsoever is *not read therein*, nor may be proved thereby, is *not* to be required of any man that it should be believed as an article of the faith, or be thought requisite or necessary to salvation.' Therefore, on the point we are debating I decline to accept as an 'article of the faith' anything which has tradition only for its support; and this, I maintain, is the case with the Trinitarian doctrine; even some high Church divines have affirmed that it has no other basis than the traditions and decrees of the Church. The judicious Hooker, without declaring so much as this, admits that this doctrine can only be inferentially obtained from Scripture. He states, 'For our belief in the Trinity, the co-eternity of the Son of God with the Father, the proceeding of the Spirit from the Father and the Son, the duty of baptizing

* *Areopagitica.* Vol. II. Bohn's Edition.

infants; these, with such other principal points the necessity whereof is by none denied (?) are notwithstanding in Scripture *nowhere to be found by express literal mention*, only deduced they are out of Scripture by collection' (*Eccles. Pol.*, Book I. c. xix. s. 2). Cardinal Newman, in his history of the Arians, says, 'The most accurate consideration of the subject will lead us to acquiesce in the statement as a general truth that the doctrines in question (the Trinity and the Incarnation) have never been learned merely from Scripture' (p. 55). My memory seems also to tell me that Keble, in his sermon on 'Tradition,' alleges that the doctrine of the Trinity is based on the 'traditions' of the Church. But, be this as it may, I challenge you, or any one else, to produce a single, direct, literal text for the doctrine. Surely, this is not too much to ask from a Church which professes itself to be based on the Scriptures, and in her Twentieth Article declares that 'it is not lawful for the Church to ordain anything that is contrary to God's word written, neither may it expound one place of Scripture, that it be repugnant to another,' and which, many times a year, declares from her sanctuaries that those who do not accept this creed 'shall, without doubt, perish everlastingly.' Again do I repeat that there may be scattered here and there a 'text' or so which may *appear* to indicate a *duality*, but not one to affirm *a Trinity* save the forgery in St. John's Epistle, which has *now* been thrust out of the New Testament as it stands revised by the greatest Greek scholars of the present century.

Vicar. The Church places the doctrine of the Trinity in the very first front of her Articles as the one primary fundamental doctrine which she expects and demands that her children should accept; and here, even if nowhere else, her Article and her Formula, the first and second Articles of her religion, and the dogmatic statements of the Athanasian Creed are in perfect accord. To dispute this doctrine, then, and to affirm that it cannot 'be proved by most certain warrants of Holy Scripture,' is an act of rebellion against the Church, is treating with disdain her 'authority in controversies of faith,' and rendering yourself liable to be 'excommunicated,' and to be regarded by 'the whole multitude of the faithful as an heathen and publican' until you 'be openly reconciled by penance and received into the Church by a judge that hath authority therein.' This is the admonition of the thirty-third of the Articles of our religion.

Parishioner. All that you have now said is most true; and I must remind you that I emphatically stated at our first interview that no honest man —and I claim to be honest—could pretend to affirm that it was *not* the clearest teaching of the Church. And I went much further than you have now done in showing how she publicly anathematizes *all* who *do not accept* her teachings in this particular. But here, as in some other matters, the Church of England is a paradox; her *theories* and her practice often contradict each other, and her 'authority' is weakened thereby. Her 'trumpet gives an uncertain sound'; nay, 'her pipes and her harps' are not only out of tune, but are made to give out *different tunes;* and the priest of one parish is ready to 'anathematize' the priest of the adjoining one. It has been my lot to hear the author of *The Christian Year* described by the vicar of his own parish as 'a blind leader of the blind,' instead of being, as Canon Liddon calls him, 'great as a poet, greater still, it may be, as a scholar and theologian, greatest of all as a Christian saint.' Indeed, the vicar of the parish and the 'Christian poet' mutually regarded each other as 'unsound in the faith,' although both were ordained priests of the Church of England. It is not pleasant to think that the good John Keble (good in purpose, but intensely bitter towards 'dissent and dissenters') was not regarded by all as a prophet 'in his own country.' Thus, during the Agricultural Riots of 1831 the reverend poet kindly endeavoured to dissuade the agricultural labourers of his neighbourhood from breaking threshing-machines belonging to the farmers and others. Their leader, a 'local preacher' belonging to the

Primitive Methodists, confronted him with a Scriptural harangue—a 'bit of the Gospel,' as he called it—and invited discussion, which Mr. Keble most wisely declined. The 'Primitive,' who had lived many years in the same parish with Mr. Keble, then acting as curate at Coln St. Aldwin's, had much to say respecting him, his opinion of the learned 'parson' being akin to that which William Taylor, the 'Model Preacher' of America, is said to have expressed respecting the philosopher Emerson—'He may be a good man, but he is as *"ignorant of the Gospel"* as Balaam's ass was of the Hebrew grammar.' But to return to our subject. The Church of England suffers in authority because of the conflict between her liturgy and her catechism and her 'Thirty-nine Articles,' her avowed 'Protestantism' and her dogmatic creeds. Her Sixth Article, which makes the Scriptures the final appeal, goes far to nullify her 'anathemas' in other directions. It is this Sixth Article which has enabled me to continue a worshipper within her material fabric and to accept with composure your intimation of 'excommunication.'

Vicar. I hope to be spared so painful a procedure; and it is somewhat ungenerous in you thus (at least indirectly) to taunt her for the reverence and deference she manifests towards the Holy Scriptures—those Scriptures which you have heretofore so warmly espoused, as transcending in authority the decrees of Councils and the statements of the Fathers.

Parishioner. And still do. What I have said is in illustration of the Church's inconsistency in speaking so dogmatically in her 'Creeds,' and, like Saul, 'breathing out threatenings and slaughter against the disciples of our Lord' who cannot accept them, and then, elsewhere, putting another authority—the Holy Scriptures—on the same plane, or higher than herself, to declare what is or what is not required 'to be believed as an article of faith.' She thus provides an *imperium in imperio* which leads to vacillation and conflict even among her priests themselves.

Vicar. You surely would not have the Church of England proclaim herself as being superior to God's Word?

Parishioner. Heaven forbid! I wish to see her in *fact*, as in *name*, *the National Church*—a Church not of catechisms and creeds and of articles, but a Church that could receive within the amplitudes of her love *all who loved God*, all who could 'worship HIM in spirit and in truth.' But there never can be a National Church—that is, a Church spiritually acceptable to devout minds until some great teacher shall arise with deep spiritual insight and energetic will, who shall penetrate behind the ordinances, forms, and ceremonies, and doctrines of 'the Churches,' 'Established' and 'Nonconforming' alike, and show forth the true and inward principle which can alone give them any value to the souls 'which hunger and thirst after righteousness.' The Fountain of the Gospel must be sought and found, if we wish to obtain the 'water of life' in its perfect purity. I cannot always sympathize with the 'Fathers,' but most certainly do I believe with Erasmus, that 'the Church was purest when its Creed was shortest.' As time went on, and as the 'Church' became thereby removed further and further from our Lord's personal presence on earth, so did the 'creeds' of Christianity increase in length and obscurity, until they reached the complex subtleties and perplexiveness of the Nicene and Athanasian Creeds. Now, no Church can become popular (or national), that is—suited to the needs and feelings of all—' the masses and the classes ' —which is based on abstruse, metaphysical, intellectual propositions, and makes the acceptance of these subtleties the condition of salvation. The heart of the poor and illiterate man cannot be comforted by such abstractions, and his needs should be considered equally with the scholastic cravings of the speculative ecclesiastic. The ' good news ' must be restored to its primitive language ; a language 'understanded of the common people,' a language as simple, clear, and plain as the language spoken by Jesus on the shore and lake of Galilee, and on the Mount of

Olivet. We need an 'Established Church' as simple in its creed and in its ritual as was the early Church at Antioch founded by Paul and Barnabas, under the guidance of the Apostles at Jerusalem, so lucidly described by Luke in the fifteenth chapter of his history of the Acts of the Apostles. I yearn and pray for the arrival of another day of 'Pentecost,' when the Holy Ghost shall come from heaven with a sound 'as of a rushing, mighty wind,' driving before it and dispersing for ever the mists and fogs and dark exhalations from the bottomless pit, which now shroud the so-called Christian Churches of the realm; so that all their 'apostles' and 'prophets' and 'evangelists' and 'pastors and teachers' may be 'filled with the Holy Ghost,' and may 'speak with other tongues as the Spirit gave them utterance'; I yearn to see an 'Established Church' where 'the weary and heavy laden' would be received, and 'rest' given to them upon terms and conditions less perplexing than this acknowledgment—'The Father incomprehensible, the Son incomprehensible, and the Holy Ghost incomprehensible; and yet there are not three incomprehensibles, but one incomprehensible'; an 'Established Church' which thundered forth no anathemas against those whose intellects were too feeble to comprehend the alleged divine arithmetical proposition, 'The Father is God, the Son is God, and the Holy

Ghost is God; and yet there are not three Gods, but one God'; an 'Established Church' which would admit within its fold, for prayer and praise and sacramental grace, and for the full membership of Christian love, all who were willing to 'keep the unity of the spirit in the bond of peace,' without the compulsory acknowledgment of any ' creed,' with vain repetition; or, more elaborate and complex than the words in which Jesus, when on the 'Mount of Beatitudes,' instructed His disciples to pray to their Father in heaven! Why need there be any theoretic religious test or 'creed' for admission and full recognition of brotherhood, other than a *prayer* in which all could join, and which Christ Himself composed and commanded? The true spirit of Christianity is a love expansive and all-embracing as the heavens, and 'creeds' should be as inclusive, and not as exclusive, as possible. Would that our 'National' or Established Church might hear and joyfully act upon the advice of the great son of Amoz : 'Enlarge the place of thy tent, and let them stretch forth the curtains of thine habitations; spare not, lengthen thy cords and strengthen thy stakes, for thou shalt break forth on the right hand, and on the left.' She should be well-nigh all-embracing. At present she is far from this. In fact, logically she is a paradox; her practice, in many particulars, is better than her creed (the very opposite of too many of us); but still she is not '*national*'; nay more, she has much of the exclusiveness and arrogance of the Romish Church, with none of her consistency, her discipline, and authority. She is a house divided against herself. She has no unity of creed (practically) or purpose; and, while frowning on 'dissent,' dissentience and strife are rampant within her own borders. In large cities there is positive rivalry between sister churches—not as to which shall best serve God, but which shall obtain the larger congregation. The very tricks of trade are employed to effect this unworthy purpose; choice music, floral decorations, gorgeous robes, pompous processions, with banners and all the resources and fascinations of song and of choral harmonies, are brought into play to achieve this end. The *words* of a hymn or a psalm are secondary to the beauties and charms of its musical composition. 'Singing with grace in your hearts to the Lord' can be cheerfully dispensed with, provided only that your voice be sweet, powerful, well-cultured, and well-controlled; for the scenic attractions of the theatre and the sensuous sounds of the opera are blended at these sabbath festivals, to attract the fashionable, the idle, the wealthy, and the crowd. Music, colour, and song are evoked to constitute 'a bright service' which should move

> Softly sweet in Lydian measures,

to lull the soul into luscious repose or 'dissolve it into ecstasies,' and make it dream, 'with sweetness through the ear,' that it was treading a flowery path to heaven. Churches crowded with fair women, and coloured dresses glittering with crosses of gold and gems, are the crowning result to human vision. But if the utterance of the name of the Most High in a thoughtless way, and only with regard to musical notation, be practically (as I believe it to be) a violation of the third commandment, then is it a scene upon which the angels of heaven must look with dismay, and One, higher than all angels, may some day say, 'Who hath required *this* at your hand, to tread my courts? Bring no more vain oblations; incense is an abomination unto me; the new moons and sabbaths, the calling of assemblies, I cannot away with; *it is iniquity, even the solemn meeting*' (Isaiah i. 12, 13).

Vicar. I am really embarrassed to understand you. At one moment you seem to me to belong to the 'Rationalists,' and to set aside the high mysteries of our most holy religion and the supernatural facts and miracles of the Gospel, or to explain them by the material or physical laws which science reveals, as, when at our first interview, you implied that there were men of such cerebral organization that they could not grasp and carry out the highest teachings of the Gospel—men whom you termed, in the language of Paul, 'vessels of dishonour'; and still lower down in the materialistic or necessitarian scheme, as when you implied that religious habits were contingent on hereditary influence; then you seem to have gone off to the very opposite pole of thought, as if you wished the Church to possess such an autocratic power that there should be no marked difference between the preachings of a priest in one parish and the preachings of the priest in another — that all should be bound in the same iron and inflexible rule as in the Romish Church; and then at the close of your remarks you exhibit all the fiery zeal of the Puritan and condemn all ornate service, forgetting the practice of the olden time, when the church or temple was, so to speak, under the immediate direction of Jehovah—the people were invited to 'praise him with the sound of the trumpet: praise him with the psaltery and harp. Praise him with the timbrel and dance: praise him with stringed instruments and organs. Praise him upon the loud cymbals: praise him upon the high-sounding cymbals. Let every thing that hath breath praise the Lord' (Ps. cl.). Yes, disregarding the command 'Let every thing that hath breath praise the Lord' would limit worship to a chosen few, and, like John Knox in the time of the Stuarts, would condemn music itself, and even banish the organ ' as a kist of whistles.'

Parishioner. I deeply deplore my incapacity to place my convictions in so lucid, logical, and consistent a form as they appear to myself. Nothing could possibly be further from my wishes than that the worship of God should be restricted to a few persons. The Psalmist himself could not be more ardent in his desire than I am that 'every thing that hath breath should praise the Lord.' My regret is that the trumpets and cymbals and stringed instruments are sounded by men who have no special desire to ' praise the Lord'; by many who 'are lovers of pleasure more than lovers of God'; by some men, indeed, who even deny his existence, but who sound the stringed instruments for mere pay—others do so 'to oblige the Vicar,' or some female friend, or to gratify their love of music, and to win praise as accomplished musicians. My objection was that this ornate service should be employed *ostensibly* ' to praise the Lord,' but really to attract a congregation to a special church. It was not the reality that I objected to, but the 'simulacrum,' the 'sham,' the formality of worship! I fear that of too many of the singers and of the musicians it may be truthfully said, 'This people draweth nigh unto me with their mouth, and honoureth me with their lips ; but their *heart* is far from me ' (Matt. xv. 8). My wish is that priest and people, pulpit and pew, employers and employed, should never forget that 'God is a spirit, and they who worship him *must* worship him in spirit and in truth' (John iv. 24). In proportion as love grows cold; in an exact ratio as the spiritual sense and the spiritual life become feeble and dull, does the craving for *external stimulants* and for *material* aid in *worship* spring up in the human heart. When jewels and gems and cosmetics are needed to make the bride attractive, then the love of the bridegroom is growing, or has grown, cold. And so with the higher, purer, deeper love of the regenerate soul to its Redeemer and its God. When 'ornate' services are a '*sine quâ non*,' when the attractions of the opera are needed to make it feel, and to say, ' I was glad when they said unto me, Let us go into the house of the Lord' (Ps. cxxii.) —then that soul has fallen, or is falling, into the condition of the Church at Ephesus, which ' had left its first love.' Alas! it is as true at this hour as when Jesus trod the flowery fields of Galilee, that 'many are called, but few are chosen.' The solemn words uttered by our Divine Lord on Mount Olivet need not to be modified, His true disciples know all too well that 'strait is the gate and narrow is the way which leadeth unto life, *and few there be that find it.*' Christ's flock is still 'a little few,' amid the thousands who 'profess and call themselves Christians.' Pure spirituality, the 'pure religion' which is 'undefiled' before God, is slow to attain popularity. That 'God is a spirit,' 'and they who worship him *must* worship him in spirit,' is comprehended slowly by the general mind. Poor, fallen, human nature seems to crave for materialism and concrete things. It is still at heart *idolatrous*, and craves for a 'golden call' in some form. Sensuous things are dear to it, although these vary in character with the culture of the individual, but, ever sensual or appealing to the senses, the emotions, and the sensual imagination only. The Church of Rome knows this well, and acts accordingly. Her extensive and deep knowledge of human nature, gained by long experience in the 'confessional' and by her intercourse with all the nations and tribes of the earth, causes her to avoid the culture of the intellect in the masses, to check absolutely all critical religious inquiry, and to cause her religious ceremonies to be full of dramatic effect, so as to gratify continually the senses of sight and hearing, and to appeal ever to the passionate emotions of the heart, to the exclusion of all intellectual exercise. Hence, the quiet acquiescence to her commands, and the tranquil enjoyment of her sensuous services, by the peasantry and inhabitants of Spain, Italy, Austria, and the greater part of Ireland. Early in her history, her penetrative sagacity caused her to retain in the Pagan Temples of Rome, dedicated to Christianity, many of the forms of the old pagan worship, and many of the names with which the worshippers were familiar. Rome in her decline abounded, as you well know, in temples to pagan gods, as modern Rome does to Christian saints ; and the shrewd ecclesiastics, after Constantine, in the fourth century, had seen the fiery cross in the heavens, and had decreed the abolition of pagan worship, and commanded that 'Christianity' should be the National Religion, took care that the change should be as gradual as possible, and that the special Christian saint to whom the pagan temple should henceforth be assigned should possess most of the qualities of the pagan god who occupied it beforetime. Thus Romulus was deified after his death, and the Romans, like the Athenians, being 'in all things too superstitious,' dedicated a temple to him ; and, inasmuch as Romulus had been abandoned in his infancy, and was subsequently providentially suckled by a wolf, he, in his deified condition, became the especial patron and benefactor of little children. Mothers brought to his shrine their sick children to be healed; and, consequently, a Christian saint was soon found who had been in a like manner abandoned, and to him, Theodorus, was the temple of Romulus assigned, and mothers brought their children in a corresponding manner, and received correspondent blessings. Thus, antecedent customs and 'hereditary propensities' received the least possible shock, and Paganism glided smoothly into the profession of the Christian faith. The most conspicuous of the Christian miracles, even at an earlier stage, were reconciled to the Pagans by comparing them with corresponding prodigies in the history of their own divinities. Thus Justin Martyr, in the early part of the second century, in his *Apology to Antoninus Pius, or Marcus Aurelius*, could write for the Divine 'Sonship,' and the immaculate origin of the Virgin, and the ascension of Jesus, as follows: 'We propound nothing different from what you believe regarding those whom you esteem sons of Jupiter'; and again, 'That the Word of God was born of God ought to be no extraordinary thing to you who say that *Mercury* is the *angelic word of God*,' 'and, if we ever affirm that he was born of a virgin, accept this as common with what you accept of Perseus,' 'and, in that we say that He made whole the lame, the paralytic, and those born blind, we seem to say what is very similar to the deeds said to have been done by Esculapius.' And to reconcile the opposing Pagans to the fact of the ascension, the pious Christian Justin Martyr writes, in the twenty-first chapter of his first *Apology*, 'What shall I say of Ariadne, and those who, like her, have been declared to be set among the stars? And what of the Emperors who died among yourselves, whom you deem worthy of deification, and in

'*A BRIGHT SERVICE.*' 217

whose behalf you produce someone who swears he has seen the burning Cæsar rise to heaven from the funeral pyre' (p. 25). Thus has it ever been, thus is it still, 'the carnal mind is enmity against God,' and 'the natural man receiveth not the things of the spirit of God ; for they are foolishness unto him.' Professing themselves to be wise, they became fools, and changed the glory of the incorruptible God into an image made like to corruptible man. . . Changed the *truth of God into a lie* and worshipped and served the creature more than the Creator, who is blessed for ever. Amen' (Rom. i.). 'Carnal ordinances,' the observation of days and months and years, 'the weak and beggarly elements' of the senses are fascinating and dear to the multitudes high and low. The things which are seen, dominate over the Unseen. And thus, true and spiritual worship is not sufficiently dramatic to meet the desires of either the 'classes or the masses,' as a whole. Hence the 'masses' crowd in their hundreds to the military buffoonery of 'General Booth,' with its drums and 'shrill, piercing-fife,' its flags, red waistcoats, sashes, marches, titles, and noise, while, on the other hand, incense and bright-robed priests and surpliced processions and banners and crosses, and the choicest and choralled chants by cultured voices, are demanded by the 'classes.' A refined taste and a cultured intellect, if not a devout heart, cause them to say—

> Let my due feet never fail
> To walk the studious cloysters' pale,
> And love the high-embowed roof,
> With antick pillars massy proof,
> And storied windows richly dight,
> Casting a dim religious light:
> There let the pealing organ blow,
> To the full-voiced quire below,
> In service high and anthems clear,
> As may with sweetness, through mine ear,
> Dissolve me into ecstacies,
> And bring all heaven before mine eyes.

All these things I deplore, as alien to the Spirit of Christ, but as to binding all in an iron and inflexible rule, you must know that this is the very exact opposite of my wishes, for no one living can be more thoroughly impressed with the belief that ' Where the Spirit of the Lord *is*, *there* is *liberty*' (2 Cor. iii. 17), and my remarks as to a 'national' Church should have caused you to refrain from hinting it.

Vicar. Why, then, draw such a picture of the trumpet, and its uncertain sound, and of the conflicting parties you say exist in the Church?

Parishioner. To show the inconsistency and the fallacy of your urging upon me to accept of a paradoxical creed (a creed irreconcilable with the reasoning faculty) upon the *authority* of the

Church, when, in fact, she has no controlling 'authority' over the preachings of her ministers and the conflicting deductions they draw from her creeds and formulas. Her inconsistency and weakness in this particular I have already pointed out, and they are almost the 'gibes' of her foes. The eloquent Cardinal Newman, in one of his *Discourses to Mixed Congregations*, says, 'Attachment is not trust, nor is to obey the same as to look up to and to rely upon ; nor do I think that any thoughtful or educated man can simply believe or confide in the *word* of the Established Church. I never met any such person who did or said he did, and I do not think that such a person is possible.' This is severe, but not more severe, and certainly not more true, than when, in again speaking of the Church of England, he proceeds : 'Does not its *essence* lie in its recognition by the State ? is not its establishment its very *form ?* What would it be, would it last ten years, if abandoned to itself'? In the same address he said : 'Strip it of this world, and you have performed a *mortal operation* upon it, for it has ceased to be. You know that, did not the State compel it to be one, it would split at once into three' [High, Broad, Low, he means] 'several bodies, each bearing within it the elements of further division. It moves because the State moves ; it is an appendage whether weapon or decoration of the sovereign power ; it is the religion not even of a race, but of the ruling portion of a race.'

Vicar. Well may you call the Cardinal eloquent; he exceeds all men in the smoothness, the rhythm, the poetry of his sentences; and his silvery voice adds to their fascination and charm. It was a great, a deep misfortune to lose him from our midst—for who could have foreseen the depths into which he has fallen! 'O what a noble mind is here o'erthrown' by credulity and superstition! How little did any of us deem that the slashing critic of the Church of Rome, the puissant pamphleteer, the trenchant 'tractarian,' the chieftain of the *British Critic*, should become the abject slave and sycophant of the Church he censured! The man of all others who exercised his mind, who applied the teachings of history with such energy and power to the intellect and reason of his fellows, now, alas! pours scorn on the noblest attribute of man, accepts with reverence the wildest credulities of the 'dark ages,' and clothes the silliest superstitions with all the graces of poetry! 'Great wit to madness nearly is allied.' Who could have thought it possible that the man who drew crowds of the most learned members of one of the most renowned universities in the world to listen to his sermons in St. Mary's, Oxford, would live to write such eloquent nonsense as the following : 'The store of relics is inexhaustible ; they are multiplied through all lands, and each *particle* of *each* has in it at least a *dormant*, perhaps an *energetic*, virtue of *supernatural operation*. At Rome there is the true Cross, the crib of Bethlehem, and the chair of St. Peter; portions of the crown of thorns are kept at Paris; the holy coat is shown at Treves; the winding-sheet at Turin ; at Monza the iron crown is formed out of a nail of the Cross ; and another nail is claimed for the Duomo of Milan ; and pieces of our Lady's habit are to be seen in the Escurial. The Agnus Dei, blessed medals, the scapular, the cord of St. Francis—*all are the medium of Divine manifestations and graces.* Crucifixes have bowed the head to the suppliant, and madonnas have bent their eyes upon assembled crowds. St. Januarius's blood liquefies periodically at Naples, and St.Winifred's Well is the scene of wonders even in our unbelieving country !' (*Present Position of Catholics*, p. 290.) Is it not most sad ? does not this very record of the signs and wonders of the Popish Church bring to mind with irresistible force the prophetic words of St. Paul : ' Then shall that Wicked be revealed whom the Lord shall consume with the spirit of his mouth, and shall destroy with the brightness of his coming: *Even him, whose coming is after the working of Satan with all power and signs and lying wonders* ' ? (2 Thessalonians ii. 8, 9). Since the Fall and the Crucifixion I know nothing more sad, more appalling in the spiritual history of man than this spectacle! Does it not shock you?

Parishioner. I am grieved, but not shocked; that is, I am not surprised, because it is the *practical* outcome of dogmatic teachings upon an inquiring, honest, and devout spirit. By inheritance, by disposition, by training, and every social surrounding, John Newman was from his earliest years imbued with a spirit of devout reverence. He has undergone three stages; but the *first* and *last* are *analogous* in this respect, that they are based on the *feelings* and sentiments alone, and hold the intellect and the reasoning powers in aversion and dread. At a time when society around was cold and worldly his home was the abode of piety and of fervid belief in the 'doctrine of grace' and 'of the new birth.' His literary guides were Venn, Simeon, Milner, Scott; and the person who was the human means of his 'conversion' and the beginning of 'divine faith in him' was Walter Meyers of Pembroke College. Of this 'conversion' he has said he 'was more certain than that he had hands and feet.' Under these influences he went to the University of Oxford; while there he became acquainted with Whately (afterwards Archbishop of Dublin), who, he says, 'emphatically *opened my mind and taught me to think and use my reason;* and thus he soon became dissatisfied with the narrowness, the fanaticism, the sour creed, and the mental mediocrity of the 'Evangelicals,' and abandoned them as a party, although their early influence on his nature abides to this hour. He then became distinguished as a polemical preacher and an ardent critic, making vigorous onslaughts on Dissent, Protestantism, and the Papacy; and as upholding Church principles (Anglican) against Papacy and 'Dissent' alike—his great dialectic work on *The Prophetical Office* being then thought a certain bulwark against the encroachments of the Papal power, as it certainly was destructive, generally speaking, in the Church of England of the 'low' views of Evangelicalism—this middle stage of his thought, like his *Via Media*, soon merged again into abject submission to dogma and authority. Whately's influence passed away; and 'to open the mind,' 'to teach to think,' '*to use the reason*,' again became as repellent to him as to any 'Evangelical.' The *fanaticism* of feeling and sentiment regained its ascendency. Hereditary influence and the plastic mouldings of childhood reasserted themselves, and the saying of Horace, '*Naturam expelles furcâ, tamen usque recurret*,' was realized. The Pope usurped the place of the Bible. This last 'conversion' (regarded psychologically) was simply a recurrence to the emotions and feelings of his earlier days. In Cardinal Newman we observe one of those impassioned souls which become 'possessed' with an idea, which thenceforth dominates over 'common sense' and every judicial attribute. His fanaticism is absolute. His judgment is as feeble as that of a child. Were the Pope to issue an 'Encyclical' to-morrow, declaring that the sun went round the earth, and that the theory of gravitation was sinful, the Cardinal would bow to it with abject submission, like as the Jesuits, when issuing an edition of Newton's works in 1742, stated that they did not accept his description of the movement of the earth *because* the Pope had pronounced it false. In him emotion and sentiment are supreme, and therefore mystic rites and ceremonies become the joy of his existence. 'To me,' he writes, 'nothing *is* so consoling, so piercing, so thrilling, so overcoming as the Mass. I could attend Masses for ever and not be tired' (*Loss and Gain*, p. 290). 'Masses' have become to Newman what wild hymns and rapturous exclamations are to the 'Salvation Army'; or the 'unction' sermons of Spurgeon on 'predestination,' 'special election,' and the like are to 'God's elect' who throng the 'Metropolitan Tabernacle.' Still, with this mental defect, John Henry Newman is an honest man, and as such to be respected. In violating his vows and in abandoning the Church of his fathers and in going over to the Church whose doctrines he once described as 'impious, heretical, and damnable,' he has consistently carried out .the teachings which in these interviews you have earnestly impressed upon me.

Vicar. When have I ever impressed upon you, or upon anyone else, such absurdities as that 'the iron crown at Monza had been formed out of one nail of the Cross,' 'that crucifixes have bowed the head to suppliants, and madonnas had bent their eyes upon assembled crowds'? Your statement as to my teachings is preposterous and most unjust.

Parishioner. You may not intentionally have wished for such results, but the acceptance of such fables as truths is the necessary corollary of your teaching. Whenever the '*reason*,' or discerning power in man, is forbidden to be exercised; whenever it is demanded that the intellect should bow to 'tradition' and to the dogmatic 'authority'; whenever *material* things are represented as the special media 'of Divine manifestations and graces'—it does not matter much whether it be 'an iron nail,' 'a bit of wood,' 'a piece of our Lady's habit,' 'a blessed medal,' or 'a piece of bread and a drop of wine'—when, in short, a man is assured, amid all the holy solemnities of public worship, that, except at the command of the 'Church,' he implicitly believes and holds a faith which *to him* is absurd and incomprehensible, '*without doubt* he shall perish everlastingly'; then there can be no limit to credulity. I myself could more easily believe in any one of the so-called miracles recited by Newman, and in its spiritual potency, than I could comprehend and believe in the phraseology, or, as it might be called, the 'logomachy,' of the Athanasian Creed.

Vicar. It is almost — nay quite—profane to compare the facts and the circumstances. In the Holy Creed only Divine Persons are referred to, not even the Virgin Mary herself, much less 'a portion' of her 'habit.'

Parishioner. On this fact we are at issue. You regard Jesus as God, and the Holy Ghost as God; and to these propositions I demur, and am not more willing to accept and use these words than I am to receive and reverence the term 'mother of God,' by which the more venerable, more powerful, and larger Church designates the Virgin. No, sir, Cardinal Newman is more consistent, and infinitely more frank, than any bishop or priest I know of in the Church of England. He is anxious to preserve the traditions, the creeds, and the authority of his Church, and he very wisely writes: *'Avoid, I say, inquiry; for it will but lead you thither, where there is no light, no peace, no hope; it will lead you to the deep pit, where the sun, and the moon, and the stars, and the beauteous heavens are not, but chilliness and barrenness and perpetual desolation'* (*Discourses to Mixed Congregations,*

p. 283). I regard these eloquent words as most wise, sagacious, and shrewd from *his standpoint;* wise as was the advice of the monk who, soon after Gutenberg's printing-type came into use, said, 'We must root out this press, or it will root out us.' There is, there can be, no alliance between the *principles* of Protestantism, which suggest 'inquiry,' and the principles of a Church which demands that all the reasoning faculties should succumb to her dogmatic 'faith'; hence the consistency of strictly forbidding all 'inquiry,' and demanding absolute submission, without any of the qualifying circumstances which, verbally, the Articles of our Church admit. As I have already stated, these qualifying circumstances are illusory and out of place so long as the 'Commination Service' and the 'Athanasian Creed' form important parts of the public worship.

Vicar. There is a bitter perverseness in your frequent comparison between the two Churches, Anglican and Roman, and their respective modes of maintaining their tenets, to the disadvantage of the former. If we had an audience, few would admit that you were sincere in affecting not to see more difficulty in accepting and believing the childish puerilities of Newman than in accepting and believing the sublime mysteries of the Creed of St. Athanasius; and I could recognize no more puerile credulity in accepting and believing the wild legends of the 'coat of

Treves,' 'the iron nail' of Monza crown, and such-like follies, than in accepting and reverencing the ineffable dogma that in the Trinity none is afore or after other, none is greater or less than another, but the whole three Persons are co-eternal together and co-equal; that in all things, as is aforesaid, the Unity in Trinity and the Trinity in Unity is to be worshipped.

Parishioner. Probably, in an audience 'few' *would* sympathize with me. The audiences I have known have preferred that others should think for them rather than they should think for themselves, and have always been ready to accept of platitudes, if they were only clothed with propriety and grace. But to myself, there is less difficulty in believing the Romish miracles than in accepting the Athanasian mystery. The miracles appear *most improbable*, but still within the *extreme* limits of the possible; and the other is not. Take the iron crown of Monza, made out of one nail of the Cross, for instance. The iron nail may have been very large, and the crown may have been small and thin, and we all know that iron is a very ductile material. But be this as it may, it certainly does not appear so difficult to believe as if it had been said: 'There were three pieces of iron, and each piece of iron was made into a nail: the first was a nail, the second was a nail, and the third was a nail; and yet there were *not* three nails, but *one* nail.'

CREDULITY AND CREED.

And even such a proposition or statement is more simple and more easily to be understood than the statement which you have given as *necessary* for a man to believe if he 'will be saved'; because there is *not* superadded to the genesis of the nails that the first nail was made of *none*, that the second was derived from the ore of the first, and that the third 'proceeded' from the other two; and yet 'none of the nails is afore or after other,' that 'none is greater or less than another, but the whole three nails are co-eternal together and co-equal.' The reverence and awe which have been transmitted to us, and the religious training of childhood, prevent us from laughing at this paradox of things; but if we had *never heard it* until our manhood, we should have been more inclined to smile at it than we should at the alleged opening of the eyes of a painted madonna in the Roman States or at the wild flight of the 'coat of Treves' over the waters. I cannot, however, conceive that the salvation of an immortal soul is contingent upon the belief of all or any of these absurdities.

Vicar. I am so distressed by your statements that I know not how to treat them. Your enthusiasm, or, I might have said, party spirit, seems to carry you away so as to cause you to palliate the errors of an apostate from his ordination vows, and actually to place the spurious miracles of the Church of Rome on a plane with the holy verities of our Church; nay worse, even to prefer them, and to regard the 'iron crown of Monza' as less of an intellectual paradox and 'stumbling-block' to an inquiring mind than the mysteries of the Catholic Faith. This is most perplexing and painful. As respects the late Vicar of St. Mary's, much as I admire his marvellous mastery over the English language, and often as I have been fascinated by his poetry and power, I cannot but feel that his 'Egoism' has been excessive, and chiefly in consequence of the profound reverence we all at one time paid him; that his self-conceit has become great; and that, in the language of St. Paul, 'for this cause God has sent him strong delusion, that he should believe a lie.' I confess that I sometimes tremble for his destiny.

Parishioner. That is strong language. The silly liquefaction of the so-called blood of St. Januarius at Naples, the bowing heads of the crucifixes, and the opening, beaming eyes of the madonnas are indeed dismal 'delusions'; and in all of these the celebrated convert has publicly proclaimed he '*believes.*' *Still*, credulity, however crass and childish, so long as it does not injure the community, or culminate in an act which is likely to do so, and remains simply as a 'crotchet' of the individual, ought, I think, to be treated with compassion. I know of no instance in Holy Scripture where credulity or creed has been condemned. In the great prophetic panorama which Jesus portrayed (as recorded by Matthew) of the Judgment Hour, the one thing, *and the one thing only*, which called forth the censure and the sentence of the Judge was, that the hungry and the thirsty and the naked and the captive had been neglected; no creeds were called for, no doctrines denounced or applauded. Not even the 'prophesying in *his name*,' or 'casting out devils,' or doing 'wonderful works in his name,' whether at the font, confessional, or altar, availed anything, but simply beneficent acts and a pure life; and, therefore, I have no anxiety respecting the ultimate destiny of one so pious and good. Moreover, St. Peter, under special illumination, declared, 'I perceive that God is no respecter of persons, but in every nation he that feareth him, and *worketh righteousness*, is acceptable with him.' These conditions the renowned Oratorian certainly fulfils, yet is he an unsafe guide in all religious perplexities. My praise, such as it was, had reference to his astuteness as a partisan, like unto the astuteness of the 'unjust steward' in the parable. I have shown by quotations from his published sermons that he is no longer a safe teacher under religious perplexity. He is the slave of dogmatic authority, and his instruction in the words 'Avoid, I say, inquiry,' are in direct contradiction to the teachings of his august Master, who said,

'*Search* the Scriptures,' do not accept any pretensions without inquiry; you have confidence in the Scriptures, 'search,' 'inquire and see whether they do not testify of me.' Newman is also practically opposed to the historian of the Acts, who declared that the people of Berea 'were more noble than those in Thessalonica,' in that they 'searched the Scriptures daily, *whether those things were so.*' It is an abject philosophy which inculcates the closing of the eyes that you may not see. And the *consequences* of 'inquiry,' 'the leading into the deep, where there is no light, no peace, no hope, no beauteous heavens, no sun, moon, or stars, but chilliness, barrenness, and desolation,' have no foundations except in the poetic and romantic mind of the writer. We know that by 'inquiry' all the material blessings of the world have been obtained, and that sun, moon, and stars were never seen in half their greatness, their grandeur, and effulgence until the telescope of 'inquiry' had been directed towards them. The writings of Isaiah and of Paul prove to us that God desireth to be honoured not with the heart only, but with the '*understanding* also,' and Hosea even declares : 'My people are destroyed for lack of knowledge : because thou hast rejected knowledge, I will also reject thee, that thou shalt be no priest to me' (iv. 6). This blind, uninquiring, passive piety, this piety of priests and ritualists, has been well described by a divine (who is as great a master of logic, rhetoric, and style as Newman himself, and far more profound in the domain of philosophy and science) as 'a refuge for the weakness, not an outpouring of the strength, of the soul; it takes away the incubus of darkness, without shedding the light of heaven; lifts off the nightmare horrors of earth and hell, without opening the vision of angels and of God.' (Martineau, *Studies of Christianity*, p. 39.)

Vicar. Dr. Martineau certainly gives us a very graphic contrast between spiritual and formal worship; but his remarks are applicable only to superstitious phases of religion, or to those abject forms of Christian devotion seen in some parts of Ireland, and in other countries where the people are very ignorant, poor, and superstitious, and where religious services are conducted in an 'unknown tongue,' as our Article states —in 'a tongue not understanded of the people.' In places and churches where this wise resolution of Paul is disregarded—'I will pray with the spirit, and I will pray with the understanding also : I will sing with the spirit, and I will sing with the understanding also. Else when thou shalt bless with the spirit, how shall he that occupieth the room of the unlearned say Amen at thy giving of thanks, seeing he understandeth not what thou sayest' ? (1 Cor. xiv. 15).

Parishioner. I am sorry, my dear Vicar, that

the resolve of St. Paul is overlooked and unpractised not only in the wild districts of Connaught, and in Basque Provinces, but much nearer home; for practically there is little to choose between 'a tongue' described as 'unknown'—or, as we may say, a 'foreign language'—and native words so connected together in sentences, and having such mystic meanings attached to them, that they cease to convey a comprehensible idea to the mind. When you, in your official robes, and in the performance of your holy office, tell your people that '*whosoever will be saved, before all things* it is necessary that he hold the Catholic Faith,' and you proceed to define that faith in the well-known manner, 'how shall he that occupieth the room of the unlearned say Amen, seeing he *understandeth* not what thou sayest'?

Vicar. I do not admit the applicability of your remarks. Every statement made by me under such circumstances is as plain and as easily to be understood as the nature of the subject admits.

Parishioner. Perhaps it might equally have been said of the shouting of 'unknown tongues' in the Church at Corinth, that it was made as easy 'to be understood' as the 'nature of the case' admitted. Nevertheless the nature of the case was such that St. Paul has himself recorded that 'he that speaketh in an unknown tongue speaketh not unto men . . . for no man understandeth him; howbeit in the spirit he *speaketh mysteries.*' The cases appear to me to be parallel. Certainly, when you are reciting the 'mysteries' of the faith one of your audience feels assured 'no man understandeth him.' Leaving myself, however, out of the question, and taking a single sentence only of that detailed 'faith' which 'except everyone do keep WHOLE and undefiled, *without doubt he shall perish everlastingly*,' how many, think you, of your congregation *understandeth* you when you admonish them 'that we worship one God in Trinity, and Trinity in Unity, neither confounding the *Persons* nor dividing the *substance*'? Even removing the incomprehensible first clause, how many 'understandeth' 'confounding the *Persons*,' or 'dividing the *substance*'? They have learnt from the Articles that 'there is but one living and true God, everlasting, without *body*, *parts*, or passions.' What, then, is their perception of 'Person' as applied to the Almighty Father? And as to *substance*, they have read in Genesis that 'every living *substance* was destroyed,' and in Deuteronomy that 'the earth opened her mouth and swallowed Dathan and Abiram up, and their houses, and their tents, and all the *substance* that was in their possession'; and in twenty other places in the Old Testament they have seen the word; but never once in that venerable Book have they read it except in a sense contrary to that in which, I presume, it is used in the above instance. In the philosophic sense, 'substance is that which underlies the attributes by which alone we are conscious of existence,' or 'the unknown, unknowable substratum on which rests all phenomena.' Thus viewed, *substance* is difficult to 'understand.' Methinks, 'trinity, person, and substance,' as they stand in your creed, with their 'confounding' and 'dividing,' may be classed among the 'unknown tongues' of the Pauline Epistles. Most certainly, as 'one that occupieth the room of the unlearned,' I am unable to say Amen, 'seeing I understand not what thou sayest'; and I think my condition would be represented by the greater portion of your congregation.

Vicar. Neither is it necessary that they should understand it. It is enough that they receive it with reverence and godly fear, and with becoming submission to their 'teachers and spiritual pastors and masters.' It is the meek and lowly who are accepted of God. Our Lord has told us that unless a man receive the Kingdom of God in the same simple spirit of trust as a little child, 'he shall not enter therein'; and the bold inquiring Thomas, who wanted such full proof, both from his senses and his understanding, of the resurrection of his Master, did not receive any special praise, but the Lord said, 'Blessed are they that have *not seen*, and *yet* have believed.' God looks at the motive, accepts the intent, and blesses the deed which springs from a loving and a grateful heart, however futile, or even silly, it may appear in the eyes of the scornful. 'She has done what she could' may be the record and the trophy in heaven of many a deed which on earth has met only with scoffing smile or stern rebuke.

Parishioner. Most true: thrice blessed are the 'poor in spirit,' and the 'pure in heart,' and the 'humble and contrite,' and all 'the weary and heavy laden' ones who pour out their sorrows before a merciful God; yea, much to be envied are those meek and lowly 'babes' to whom has been 'revealed' these 'things' which 'the wise and the prudent' have failed to perceive and to grasp. They may not be able to syllable a prayer, and yet, with a deep consciousness of need and an unfaltering faith and trust in some great Helper of the helpless, may 'count their beads' even in the poor mud huts on the wild moorlands of Connaught or elsewhere, as a religious and prayerful act acceptable to the Great Spirit 'in whom they live and have their being,' and *not count them in vain.* But then, what becomes of your previous remarks which called forth mine? St. Paul never said, and I am sure I never thought, that *prayer* in an 'unknown tongue' was unheard by the great Hearer and

Answerer of prayer; but it becomes the *teacher* to speak with 'understanding,' and *not* in an *unknown tongue*, lest 'he who occupieth the room of the unlearned should not be able to say Amen, seeing he understandeth not what thou sayest.' Moreover, there is no possible contact, *there is no semblance of similarity between the acceptance of a paradoxical creed as a condition of salvation, and the outpourings of a 'broken and a contrite spirit' seeking pardon and solace from its Maker and its God.* No, sir, I feel that your antipathy to Roman Catholicism, your mental vision of 'relics' and all the paraphernalia of superstitious worship, coupled with a sense of desertion and wrong inflicted by a once powerful advocate of your own Church, caused you to confound creed and prayer, and to obtrude upon and to censure me for notions which I never entertained. Most heartily do I accept and adopt all that you say respecting the meek and the lowly; and I will go further and say that a bold and arrogant spirit never *can* learn the lore of 'the kingdom of heaven.' It is the humble mind and the loving heart to which are revealed things hidden from the wise and prudent. It was to shepherds in the field rather than to the philosopher in his study to whom the 'good-tidings of great joy' first came. I think there is a divine truth, as well as sweet poetry, in the lines of Coleridge—

> He prayeth best who loveth best
> All things both great and small;
> For the dear God who loveth us,
> He made and loveth all.

Vicar. You brought forward two distinguished clerical authors to sustain your assertion that in the whole range of Canonical Scripture there was not a verse which, *per se*, clearly established the doctrine of the Trinity; proved it, that is, in an unequivocal manner such as might be expected in a book pronounced to be 'a *revelation*,' and 'the New Testament of our Lord and Saviour Jesus Christ'; therefore, I felt it my duty to point out to you that one of these divines was untrustworthy and to be avoided, inasmuch as, although he was once 'numbered with us, and had obtained part of this ministry,' yet had he forsaken that 'ministry,' become a 'false teacher,' 'bringing in destructive heresies,' and otherwise proving himself an apostate from the true faith.

Parishioner. Yet, nevertheless, as he was, and *is*, like Apollos of Alexandria—'an eloquent man and mighty in the Scriptures'—his authority for the purpose I quoted remains unimpeached, and is *the more* weighty and 'mighty' from the fact that he, Newman, of all persons, is the most determined opponent of the views I hold. On this especial subject he is severely indignant. It accords with the character I have assigned to him that he should be so. As the Athanasian Creed is the most mystic and incomprehensible of the creeds of the Church, it becomes *ipso facto* the subject of his most rapturous praise. He tells us that 'it is a hymn of *profound self-prostrating homage;* it is the war-song of faith. *For myself*, I have ever felt it as the *most simple* and sublime, the *most devotional* formulary to which Christianity has given birth, *more so* even than the Veni Creator and the Te Deum' (*Grammar of Assent*, p. 128). But, Newman and Keble aside, I repeat that with the exception of the verse which the Revisers of the New Testament have thrust out as spurious, there is no verse, or consecutive verses, which in their plain, grammatical, and vernacular sense show forth a Trinity. It is this fact which emboldens me to declare that it is presumptuous audacity in any man or priest to declare that whosoever doth not accept that creed, '*without doubt shall perish everlastingly.*' I maintain that so '*fundamental*' a doctrine would have been—nay, *in accordance with the eternal princples of justice must have been*—made as plain as the decrees of the Decalogue; made as emphatic, unequivocal, and explicit as were the words of Jesus when He 'lifted up his eyes to heaven, and said, Father, the hour is come; glorify thy Son, that thy Son also may glorify thee: as *thou* hast GIVEN HIM power over all flesh, that *he* should *give* eternal life to as many as thou hast given him. And THIS IS life eternal, that they might know THEE the ONLY TRUE GOD, and Jesus Christ, whom THOU hast SENT" (John xvii. 1, 2).

Vicar. I am not surprised at your bringing these verses with the same emphasis as heretofore, but they must be interpreted by other texts, which modify and explain them. I am myself astonished that during our long colloquies I have not brought under your notice the clear statement of St. Thomas as to the Divinity of our Lord, recorded by St. John (xx. 28). The emphatic words, 'My Lord and my God,' of the once sceptical but now believing disciple ought to dispel your doubts and restore your faith in the blessed Trinity. In those few expressive words St. Thomas furnishes us with a perfect 'catena' of theology, a terse summary of the orthodox creed. I hope that these words of the once doubting disciple will be blessed to you, as was the testing of the wounds in the hands and side of Jesus to him, and cause you also to receive the faith which is 'necessary to salvation.' Let me earnestly remind you that in his adoration, St. Thomas recognized alike the Humanity and the Godhead of Christ, by the two distinctive words, 'My Lord (Κυριος) and my God' (ο Θεος). In your professed reverence for the words of Scripture, I base my hope that in this pregnant sentence you will find a solution for all your doubts, and that henceforth you will become a partaker in all the rites and ceremonies of the Church so much loved by your forefathers.

Parishioner. This expression of St. Thomas never impressed itself strongly upon my attention, inasmuch as it seemed an exclamation common enough in a moment of intense surprise and wonder. I have been accustomed to hear such expressions in moments of intense alarm. Not long since, a mother seeing her young child rushing from the cottage with her clothes on fire, exclaimed, in her agony, 'O, my God, my child'! The labouring classes, when suddenly surprised, so often couple the sacred name with other names and things, that the words you have quoted seemed to me simply an instinctive exclamation on the part of the astonished Apostle. It was not until I had heard the utterance used for controversal purposes, and for the defence of the doctrine for which you have now used it, that I gave the words any special attention. As I have said, the frequency with which the Holy Name is uttered caused the sentence to be read and understood by me as a simple exclamation under intense surprise; although, of course, it showed that this direct appeal to the evidence of his senses had removed the previous doubts of Thomas as to the identity of Jesus and the Vision which had appeared to 'the other disciples.' After most careful consideration, and after all that you have now said, I am unable to conclude that these words *prove* a recognition on the part of Thomas of the Godhead of Christ. Admitting that the words *may* imply the acknowledgment of some previous error on the part of Thomas, this clearly had reference exclusively to the identity and re-appearance of Jesus. The Apostle had possibly heretofore regarded Him as the Messiah and Redeemer of Israel, and His death had frustrated these hopes—hopes which came rushing back on beholding his risen Lord. He could never have regarded Jesus as God Almighty, or he could not have felt so strong a doubt of his re-appearance to 'the other disciples' when reported by them to him. Moreover, I cannot fail to remember that in the later months of Thomas's intercourse with his Divine Master, the true relation of Jesus to 'the Father' had been often dwelt upon, and he had been accustomed to hear the two names of Jesus and God associated; he had been in the habit of calling Jesus 'Lord,' and had received approval for the same: 'Ye call me Master and *Lord*, and ye say well, for so I am' (John xiii. 13). And hence the two ideas rush into his mind at this startling crisis. A very short time indeed before His crucifixion Jesus had most tenderly besought Thomas and the other disciples in the words, 'Ye believe *in God*, believe *also in me*,' and in the joyous flush of his returning belief '*in me*,' no marvel that this pathetic entreaty should occur to the mind of the Apostle, and that he should have exclaimed, 'My Lord and my God'; thus fulfilling the almost 'dying' request of his 'Master and Lord,' and doubtless not forgetting that when he was entreated to believe 'also' in Jesus, because he believed 'in God,' he and the other disciples were, on that very occasion, informed that if they loved Him they would rejoice, because He (Jesus) said, 'I go unto the Father, for *my Father is greater than I*' (John xiv. 28). This exegesis is, I think, decisive; but admitting as a passing argument your inference, the words or exclamation would fall under the category of those 'texts' which may possibly imply a duality, but would be futile as an argument to sustain the Trinitarian assumption. In no court of honest judicial inquiry would these hasty words of the Apostle outweigh the testimony which the Scriptures afford of the fallacy of the paradoxical Creed or 'Faith' of which the Church of England declares, 'except everyone do keep whole and undefiled, without doubt he shall perish everlastingly'! The first thing that struck me in examining the passage under these new conditions, was that the cry was not in the vocative case, as a direct prayer in classic Greek would have been, and the absence of which has caused some expositors to consider the words merely as an exclamation. This, however, may be waived, inasmuch as the New Testament language varies much and

THE TRINITY TEXTLESS.

frequently from the Greek of Herodotus or Homer. Moreover, the words 'said unto him' (εἶπεν αὐτῷ) are decisive that Jesus was addressed by Thomas. Still, the words show no more than that Thomas recognized in the person before him 'The Lord' (ὁ Κυριος), the Master, whom he had loved and followed; and in His resurrection the power and almightiness of the God (ὁ Θεος μου) who had raised Him, as Lazarus also had been raised by the prayer of Jesus to the same God. Jesus, in His message to the disciples conveyed by Mary Magdalene, had informed them that He was about to ascend 'unto my Father, and to your Father; and to *my God*, and *your God*,' so that we need not be greatly astonished at the fervour of the Apostle's language at again seeing his beloved 'Κυριος' in the flesh, and in recognizing the power of HIM who, in the language of Peter subsequently, '*hath raised him* from the dead; whereof we are witnesses' (Acts iii. 15). While candidly admitting, then, that an exclamation common enough among the villagers of the Cotswold hills *would be* an unusual thing in Judea, where the name of the All Holy One is rarely pronounced—foregoing for the present what others, in common with myself (even very able men), have maintained that it was the mere instinctive utterance of agitated surprise—I yet maintain that when all the circumstances are rightfully considered, the words do not admit of the 'exegesis' you have given to them; and although not baseless, visionary, and false as the alleged statements of St. John, that there are three that bear record in heaven, and that 'these three are one,' yet are they useless for your purpose; and the readiness with which such words are brought forward by 'Trinitarians' testify how exigent is their need of scriptural 'texts' to uphold their theory. But, in respect to Church authority, decrees of Councils, and more especially the vast majority of professing Christians holding the doctrine, these facts have impressed me deeply, and, as I have repeatedly said, long delayed my utterance of vital truths.

Vicar. These quotations of yours from St. John as to the 'only true God and Jesus Christ whom he has sent,' and your plausible explanation of the words of St. Thomas, if they stood alone, would almost compel me to fall back exclusively upon the authority of the Church and the Fathers for the grounds of my Faith. Indeed, it would be well, perhaps, if we all possessed the deferential spirit of St. Augustine, who said, 'I should not believe the Gospel were I not moved by the authority of the Catholic Church.' *This*, moreover, is the safer guide amid the conflicts, the discrepancies, the deficiencies, and the literal errors of the Scriptures themselves, as we now possess them. But in respect to the especial matter before us, I have only to remind you that our Lord on finally leaving His disciples, commanded them, 'Go ye, therefore, and teach all nations, baptizing them in the name of the Father, and of the Son, and of the Holy Ghost.' This of itself is a complete refutation of your position on scriptural grounds ; and the command has been carried out through all the Christian centuries to this hour, so that it reaches us with the combined authority and weight *of the Scriptures* and *of the Church.*

Parishioner. I have heard that a distinguished Unitarian—[I dislike the term as I do that of Quaker, Baptist, Methodist, and the various other nicknames under which many so-called Christians carry on their petty strifes and warfare—] had said that this was the only statement in Holy Writ that gave him any anxiety. Why this in its isolated peculiarity should have done so I know not, even if it had been more distinctive of the three-in-one and one-in-three theory than it is. The record comes down to us with some suspicious circumstances. 'Some' of the disciples who were present on the occasion '*doubted*'; and further, there is no distinct record (that I know of) of the formula having been used by the immediate disciples of Christ ; and neither Mark nor Luke, in describing the Ascension, reports the words ; and John, I need not say, omits the circumstance of the Ascension altogether from his narrative. It would have been much strengthened as an authoritative statement if in the early baptisms recorded by Luke in his 'Acts of the Apostles' the formula had been repeated. On the Pentecostal occasion, however, when 'about three thousand souls' were added to the Church, we read only that they had been called upon to 'repent' and to be 'baptized, every one of you, in the *name of Jesus Christ* for the remission of sins.' The name only of Jesus appears to have been used. The baptism of Simon the sorcerer, and also those of the people of Samaria to whom Peter and John were sent, appear to have been conducted solely 'in the name of the Lord Jesus.' The special condition which Philip exacted from the distinguished officer of great authority under Candace, Queen of the Ethiopians, in order that he might be baptized, was that he should 'believe that Jesus Christ is the Son of God.' When Ananias restored Saul's sight we learn that Paul arose and 'was baptized,' but we have no detail of the ceremony. When under the preaching of Peter the 'Holy Ghost fell' upon many people in Cæsarea, the Apostle commanded them 'to be baptized in *the name of the Lord*.' In none of these primary baptisms have we the triple combination of 'Father, Son, and Holy Ghost.' Again, the people at Ephesus whom Paul baptized 'in the name of Jesus' had not so much as heard that 'there be a Holy

Ghost.' These three names do not prove the theory of three-in-one, still less a 'Trinity' as defined in the Athanasian Creed. No great Act of Parliament is valid—that is, it does not become a part of the statutory laws of the realm—until it has been passed 'in the name of the Queen, the Lords, and the Commons'—analogous to the form you have given as necessary for the due fulfilment of the baptismal rite; but this fact does not prove the *equality* of each body or determine anything beyond the fact that the *consent* of the three powers which constitute the one government is necessary for the permanent ordination of a law. The parallel seems to me to be complete. The argument is powerless for the purpose you quote it, inasmuch as the words Jesus used, immediately preceding this parting instruction, set aside wholly and absolutely all pretensions of an inherent, underived, co-eternal and co-equal Godhead. His precise words were: 'All power *is given unto me* in heaven and in earth'; thus forcibly reiterating at the very close of His ministry what He had told some of His disciples at its commencement—'as the Father hath life in himself, so *hath he given the Son* to have life in himself; and hath given him authority to execute judgment also, because he is the Son of man' (John v. 27).

Vicar. The manner in which you, and others, bring one passage of Scripture into collision with another, and thus, as it were, throw a suspicion on both, convinces me that Luther and the so-called reformers erred greatly in giving the Scriptures precedence over the authority of the Church; and never was a more unfortunate aphorism than that of Chillingworth, which became almost a war-cry among the 'Evangelicals'—'The Bible, I say, the Bible only is the religion of Protestants,' for in tens of thousands of instances it has caused that Book to become, as it were, a charm, a 'fetish,' and as much an object of superstition, as you have already stated, as a relic of St. Peter, or a 'rosary,' or a cup of 'holy water'; but still, where its enunciations are clear and harmoniously sustained throughout, they must be authoritative with all professing Christians. I must therefore again impress upon you this clear statement of St. Matthew, and correct you in your notion that it is isolated or unsupported, for we have a corresponding statement in many places, and especially in this striking passage of St. Paul in his second Epistle to the Corinthians: 'The grace of our Lord Jesus Christ, and the love of God, and the communion of the Holy Ghost.'

Parishioner. There is an aspect in which I can sympathize with you in your remarks as to the supremacy given by Protestants to what they call the Bible; but to 'the law and the testimony' is my *present* appeal, and I must not be carried away by a side issue. You have quoted, in vindication, or rather I ought to say, as an *enforcement* of the 'Athanasian Creed,' the baptismal formula as given by St. Matthew; and I admit that it is, among weak ones, the most weighty text for its authority that I am acquainted with; but, as I have already said, not so overwhelming as to crush the numerous 'texts' which have a different issue, and more especially as the precise words are not again repeated; and, so far as we know, every baptism reported in the Scriptures was performed without them. Baptism was certainly the initiatory rite into many forms of religion; was, in fact, the outward seal that the special faith or religion had been adopted, as when John baptized. But that it had *not* the full significance and vital importance with which the Church of a later age has invested it, becomes, I think, clear, from the fact that Paul even '*thanked God*' that he had *baptized none* of them except Crispus and Gaius and the household of Stephanas. Moreover, the Jews, 'all our fathers,' as Paul called them, were 'baptized unto Moses.' This baptism *unto Moses* shows, with other things, that being baptized in the name of a person does *not establish the divinity of that person*. On the contrary, it brings forcibly to mind the prophecy recorded by Moses of the coming Christ, which *nullifies* the idea you wish to enforce by the text; for the Lord said unto

Moses, 'I will raise them up a Prophet from among *their brethren, like unto thee,* and will *put my words* in *his* mouth; and he shall *speak unto them* all that I shall command him.' Thus Jesus was to be '*like unto Moses,*' selected from the brethren, and what He should speak was to '*be put into his mouth,*' and He would speak all that *God* should *command* Him, *and no more;* and then, after centuries had rolled away, and the Prophet Jesus had been raised up, we hear Him saying, in exact fulfilment of the above prophecy: 'Then shall ye know that I am he, and that I *do nothing of myself;* but as my *Father hath taught me,* I *speak* these things' (John viii. 28). This, I think, is *demonstrative* evidence that the verse *cannot* sustain the doctrine you wish to inculcate. The order of the names may signify the distinctive precedence of the Holy Beings named—the Father first, as the primary source of all power; the Son and the Holy Ghost following, as the recipients and dispensers of that power. Be this as it may, it is to me a most impressive fact that although Peter must have been present on the occasion referred to by St. Matthew—and it is almost morally impossible that *he* should be included in the phrase 'some doubted'—yet did he not use the formula on the memorable occasion at Cæsarea, but '*commanded* them to be baptized in the name of the Lord.' This circumstance cannot be otherwise than most weighty to any honest and discriminative person. It would, I firmly believe, be *conclusive* to any judicial mind before which the question came, untainted by previous education. Ponder, reflect! There is the chief of the apostles, the one especially selected by Jesus to build up His Church, to whom the very 'keys of heaven' had been given, performing or directing the rite of baptism soon after the alleged utterance of the command and the Ascension of his Lord. Is it in the least degree probable—I had almost said, Is it morally possible—after his marvellous experiences, after his thrilling ecstasy of joy on the Mount of Transfiguration, and his anguish and remorse in the palace of the high priest, that he should, in his very first official administrative act as chief of the apostles, fail to carry out faithfully, implicitly, and exactly the instructions of his beloved Master? Utterly improbable! Moreover, what he did subsequent to their conversion was in exact harmony with his speech which 'pricked their heart'—a speech which nullifies all the subtle dogmas and all the 'damnatory' creeds of the after-ages of the Church—a speech which sets forth in simple yet graphic and lucid language the real nature of 'Jesus of Nazareth,' His mission, and His destiny. 'Ye men of Israel, hear *these* words; Jesus of Nazareth, *a man approved of God among* you by miracles and wonders and signs, which *God did by him* in the midst of you, as ye yourselves also know: Him, being delivered by the determinate counsel and foreknowledge of God, ye have taken, and by wicked hands have crucified and slain: *whom God hath raised up*, having loosed the pains of death: because it was not possible that he should be holden of it' (Acts ii. 22-24). I must ask you to pardon this long disquisition; the *apparent* force of the verse long since impressed me, and gave me much prayerful study; and the result I have now given. There is but *one* other verse which has presented so great a perplexity, and that one is still 'nebulous,' yet—cannot upon any 'doctrine of probabilities' be made to outweigh 'the cloud of witnesses' which testify that Jesus knew 'that the Father *had given* all things into his hands, and that he was come *from* God, and went *to* God' (John xiii. 3).

Vicar. To what text do you refer?

Parishioner. To the first verse of the first chapter of John, in connection with the fourteenth verse of the same chapter; for although it is insufficient to sustain the Trinitarian theory—in other words, the Athanasian Creed—yet do these first fourteen verses require the illumination of many others, and of much reflection on the sacred history for their full elucidation. Individually, I do not care to shun the difficulty by asserting—with Bretschneider, Schwegler, and Strauss—that the Gospel is of late date and has not apostolic authority; for, although it is certain that the writer has been influenced by the philosophy of Alexandria and the writings of Plato, yet is he full of the true spirit of Christ; and if his introduction be mystic, yet are his subsequent statements so lucid and plain that to forego them would be a great loss to my argument.

Vicar. Certainly the fourteenth verse with the peculiarly Johannine expression '*sarx egeneto,*' is a strong scriptural basis for the faith, but not more so than the assertion of Paul to Timothy— 'Without controversy great is the *mystery* of godliness: God was manifest in the flesh, justified in the Spirit, seen of angels, preached unto the Gentiles, believed on in the world, received up into glory' (1 Timothy iii. 16); or his equally clear statement to the saints and brethren at Colosse, as to how anxious he was that 'their hearts might be comforted, being knit together in love, and unto all riches of the full assurance of understanding, to the acknowledgment of the *mystery of God,* and of *the Father,* and of *Christ;* in whom are hid all the treasures of wisdom and knowledge' (Colossians ii. 13).

Parishioner. To those who have seen only their English New Testaments, and are in happy ignorance of *how* their Bibles and Testaments reached them—who to this moment read with implicit faith in St. John's Epistle, that there are three that bear record in heaven, and that 'these three are one'—the address to Timothy would be very weighty, and approximative to the verse I have referred to. But ἐφανερώθη ἐν σαρκί is a very different expression to σὰρξ ἐγένετο; and, sad to tell, in the verse you have given the word 'God' is not present in the best texts. Our good Bishop Ellicott, with all his strong Trinitarian faith, after minute personal inspection of the Alexandrian manuscript, declares implicitly for 'who' (ὅς), and no other uncial manuscript pretends to have the word. In no very ancient version can it be found, nor in the quotations by the earliest Fathers of the Church. Mr. Sheldon Green, in his very excellent text and translation, published by Bagster, gives the words 'He that was manifested in the flesh'; and in the 'Revised Version' —which, unfortunately, comes slowly into general use—we read, 'He who was manifested in the flesh'; and thus it loses every atom of power for the purpose you have quoted it. Nor has the latter quotation, for the readings of the most ancient manuscripts differ exceedingly, some excluding the word 'Christ,' many the word 'Father,' besides arranging the order of the words differently. Mr. Green, to whom I referred just now, gives this passage 'unto acquaintance with the mystery of God; in which are all the treasures of wisdom and knowledge in hidden store'; and the most learned Revisers, who have recently finished their labours, omit the word 'Father' from the sentence, and assure us that the ancient authorities vary much in the text of this passage.

Vicar. All these facts show the necessity and the wisdom of the Roman Catholic Church in decreeing that the Church should be the sole interpreter of the Scriptures, and fully justify the warmth with which Pope Pius the Ninth combated the 'Bible Societies' and forbad the reading of the Scriptures by the laity except under the immediate guidance of the priests. I have never felt this so strongly as since our discussion. When it is known that the oldest manuscripts we possess, from which our New Testament *Gospels* have been derived, date nearly or quite four hundred years *after* the Christian era; when we ponder on all the possible—nay probable—sources of error in the copying of so large a mass of writing; when we reflect on the fact that the oldest, or 'Uncials,' are written wholly in capital letters, without any kind of pause to mark the termination of a word, and remember how strongly religious *feeling* biases the mind, and that this feeling was manifested even in the days of Peter and Paul, and led to their disagreement and separation; when to these facts we add that the first written Gospel did not appear until some fifty years after the death of Christ, and that a message conveyed through many persons for many years does, by default of memory or trick of the imagination, become greatly modified or changed: then must we acknowledge the great need there is that the *Church* should be our guide and teacher in all these matters; nor can we be too thankful for the promise of Christ that He will be with her even unto the end of the world.

Parishioner. The Church of Rome in this, as in many other matters, is sagacious, consistent, and logical; but we are bound, as members of the Church of England, if we are loyal to her Protestant origin, to maintain the supremacy of the Scriptures. There is, however, no gainsaying the truth of your statements respecting the many sources of error in the transmission of these documents, and the last few years have shown how countless these errors *have practically been.* Indeed, it seems the condition of things that errors should creep in when the structure of ancient Greek MSS. is understood. The equal size of the letters in a word, their continuous lines and close contiguity without any distinctive punctuation or pause. The mistakes which are possible and probable from confusing the marginal notes of some previous amanuensis, from imperfect dictation by a reader, or the imperfect hearing of a copyist, or defective formation of letters and words in the MS. copied, and scores of other causes. No one who has himself copied much from the writings of others, or has had others copy from his dictation, or has received 'copy' of his own writings from printers, will be surprised that errors have crept into ancient MSS. from each of these causes (except that of the printers, who were non-existent). Unintentional errors have changed the entire purport of a document as completely as the wilful design of the dishonest copyist. Witness the printer's error in 'King James's Bible' printed by Barker and Bill, in 1631, in which the word 'not' is left out in the seventh commandment (Exod. xx. 14), and in some others, where the word 'righteousness' occurs in Romans vi. 13, in the place of 'unrighteousness,' making it to read— 'neither yield ye your members as instruments of righteousness.' The very expressive little word 'not' has been omitted, even in works treating of the revision of the Holy Scriptures; for example, in the learned work by Drs. Milligan and Moulton, entitled *International Revision Commentary on St. John's Gospel*, it is there written, 'yet we should overlook,' instead of 'yet we should not overlook' (p. 341). And, as for oral transmission, no one could accept it as unerring [who has observed much of human habits] after it has passed through many minds and for over long periods of time. There is a 'parlour game' which illustrates this forcibly. A short phrase is *written* on paper and read to the first silently; this person transmits it in a whisper to the second, the second to a third, and so on to a dozen persons; and I have rarely known it to be accurate when given out aloud by the last person. How much more inaccurate would it have been had the message from one to the other extended over months and years instead of as many minutes? Everyone is familiar with the illustrative tale in which 'something as black as a crow' became by transmission '*three black crows.*' As regards the great lapse of time between the appearance of the Synoptic Gospels in a written form and the occurrence of the facts recorded in them, we are relieved very much by the circumstance that St. Paul's Epistles reach us, as it were, contemporaneously with their issue from his pen, or the pen of his amanuensis.

Vicar. As you attach this importance to the Epistles of St. Paul, permit me to draw your attention to his positive assertion of the Divinity of our Lord in his address to the Philippians— 'Let this mind be in you, which was also in Christ Jesus: who, being in the form of God, thought it not robbery to be equal with God' (Philippians ii. 5, 6); and further, to an equally strong expression in his Epistle to the Colossians —'For in him' [Christ] 'dwelleth all the fulness of the Godhead bodily' (Colossians ii. 9).

Parishioner. We both of us have had occasion to remark that by isolating a 'text' from its context great liability to error is incurred. This is especially the case in your quotation from St. Paul's letter to the Philippians. The very tone of the passage shows that there is some *moral* to be inculcated; and by reading the four verses preceding the two you have given we learn that in this portion of his Epistle the Apostle is earnestly imploring the saints and the bishops and deacons of Philippi to live in amity together, to banish strife, to be like-mindèd, and to cultivate the grace of *humility*, and each to 'esteem others better than themselves'; and to enforce these precepts he brings forward the example of Jesus, who, although He was the 'first-begotten Son of God, in whom HE was well pleased,' yet 'made himself of no reputation, taking even the form of a bond-servant' (δοῦλος), nor considering it 'a prize' or 'a thing to be *grasped at*' (as some versions have it) to be on an equality with God. As it pleased the Most High that in Christ should 'all fulness dwell,' and that men should 'honour the Son even as they honour the Father,' there could be no 'robbery' in his claim; and as to being in the form, or shape, or image of God, this statement can hardly be startling, still less confirmatory of any special divinity, to those who 'believe their Bibles' and have learnt therefrom that 'God said, Let us make *man in our image*, after our likeness . . . *so* God created *man* in his own image: in the image of God created he him' (Genesis i. 26, 27). This explains all that is implied in the words being 'in the form of God';

while his words to the Colossians which you have given would be fully understood by them in consequence of what he had *previously* said in the same Epistle ; for after having described Jesus as 'the image of the invisible God,' he instantaneously adds 'the first-born of *every creature.*' This idea was also present in the mind of the writer of the Apocalypse, for he calls Jesus 'the faithful and true witness—the *beginning* of the Creation of God' (Rev. iv. 14). St. Paul proceeds to call Jesus also the 'head of the Church,' as well as 'the first-born from the dead.' [This phrase is somewhat perplexing, because it would almost seem that Paul was ignorant of the many persons who had been raised from the dead prior to the resurrection of Jesus—such as by Elijah, by our Lord himself, and others]; 'that in all things he may have the pre-eminence,' '*for*' [mark the word] '*it pleased* the Father that in him should all fulness dwell.' Thus the Colossians could by no possibility have been impressed with the idea, which possessed your mind when you quoted to me the words you have done. Moreover, he earnestly implored them to continue in Christian fellowship, and prayed that their hearts may 'be comforted, being knit together in love, and unto all riches of the full assurance of understanding, to the *acknowledgment* of *the mystery of God*, and of the Father, *and of Christ ;* in whom are hid all the treasures of wisdom and knowledge.' Here you cannot fail to notice the pre-eminence and the distinctiveness given to 'God,' and also the *source* from which Christ *obtained* the '*pre-eminence in all things*'; and whatever the '*fulness of the Godhead*' may mean, it was a *virtue* which Paul earnestly hoped might be possessed by '*the saints* and the *faithful* in Christ Jesus' at Ephesus, for in his Epistle to them he said that 'he bowed his knees unto *the Father* of our Lord Jesus Christ,' that they 'might be *filled with all the fulness of God*' (Ephesians iii. 14, 19). These statements of St. Paul are (if possible) more weighty because of his known learning, his zeal, and above all the honesty of his character. We feel assured that St. Paul was not willingly reticent of any important fact in the Gospel scheme. When at Miletus, in his most touching appeal to the elders of the Church in Ephesus whom he had called unto him, he said, 'I am pure from the blood of all, for I have not shunned to declare unto you *all* the counsel of God . . . and kept back *nothing* that was profitable unto you' (Acts xx. 20-27). St. Luke in his Gospel, and more especially in his history of the Acts of the Apostles, shows to us that verily Paul 'kept nothing back' that was profitable to the followers of Jesus. As a man of consummate wisdom, he adapted himself to circumstances, and 'made himself servant unto all that he might gain the more'; and he informs us that, 'unto the Jews I became as a Jew, that I might gain the Jews.' So passionately did he yearn for their salvation, that he actually tells the Church in Rome, 'I could wish that myself were accursed from Christ for my brethren—my kinsmen according to the flesh' (Rom. ix. 3). To these Jews, therefore, he must have been especially anxious so to present Christ, that they should form a correct idea of His (Christ's) relationship to God; and he has so presented Christ, that they, the true believers in the 'only true God,' are without excuse in rejecting 'Him whom God did send,' even Jesus Christ (John xvii. 3). From these statements to the Church at Colosse, as to Ephesus, and from the large numbers of like utterances which I have given from time to time from these and other sources, it is evident that the followers of Jesus became blessed by God with the same or like privileges with which HE had endowed the 'first-born,' thus realizing the pathetic and impassioned prayer of Jesus and consummating His tender utterance, 'The glory which *THOU gavest me I have given them;* that *they may be one,* even as *we are one:* I in them and thou in me, that *they* may *be made perfect in one;* and that the world may know that thou *hast sent me,* and *hast loved them, as thou hast loved me*' (John xvii. 22, 23).

Vicar. I have listened with patience and, indeed, with interest to your interpretation of the texts I gave to you, and to the collateral texts by which you strengthened your arguments; and I did so because all your remarks have tended to help me to a decision on a point about which I have for some time been doubtful, namely, the value of the Scriptures as a *final appeal* in matters of doctrine apart from the interpretations and decrees of the Church thereon. Our discussion has convinced me it is a mistake, and the sooner we claim and adopt the principle of the Roman Catholic Church in this particular the better for ourselves, our people, and the common Faith. Your illustration derived from so common or humble a source as a parlour game is demonstrative, in my opinion, of the improbability of oral tradition being quite accurately conveyed through many individuals for long times, and also of any manuscripts being copied faithfully for many years in succession. It is obvious that it would require a *perpetual miracle*—an 'infallibility'—based on a stronger assumption than the Church claims, as the teacher and guide of mankind in spiritual things, to have secured for us an exact and literal transcript of the words and acts of Christ and His Apostles, as tens of thousands of Protestants regard the 'Bible' to be. Their opinion rests upon the most profound ignorance; and of those who become enlightened by history, research, and common sense, and learn the true nature of the Bible, too many of them at once fly off into absolute scepticism on all matters of religion; just as the French people, on finding out the fables and mummeries of Papacy, declare at once, 'There is no God!' and become Anarchists in all things. Your arguments have not influenced my judgment in the deep mysteries and verities of the Faith; but they have certainly proved to me that the Queen and Convocation erred when, in drawing up 'The Articles of Religion' for the 'Church of England,' they gave so much supremacy to Scripture as to declare that it should 'not be required of any man to accept as an "article of faith" whatsoever is not read therein, or may be proved thereby,' without having declared more distinctly and sharply *with whom* 'the proof' should finally rest; for at the present moment we have one bishop proclaiming the falsity of the Pentateuch, and another denouncing him as a heretic for his assertions! Can a house be more 'divided against itself'?

Parishioner. Nothing can be more true than that the wild views held respecting 'inspiration' and the idolatrous reverence for the Bible inculcated by the 'Evangelicals' and the founders of 'the Bible Society' upon the rising generation of the first half of the present century, begat a state of religious feeling and opinion, unfavourable to manliness and morality. It diffused a morbid and morose feeling, engendered pharisaism and spiritual pride, banished all æsthetic feeling and appreciation of art, created a dislike to intellectual research of all kinds, gave rise to set phrases in religious discourse which culminated in cant, and caused religion to consist in emotion, sentiment, and a fixed '*doctrine*,' to the discouragement of practical piety and usefulness. Further, it transformed the 'Bible' into something more hallowed and potent than 'the Ark of the Testimony'; a sealed book in its meanings to the myriads, although clear and infallible to 'the children of grace'; and thus it became a kind of 'fetish' to that large class, the lower middle class, whom Matthew Arnold calls 'Philistines'; the practical outcome being that the artisans, mechanics, and labourers of our large towns capable of reading and fond of listening to voluble and frothy demagogues have become 'secularists' and scoffers on finding that the idolized 'book' was not, as they had been taught to regard it, 'the immediate, unadulterated, unchanged, and infallible Word of God.' Mischief of the direst kind has befallen our operative classes from this cause. In the past generation the 'plenary inspiration' of the Bible, that is, that every word was Divine, was everywhere taught. To demur to the statement excited the greatest indignation among the followers of Simeon, Venn, and Scott. It was to the 'Evangelical' as profane a thing as to doubt the bodily presence of Jesus in a 'consecrated' wafer would be to a devout 'Anglican priest' at the present time! When the spread of education through Board schools and other influences caused men to know that the 'Bible' was an aggregation of books, written some of them hundreds of years apart, containing the history and the poetry of various individuals in various nations; that they had been *translated* from several languages, and, therefore, subject to the same errors as other books which have been written and printed in one language, and after the lapse of years have been translated, and written, and printed in the language of another country, the effect was most sad. The pious error zealously fostered by earnest and ignorant men has (as is always the case with falsehood) culminated in calamity. The scientific errors, the histories of immorality and crime, which are to be found within its pages, have been distorted and exaggerated, and the volume which was once reverenced as a sacred thing is treated with scorn, even as a savage has battered to pieces some 'graven image' to which he had prayed in vain for rain, food, or revenge on his foes. The 'Bibliolatry' of the past, this mistaken fanaticism, has produced such a revulsion of feeling that it has now come to pass that the grandest, the best of books, the book verily containing the words of God, is treated by tens of thousands of persons with neglect, and by hundreds with ridicule or scorn.

Vicar. The picture you have drawn is a sad one, dark 'as earthquake and eclipse,' but I fear that it is a true one. The literature of the day, whether we look at the daily newspapers, the monthly magazines, or the quarterly reviews, is marked by a 'scepticism' which would have shocked our forefathers. If we listen to conversation at the clubs by leading politicians, judges, barristers, and physicians of the day, we cannot but observe that the old reverence for, and belief in, many of the statements of Holy Writ have passed away. The vulgar scoff of the early Georgian era may not be heard (the courtesy which high culture creates forbids this), but it would be sheer folly to conceal the fact that many a Biblical record received with reverence by our forefathers is relegated to the chronicle 'of old wives' fables' by the cultured minds of the present generation. No marvel, then, that smatterers in science, whom 'a little knowledge puffeth up,' that designing demagogues and 'agitators' should inflame and intoxicate the minds of the ignorant and discontented with statements and theories calculated to subvert and destroy respect for all order and authority, whether religious or social. The outlook of the future is most gloomy, but may the Great Controller of all events, who can cause 'the wrath of man to praise him,' and 'hath made all things for himself, yea, even the wicked for the day of evil,' direct it to His glory, and the happiness of mankind.

Parishioner. Deeply and devoutly do I respond to the words you have just spoken. The moral outlook of the future is, indeed, gloomy. In all our large cities the revulsion from religious credulity is excessive and widespread. It is, indeed, correspondent with that great law of physics which enforces that the rebound shall be proportionate to the momentum of the original force applied, and the fanaticism in respect to the immediate verbal inspiration, and consequent sacredness of the 'Bible,' was extreme. *Bibliolatry*—for this *it was*—prevailed almost universally. To be engaged reverentially in any manner with the Bible, no matter how mechanically, was deemed a pious act; a work not simply 'well pleasing in the sight of God,' but more so than a faithful performance of the secular duties of life; and consequently they employed themselves in counting its chapters and verses and duly recorded them. Nothing in relation thereto was frivolous, but all was 'holy.' Consequently we are gravely informed that the conjunction 'and' occurs thirty-five thousand five hundred and thirty-five times in the pages of the

Old Testament, and that in the New Testament it occurs ten thousand six hundred and eighty-four times. Further, we have been told that the twenty-first verse of the seventh chapter of Ezra contains all the letters of the alphabet; and, not contented with numbering the books, chapters, and verses, devotees have assured us that there are seven hundred and seventy-three thousand words; and, further still, that there are three million five hundred and sixty-six thousand four hundred and eighty letters in the 'Holy Bible.' 'Churchmen' and 'Dissenters' alike smile or pity, according to the depth of their Christianity, when such things are told of Mohammedans in respect to the 'Koran,' wholly unconscious in respect to this kind of idolatry, of 'the beam in their own eye,' while so very cognisant of 'the mote' in the eye of their Mohammedan brother. The revulsion has, however, set in, and the sceptical feeling is evident, more or less, in all classes. From the theories and conclusions of scientific men, even atheistic notions have been deduced; but, as you justly observe, the smatterers, whom 'a little knowledge puffeth up,' have been chiefly conspicuous in diffusing their platitudes, and have not hesitated to deduce atheistic notions from the writings of Darwin, and to publish them as essays in magazines, or to proclaim them in discourses at lecture halls; although the great philosopher himself has not authoritatively announced such conclusions. Indeed, so far from avowing atheism as his creed, this accurate observer in his monumental work on *The Origin of Species*, in its third edition, writes, 'I see no good reason why the views given in this volume should shock the religious feelings of any one. It is satisfactory to know, as showing how transient such impressions are, to remember that the greatest discovery ever made by man—namely, the law of the attraction of gravity—was also attacked by Leibnitz "as subversive of natural, and inferentially of revealed religion." A celebrated author and divine has written to me that he has gradually learnt to see that it is just as noble a conception of the Deity that he created a few original forms capable of self-development into other and needful forms, as to believe that HE required a fresh act of creation to supply the voids caused by the action of his laws. . . . To my mind it accords better with what we know of the laws impressed on matter by the *Creator*, that the production and extinction of the past and present inhabitants of the world should have been due to secondary causes like these determining the birth and death of the individual' (pp. 515-24). No 'atheism' is to be found in these grand words, nor do I think that the speculations of biologists have been half so mischievous as the wild theories of theologians, and the perversion of the true meaning of words to sustain a pre-conceived or accepted belief. It has been chiefly through theories of the Divine Government, which shock the moral sense and disgust the rational and instinctive attributes of mankind, that the widespread atheism of the hour has taken its rise, and finds its sustenance. Let us hope, however, that the swing of the pendulum will right itself; that the darkness may be the precursor of a purer and greater light ; that the widespread infidelity may be of short duration ; and that the removal of this vast Biblical error will be like the removal of some huge tumour by a skilful surgeon, which, although painful and bewildering in its immediate action, is followed by vigorous health and lasting vigour. The Great Arbiter doeth all things well. I often think that great poets are true prophets, for even the timid and despondent Cowper, despite his Calvinistic creed, could in his wiser moments write :

> *Heavenward* all things *tend.* For all were once
> Perfect, and all must be at length restored.
> *So God has greatly purposed ;* who would else
> In his dishonoured works himself endure
> Dishonour, and be wronged without redress.

These lines seem to convey a sublime truth, however much we may demur to the incidental statement 'for all were once perfect.' The modern teachings of 'biological' science assure us that Tennyson was the more accurate, who, while accepting the theory that heavenward all things tend, tells us—

> They say,
> The solid earth whereon we tread
>
> In tracts of fluent heat began,
>   And grew to seeming-random forms,
>   The seeming prey of cyclic storms,
> Till at the last arose the man;
>
> Who throve and branch'd from clime to clime,
>   The *herald of a higher race,*
>   And of himself in higher place,
> If so he type this work of time
>
> Within himself, from more to more;
>   Or, crown'd with attributes of woe
>   Like glories, move his course, and show
> That life is not as idle ore,
>
> But iron dug from central gloom,
>   And heated hot with burning fears,
>   And dipt in baths of hissing tears,
> And *batter'd with the shocks of doom*
>
> *To shape and use.* Arise and fly
>   The reeling Faun, the sensual feast;
>   Move upward, *working out the beast,*
> And let the ape and tiger die.

Vicar. The lines you quote teem with thought and poesy; but I must protest against them as most erroneous and heterodox, warring against the very first principles of our faith, against the teachings of the Bible as to the creation and the prime perfection and fall of man; and as a corollary, against the great Atonement as a propitiation for sin, and the redemption of mankind from the consequences of the Fall.

Parishioner. As you have already said, the Bible needs an interpreter. If we sought in its pages for an authentic statement of the creation of man, where should we look—to the first chapter of 'Genesis,' or to the second chapter of that book? for the description of the creation differs in each, and has evidently been written by two distinct historians. I will not, however, attempt to disguise from you that I accept neither as accurate literal descriptions of the creation and fall of man. I look upon the story as an imaginative narrative akin to that of *Paradise Lost*, which Milton has based upon it. No geologist of repute will admit that this world is not six thousand years old, as the chronology of our Bibles would imply. Indeed, most of the 'defenders of the faith' have given this up as a baseless proposition; and to reconcile the statements of the Bible with the known facts of geology various devices have been resorted to. As in aid of the doctrine of the Trinity words and verses have been forged and added to the manuscripts, so to reconcile the first chapter of Genesis with the indisputable facts of science, *word-torture* has been used. 'In the beginning' has been wrested from its context and *made* to mean or signify a period of æons, prior to the creation of day and night. The word 'day' has been made to do duty for thousands of years, or any indefinite time; although we are distinctly told that the 'evening and morning were the first day,' and so on through a consecutive series of days and creative acts until we reach the seventh day; and then we learn that 'God blessed the seventh day and sanctified it, because that in it he had rested from all his work which God had created and made' (Genesis ii. 3). This perversion and trifling with words for theological purposes has been sanctioned by the highest dignitaries of the Church, notwithstanding that the same Moses* who tells of this procedure of creation *also* tells us after his interview with God on the top of Sinai that the seventh day was to be hallowed for ever, because God had in *six days* created the world and its denizens, and rested on the seventh day. For centuries this commandment has been literally observed by the Hebrews, to whom it was given, in whose *language it was written*, and the word 'day' has been by them regarded as the time between the rising and setting of the sun. A book that needs *such* manipulation cannot be of Divine origin. To 'reconcile' *known facts* with Biblical history, Dean Buckland, in his great Bridgewater Treatise, resorted to this tricksy expedient; and to reconcile the irreconcilable, the scholarship of many divines (good Bishop Ellicott among the

* Exodus xix. 20.

number) and the marvellous talents and skilled geological labours of Hugh Miller have been employed in vain. 'The testimony of the rocks' was adverse, and the zealous advocate of a 'pious' theory died overwhelmed with despair. As the sunlight first illumines the mountain-peaks, and then diffuses itself over the less elevated regions, and subsequently sheds its splendour over the valleys, until every knoll and every rivulet are bathed in light, so is it with the birth and diffusion of knowledge. The light of science is now radiant in the higher regions of human thought, and here and there we have even bishops, who can gaze upon it without flinching, while others, owlet-like, hover in the twilight, or shut their eyes in dislike or dismay. Knowledge, like light, is diffusive, and ignorance and falsehood disappear before it, as darkness melts into the sunshine. Superstition recedes, as the ghostly fears of children vanish with the approaching day, and thus it comes to pass that the awe with which the 'Bible' was regarded, and the dread of investigating any of its statements, are disappearing in the cultured classes. The good Bishop Colenso, long since, had the honesty and the courage to declare in a missionary address 'It is *impossible* to believe in that traditionary notion, in which, I suppose, we have most of us been trained, of the whole human race having sprung from the three sons of Noah about four thousand years ago, as well as of all animals having been derived from those which were preserved with Noah in the ark, when we know that on the monuments of Egypt, dating shortly after the scriptural date of the Flood, if not even before it, there are depicted the same distinctly marked features as characterizing the different races of men and animals just exactly as we see them now.' There is nothing new in this statement, except as having been spoken by a bishop of the Church of England, and hence will arrest an attention from hundreds who look to 'clerical' authority for guidance; reflected from such a mountain-peak, the peasant in the valley may observe the light, and profit accordingly. It is in this region that I have hope; tradition, education, custom, and 'caste' make such enlighted dignitaries rare; yet still, as one great mind after another becomes imbued with some individual truth, and has the courage to enunciate its opinions, the light must increase and the darkness disappear in a corresponding degree. The 'morning stars' visible, are as yet few, but they are of the 'first magnitude,' and Farrar, and Jowett, and Colenso, and Stanley, augur the approach of day; at present, however, the dawn is feeble, for their ecclesiastic brethren as a class, like dense clouds, intercept their beams. As the cultured secular mind has become tolerant of the idea, that for untold millions of years this earth has been the theatre of life and death, foolish expedients have been resorted to, as I have shown, to reconcile such statements with the Mosaic record, and very recently, I am quite sorry to say, forty bishops and scores of clergymen have testified their approval of the book of a pseudo-scientist, who, adopting the pretty theory of Kurst, of a series of panoramic visions passing before the mind of a tranced seer, has daringly stated that the description ascribed to Moses harmonizes in every particular with the facts of geology and biological science. By such expedients the tales of Baron Munchausen and the travels of Samuel Gulliver may be made to appear as veritable history.

Vicar. When I said that many a Biblical record accepted as a fact by our forefathers had been relegated to the regions of 'old wives' fables' by scientific persons, I did not anticipate that *you* would throw aside the authority of Revelation, because throughout our discussion you have persistently said to 'the law and the testimony,' and by the Scriptures, and the Scriptures only, you declared that you would justify your non-acceptance of one of the oldest creeds of the Holy Catholic Church. Am I to understand that you have ceased to regard the Book as Divinely inspired—as being, in fact, *the Word of God?*

Parishioner. I think I have already proved—*demonstrated*, in fact, as far as words can demonstrate anything—that the Holy Scriptures give no support to what is called 'The Athanasian Creed.' I have shown from its hallowed words—hallowed by age and by the reverence and the love of the highest and purest minds of our race—that the doctrines or ideas contained in that Creed are opposed to the words and the acts of our blessed Lord, to the sayings of the Evangelists, to the teachings of Paul and Peter and James, and to the inspired utterances of the sages and prophets of the Old Testament. I have shown conclusively from the Gospels and Epistles of Holy Scriptures—that the Athanasian Creed is Antibiblical. That in the 'Law and Testimony' it finds no support. It is wholly textless, and without an atom of Scripture Authority—and by the Scriptures and the Scriptures in their entirety, I have justified, and that most fully, my non-acceptance of the creed—which you are pleased to call 'one of the oldest creeds,' although, as a matter of historic accuracy, you might have called it 'one of the youngest.' But as respects the Bible, as it is *not*, as its name implies it to be, one book but many books, written by various writers; as the writers of some of the books are unknown; as they were written in different places and hundreds of years apart; as some of them contain descriptions of things which we now know, from like things under our own immediate observation, to be inaccurate; as the books vary in moral qualities, and are sometimes contradictory the one to the other; as they have been changed verbally in most important particulars by passing from one language to another, and by the design as well as by the unintentional errors of copyists: as some of the acts applauded therein are revolting to the highest and purest feelings which Christianity inculcates and fosters, I cannot regard the whole Bible as '*the* Word of God,' although I most sincerely believe that in no other book in the world can we find the words of God so frequently and so clearly enforced.

Vicar. St. Paul, in his second Epistle to Timothy, distinctly writes that '*all* scripture is given by inspiration of God, and is profitable for doctrine, for reproof, for correction, and for instruction in righteousness' (iii. 16).

Parishioner. There again is an illustration of the need of an authentic interpreter of the Scriptures, and also an illustration of how fallacious the Bible may, and has, become in the hands of the masses. The text you have given is most misleading through an erroneous translation; it should *not* have been printed '*All scripture is given* by inspiration,' but, as it was written by Paul, '*Every scripture inspired of God is profitable,*' which is a very different matter. I joyfully and most gratefully accept the fact recorded by James, 'that every *good* gift and every perfect gift is from above, and cometh down from the Father of Lights, with whom is no variableness' nor 'shadow of turning.' Not only in the 'old time,' but *in the present*, do I firmly believe that 'holy men of God spake as they were moved by the Holy Ghost' (2 Peter i. 21). God is 'the same to-day, yesterday, and for ever'; and as His wisdom is infinite, His power boundless, and His love such that 'his mercy endureth for ever,' *what HE inspires* must ever be in principle *changeless*, harmonious, and consistent with HIS own attributes of justice and truth. His decrees cannot be contingent on circumstances, or change with clime or time. But it seems to me absolutely monstrous that men and women should, as they practically do, bow with slavish fear to every word contained in a bundle of numerous books which, being bound in one cover, is called 'The Bible,' written they know not when or by whom, *and yet at the same time believe* that the operation and teachings of the Most Holy Spirit of God were limited to the land of the Hebrews, and to an epoch which ended with the life of the writer of the mystic book called 'The Revelation of St. John the Divine.' This 'Bibliolatry,' this clinging to mere material forms, this reverence for a printed book, this training, this union of superstition and ignorance, have caused 'Christians' (as I have shown) to equal the lowest savages in barbarous feelings. Few savage lands have more painful records than has ours in *Foxe's Book of Martyrs;* and in *The History of Witchcraft* we have also an equally painful record of the effects of an exaggerated and erroneous view of 'Inspiration,' and the consequent idolatrous reverence for every word contained in the Bible. 'Bibliolatry' has exacted its victims, and subjected them to cruelties as barbarous as has 'Idolatry.' In Protestant England, yea, even in Protestant Scotland, have hundreds of persons been put to death by the most excruciating tortures under the belief that they were 'witches,' and therefore to be destroyed, in obedience to the inspired (?) Mosaic Law, 'Thou shalt not suffer a witch to live' (Exodus xxii. 18). Instead of testing the Divine origin of *a book* by the *eternal laws of justice*, the laws of justice have been made conformable to the statements contained in a book alleged by its votaries to be in every syllable the 'Word of God,' although admittedly derived from a language other than their own, therefore necessitating a *translation*, and as a corollary, the inspiration of the translator. Even so honest, and legally so learned a judge as Chief Baron Hale could tell a jury: 'That there *are* such creatures as witches I make no doubt at all; for, first, the Scriptures have affirmed so much; secondly, the wisdom of all nations hath provided laws against such persons, which is an argument of their confidence of such a crime.'

(Campbell's *Lives of the Queen's Justices*, Vol. I.) The two poor women were hung accordingly. Luther had heartily advocated the burning of witches on the same grounds. For a time, in our own country, the iniquitous laws demanding such barbarities were repealed in the reign of the Roman Catholic Queen Mary; but during the reign of 'Good Queen Bess,' at the instigation of bishops and priests, the cruel laws were re-enacted. In Bishop Jewel's sermons, published by the Parker Society, we learn this: preaching before Her Majesty, he said: 'May it please your Grace to understand that witches and sorcerers within these few years are marvellously increased within your Grace's realm. Your Grace's subjects pine away even unto the death: their colour fadeth, their flesh rotteth, their speech is benumbed, their senses are bereft'; and then, with consummate cunning, the wily bishop adds: 'I pray God they never practice *further than upon the subject.*' Well might this 'pious' prayer startle Her Majesty. No marvel that after this appeal hundreds of aged, ignorant women were condemned to death. Hanging and burning were sometimes, nay often, preceded by ingeniously contrived, excruciating torture. Pitcairn's *Criminal Trials of Scotland* contain harrowing details. One case will suffice as detailed by Lecky in his *History of Rationalism in Europe*. One Dr. Fian was suspected of having aroused the wind, and a confession was wrung from him by torture, which, however, he almost immediately afterwards retracted. Every form of torture was in vain employed to vanquish his obduracy. The bones of his legs were broken into small pieces in the 'boot.' All the torments that Scottish law knew of were successively applied. At last the King, James I. (who personally presided over the tortures), suggested a new and more horrible device. The prisoner, who had been removed during the deliberation, was brought in, 'his nails upon all his fingers were riven and pulled off with an instrument called in Scottish a turkas, which in England we call a pair of pincers, and under every nail there were thrust in two needles over even up to the heads.' Notwithstanding all this torture, the quaint contemporary narrative adds, 'so deeply had the devils entered into his heart, that he utterly denied all that which he had before avouched,' and he was then burnt unconfessed. The storm which this doctor was said to 'have raised' was one which hindered the matrimonial arrangements of King James with the Princess of Denmark, by driving back the Princess, after putting to sea, to Upslo, in Norway. A great foe to witches was James; and soon after his accession to the throne, a law was enacted which subjected witches to death on the first conviction, 'even though they should have inflicted no injury upon their neighbours.' Twelve bishops sat upon the Commission to which this law was referred; but, sad also to say, that even under Cromwell the same system prevailed; in fact then, and long after, such cruel persecutions were deemed expedient and just by all who regarded the Bible, presented in our own language, as verily and actually in every word the command of the Almighty and Eternal God, and tens of thousands still so regard it. Hence it often happened that an unfortunate old woman, ugly, deformed, or insane, was deemed to be a 'witch,' and therefore it became wicked that she should 'be permitted to live,' and holy men like unto Richard Baxter rejoiced in their destruction. In his book, *World of Spirits*, he almost revels over the death of 'an old *reading parson* (reading is usually an antidote to witchcraft) named Lowis, not far from Framlingham,' who was hanged as a witch. By that ghastly perversion of logic and sound reasoning, namely, testing the soundness of a doctrine by the tenets of an ancient book, rather than the truthfulness of the book, by the common sense and justice of its tenets, all the said miseries came to pass; and even the saintly John Wesley has left on record in his Journal, 'the English in general, and indeed most of the men of learning in Europe, have given up all accounts of witches and apparitions as mere old wives' fables. They well know (whether Christians knew it or not) that *the giving up witchcraft is in effect giving up the Bible.*' Yet has this manner of 'giving up the Bible' by the 'giving up of witchcraft,' saved the lives of tens of thousands of persons. It is appalling to know that in one year, in the district of Como, one thousand persons were burnt as witches, and that this stupendous crime was common to all 'Christian' countries. During the 'Long Parliament' in England, three thousand witches are said to have been destroyed; and from 'first to last in Presbyterian Scotland some four thousand,' and this murderous thing would have gone on even until now had not 'sceptics' (that is, men so called by others whom the said 'sceptics' might pity as 'fanatics') protested against the further continuance of the Mosaic Law: 'Thou shalt not suffer a witch to live.' With the abolition of the law the witches have disappeared, although they were said to have existed by thousands in Europe during the Middle Ages, and by hundreds in England and Scotland during the reigns of Elizabeth and James, and the Commonwealth; and those who doubted their existence were deemed by the clergy, and even by so intelligent a layman as Sir Thomas Browne, to be sinful people, or, in the words of the latter, 'a sort not of infidels but atheists.' [The said nomenclature applied to the 'unbelievers' in witches is still retained for use to those who are unable to comprehend that 'three are one' and 'one is three.'] As wolves and other noxious creatures have disappeared in this country under 'the resources of civilization, even so have the grosser phantoms of the mind vanished under the tuitions of observation and science; so, in due time, will also the baseless subtleties and irrational paradoxes of the creed of St. Athanasius. Our Divine Lord in His day abrogated the Mosaic code of 'eye for eye, tooth for tooth, foot for foot, burning for burning, wound for wound, stripe for stripe' (Exod. cxxi. 24, 25); and, guided by His teachings, and His practice, the more courageous and truthful of His disciples have in process of time rescinded the companion law of 'Thou shalt not suffer a witch to live' (Exod. xxii. 18). Thus truth and justice survive and triumph. Thus do mischievous fallacies ultimately fade from the minds of men, whether they exist under the name of witchcraft, or 'inspired texts,' or the 'Catholic doctrine' of the Trinity. Neither our blessed Redeemer, who abrogated the vengeful code of 'eye for eye, tooth for tooth,' or His faithful and true followers who enforced the repeal of the death-sentence in witchcraft, could have accepted the theory of the 'plenary' inspiration of the Bible, as understood by the 'Evangelical' section of the Church of England, or by the crowds which hang upon the lips of Charles H. Spurgeon, or follow the drum and banners of 'General' Booth. Jesus came to fulfil and not to destroy the law of His God, and therefore would not have dared to condemn that which had been directly commanded by HIM. Christ knew full well that the command issued by Moses was finite in its nature and its purport, and therefore was not 'the Word of God' in the rigid sense taught by enthusiasts. God is omniscient and Almighty, and therefore His words and His laws are changeless and eternal. Jesus would have said with Isaiah: 'The grass withereth, the flower fadeth; *but the word of our God shall stand for ever*' (Isaiah xl. 8). These clear facts being so distinctly impressed upon my mind, I marvel that it has not aroused hundreds of others besides George Fox into a state of spiritual indignation and frenzy that men should thus limit to place and time the operations of that Divine agency which Jesus told Nicodemus 'bloweth where it listeth.' Moreover, it seems verging on profanity that the external works of God, the eternal laws of justice and morality, the voice of conscience, and the teachings of nature should be tested exclusively by this ancient volume, composite in language and theme, rather than that these great principles should in themselves be the tests of the truthfulness or untruthfulness of a record written by many men at various times and various places. God is revealing Himself continuously throughout the ages, and therefore the present, as compared with any preceding age, is one of light and revelation, and has a higher claim to the phrase of 'wisdom of antiquity,' as being in reality the more 'ancient,' or aged.

Vicar. My fears are greatly intensified by your remarks. I regret deeply that you do not regard the whole of the *canonical* books as received by the Church of England as directly and exclusively inspired, and not to be contravened by anything whatever. Certainly it would have been better for the avoidance of confusion and the check of schism if the *interpretation* or *meaning* of the Scriptures had been exclusively vested in the Church; but I shall be unable to recognize you as a Christian, still less as a member of the 'holy Catholic Church,' if (as I understand) you do *not* accept *the general sense* of all the canonical books as undoubtedly inspired and every way indisputable. I hope I may have misunderstood you in this matter.

Parishioner. In frankness I must say that you have not misunderstood me. My desire is to be lucid and plain. Truth is dear to me as life itself. To use Bacon's metaphors, I am battling for no 'idol,' whether of the 'den,' the 'market,' or the 'theatre.' I have now no theory to uphold. The superstitions, dreams, and convictions of my youth and middle age have been wrenched from my soul; a 'new birth' has been realized with sobbing and pain, as all births are. But this is past. I have learnt to know that God is ever ready to commune with the spirit of man, 'to send forth his light and his truth' to all who yearn for them, inasmuch as 'God is Love,' and since 'God is our Father in Heaven,' this *necessarily* must be so, and one is not now surprised that Paul should have told the Athenians that 'in him we live and move and have our being, as certain even of your own poets (Aratus) have said, "for we are also his offspring."' The great Apostle of Christ thus endorsed the utterance of the secular poet, and used it to illustrate his own inspired statement. God has spoken in all ages to the listening soul. Even Seneca, born though he was before the Christian era, could write, 'Ita, dico, Lucili, sacer intra nos Spiritus sedet, malorum, bonorumque nostrorum observator et custos. Hic prout a nobis tractatus est, ita nos ipse tractate. Bonus vir sine Deo nemo est' (Epistle 41); and centuries after the days of Seneca there arose in another land a great teacher, Mahomet, who, in summing up his teachings in the eighteenth chapter of the Meccan series of the Koran, writes, 'Say, I am *only a mortal like yourselves, I am inspired* that your God is only one God. Then let him who hopes to meet his Lord act righteous acts.' To worship 'only one God, and to act righteous acts' was the sentence or commandment which Mahomet considered he was 'inspired' to utter, and we learn from trustworthy historians that his teachings have been accepted by tens of thousands, and are the guide through life and the solace in death of most of the inhabitants of Turkey, India, and many other parts of Asia and Africa. Thousands of Her British Majesty's subjects in India live and die in the 'Mohammedan' faith—the faith which Mahomed claims to have been given by inspiration from God, although carefully avowing himself 'a mortal like unto yourselves.' But, leaving this illustrative passing thought of the inspiration of the great 'Prophet of Arabia,' I maintain that the Spirit of God is a continuously operating power, that the inspiration of the Almighty is ceaseless, and as efficacious and as immanent now as ever it was in the grey morning of the world. Did I not believe this I could not, as now, pray in your church for 'the healthful spirit of God's grace'; I could not, as I do now, almost daily adopt the words of David, 'O send out thy light, and thy truth—let them lead me,' 'Open thou mine eyes that I may behold wondrous things out of thy law'; I could not gather, as now, cheerfulness and comfort from the belief that Christ is 'a true light which lighteth every man that cometh into the world'; that 'God who commanded the light to shine out of darkness hath shined in our hearts to give the light of the knowledge of the glory of God in the face of Jesus Christ'; that, as in the olden time there were prophets, so are there now many 'who are light in the Lord'; and as Bezaleel was 'filled with the spirit of God, in wisdom and in understanding, and in knowledge, and in all manner of workmanship, to devise cunning works, to work in gold, and in silver, and in brass' (Exodus xxxi.), so are men now, in like manner, filled with 'the Spirit of God' to do great and good acts for the benefit of their kind. Yes, that good Spirit speaks to pure and receptive souls at the present time as clearly and as fully as HE did when the young Samuel, from his sleeping cot in the temple, cried, 'Speak, Lord, for thy servent heareth.' But there are delusive voices as there are 'lying spirits,' and it becometh the wise not to believe 'every spirit, but try the spirits whether they are of God : because many false prophets have gone out into the world' (1 John iv. 1); and one infallible test is *consistency*, the never-failing consentient harmony between *all* the words and all the works of God 'in all places of his dominion,' whether in the domain of nature, or the spiritual kingdom, or the heart of man. You speak of 'canonical books' as 'inspired.' Who decreed, out of the numberless 'gospels' which existed in the earliest centuries of Christianity, which of the many should be 'canonical' and which excluded? Perhaps one of the most august, certainly one of the most influential, of the numerous 'Councils' of the Church was the eighteenth, or General Council of Trent, which assembled in A.D. 1545, and continued (with interruptions through the pontificates of Pope Paul III., Julius III., and Pius IV., to 1563. This Council decreed what books out of the mass of so-called 'Scriptures' before them should be *canonical*, and pronounced an anathema of eternal condemnation upon all who decline to accept any one of them so decreed. The *Church of England* has *excluded* several of the books *thus authorized* from '*canonical*' rank, and yet, with her accustomed inconsistency in spiritual things, she authorizes some of these very 'uncanonical' books (canonical according to the Council of Trent) to be read at her *daily* services, but will not allow them to be read on the Sabbath Day. Do you expect me to accept these books, which are sufficiently good to be read on 'week-days,' but not sufficiently 'holy' to be read on Sundays, as '*inspired*'?

Vicar. Most decidedly not. I distinctly said the whole of the '*canonical books*' as *received by the 'Church of England,'* and *not* to accept them is, *ipso facto*, to exclude yourself from the ranks of her sons.

Parishioner. The Church of England has deliberately refused to accept into her canon as *inspired* several books which the more ancient Church (from whom she derives all her pretensions to be regarded as a Church having apostolical succession and all that it involves) declares to be 'canonical,' nay, assures us that they 'have been dictated either by Christ's own word of mouth or by the Holy Ghost, and preserved by a continuous succession in the Catholic Church,' and has declared with the same emphasis as the younger Church has of the Athanasian Creed, 'If anyone receive not *as sacred* and canonical these same books entire, with all their parts, let him be anathema!' As an individual, upon 'Protestant' principles, *i.e.* the right of private judgment, I claim the same privilege of selection as did the 'Reformation' Committee upon the books which the ancient Church had in the most solemn manner declared to have been derived from 'Christ's own word of mouth' or 'by the Holy Ghost.' I do so because, after all, both in the 'Council of Trent' and the 'Reformation' Chamber the reason or judgment of man was the final appeal as to which of the books were 'inspired,' and which were not, and most certainly some of the books which the 'Protestant' Church *refused to receive* into her canon are far 'more profitable for doctrine, for reproof, for correction, and for instruction in righteousness' than others which she has accepted, and which you call upon me to receive as directly and wholly the inspired Word of God.

Vicar. What can you mean by such a daring

statement? Surely you do not presume to say that the 'books of Maccabees' and the history of 'Bel and the Dragon' are to be compared, for the purposes described by Paul to Timothy, with the writings of Isaiah and David?

Parishioner. No, but I say that the 'book of Solomon' and 'Ecclesiasticus,' approved by the Council of Trent, are better adapted for such purposes than is 'The book of Canticles,' which has been preferred before them, which has been retained as 'inspired,' while the other two are denied that distinction. It is an insult to common sense to hold up the Canticles as the direct 'Word of God.' I know what to expect from the credulous, the ignorant, and the fanatical in speaking thus of this book; a book which, by-the-bye, used to be an especial favourite among the 'Evangelicals,' and over which I have known more than one young lady go into *hysterical* raptures. The two books I have named abound in sublime thoughts and words full of wisdom, whereas the 'Canticles' read like voluptuous love-songs, and never could have been considered anything otherwise than an amatory poem had not some interpolator introduced parenthetically into a manuscript the words 'Vox Christi,' and some other 'pious' copyist divided the songs into chapters, and put plausible 'headings' to each chapter, by which Christ and the Church are made to take the places of the lover and his beloved. Origen calls it an epithalamium in the form of a drama: he soon, however, clothes it with allegory. Theodore, Bishop of Mopsuestia, the friend and schoolfellow of St. Chrysostom, wisely sets aside the allegory, and regards them as a series of amatory poems written by Solomon to win the affections of an Ethiopian princess; a description which the entire language of the book fully justifies. Be this as it may, when two great Churches like the Western and the Anglican differ as to which books of the Bible *are* inspired, and which books are *not* inspired, a prudent and conscientious man will exercise his own judgment as to which of the decrees he shall accept. In Solomon's Song I recognize strong and passionate love, exquisite poetry, and most voluptuous imagery—imagery not exceeded in lyric sweetness by Anacreon or Moore. What more amatory than, 'Behold, thou art fair, my love; behold, thou art fair; thou hast doves' eyes within thy locks : thy hair is as a flock of goats, that appear from Mount Gilead. Thy teeth are like a flock of sheep that are even shorn, which came up from the washing; whereof every one bear twins, and none is barren among them. Thy lips are like a thread of scarlet, and thy speech is comely : thy temples are like a piece of pomegranate within thy locks. Thy neck is like the tower of David builded for an armoury, whereon there hang a thousand bucklers, all shields of mighty men. Thy two breasts are like two young roes that are twins, which feed among the lilies. Until the daybreak and the shadows flee away I will get me to the mountain of myrrh, and to the hill of frankincense. Thou art all fair, my love; there is no spot in thee.' Do not these words breathe of 'the clime of the East, the land of the sun'? The metaphor of the 'two young roes that are twins, which feed among the lilies,' seems to me unsurpassed for sensuous beauty in the odes of Horace, the poems of Byron, or the songs of Sappho; but, in the words of St. James, 'this wisdom descendeth not from above, but is earthly and sensual,' whereas in the thirteenth chapter of *The Wisdom of Solomon* I read noble words, which, like Adam's morning hymn in Milton's *Paradise Lost*, appear instinct with 'inspiration' of the highest kind. 'Surely vain are all men by nature who are ignorant of God, and could not out of the good things that are *seen* know him *that is;* neither by considering the works did they acknowledge the workmaster, but deemed either fire, or wind, or the swift air, or the circle of the stars, or the violent waters, or the lights of heaven *to be the gods* which govern the world; with whose beauty if they being delighted took them to be gods, let them know *how much better the Lord of them is*, for *the first author of beauty hath created them*. But if they were astonished at their power and virtue, let them understand by them how much *mightier he is that made them. For by the greatness and beauty of the creatures proportionally the Maker of them is seen.*' Here is the philosophy of Paley and Ray, and the best of the Bridgewater Treatises condensed in a passage of poetic prose which clings to the memory for ever.

Vicar. You seem to forget that the 'Canticles,' which you regard as simply a human composition, have been accepted as '*canonical*' by *both Churches*, and ought therefore to be received by you with reverence and unquestioning faith. Moreover, the one from which you quote with approval has been dismissed as apocryphal by your own Church. It grieves me, however, to observe that you make so little distinction between what is ordinarily called 'genius' and that which Christians of all denominations regard as 'inspiration,' namely, the infusion of ideas into the mind by the holy Spirit of God; your reference to Milton's poem, for instance, and again the fearlessness with which you bring the most solemn records to the test of some experiment or the facts of physical science.

Parishioner. A *fact is a fact*—nothing *can* gainsay or overthrow it. I *do* say *fearlessly* and *confidently* that if a legend, tradition, or 'historic statement' come down to us, no matter for how long a period or under whatever *authority*, alleging something which is contrary to the evidence of our senses as corrected by experience, by mental analysis, and by all the tests which cumulated science has provided for that end, an honest, God-fearing man cannot do otherwise than *disbelieve it.* No matter how loud may be the cry, 'Touch not, taste not, handle not,' he will not be 'beguiled' by a show of wisdom in will, worship, and humility; for he will be unable to feel that there is *true reverence* in accepting such legends, 'such ordinances,' as St. Paul says, 'after the commandments of men,' or, as Isaiah puts it, 'as is taught by the precepts of men.' A legend, tradition, or command opposed to *such* evidence is *human*, and *not divine*, no matter how clothed with seeming sanctity, hoary antiquity, and priestly authority. The *words* and the WORKS of the Almighty *must be* consistent and harmonious. In the very nature of things—from the absolute perfection which is inseparable from Godhead—they *cannot* contradict each other. The child of God recognizes in this great truth the handwriting of *his Father*, and knows therefore the alleged 'inspired' tradition, which is in conflict or contradiction to some known natural fact, to be a human fallacy or a forgery. To accept it would be to dishonour his Father, to place himself in a like position to the Scribes and Pharisees of Jerusalem to whom Jesus said, 'Ye have made the *commandment of*

God of none effect by *your tradition*' (Matt. xv. 6). So long as we are ignorant of the facts which do stand in opposition to the alleged inspired tradition, as is the case with thousands of simple believers, *then* is our faith honest and sincere, and cannot be offensive to a just God ; but when *the fact* and the *alleged* word *are known* to be irreconcilable, then to accept the latter becomes 'voluntary humility' to a mere human decree ; it is 'to bow down his head as a bulrush,' to the mere 'ordinances of men'; it is to *reverse* the noble conduct of Peter and the other Apostles who answered and said to the Council and High Priest, 'We ought to obey God rather than men.' Yea, it is as wrongful a thing as to worship 'the circle of the stars, or the violent waters, or the lights of heaven' rather than 'the Author of beauty who has created them.' For a geologist to ignore the *facts* of geology because they war against the legend of Moses is to honour Moses rather than the Great Creator of whom Moses wrote.

Vicar. Am I to understand you that if Charles Lyell or Charles Darwin say one thing, and Moses or Ezekiel state something which is not in accordance with the theories of these philosophers, then the assertions of the prophets are to be disregarded ? This is indeed displacing the Bible from the high place it has held for centuries and clothing it with dishonour.

Parishioner. I took great pains to emphasize the word '*fact*,' because, with the distinguished German scientist Virchow, I affirm that the speculative ideas of philosophers should be kept wholly distinct from scientific *facts*. Their theories do not come within the assured domain of science; they may contain possible truth, but cannot be regarded as *truth* until they have passed the region of speculation, and by accurately tested demonstrative evidence—evidence sifted and tried under every possible condition—are shown to be not ideas only, but *facts*, or *truths*. David tells us in the nineteenth Psalm in respect to the sun, 'His going forth is from the end of the heaven, and his *circuit* unto the ends of it'—whilst most intelligent persons know, from the teachings of astronomers, that the Psalmist was in error; that the sun makes no such circuit, but the *earth* revolves around the sun. Joshua and Habakkuk also tell us that 'the sun stood still.' The former writes :—' The sun stood still, and the moon stayed, until the people avenged themselves upon their enemies. Is not this written in the book of Jasher? So the sun stood still in the midst of heaven, and hasted not to go down about a whole day. And there was no day like that before it or after it, that the Lord hearkened unto the voice of a man, for the Lord fought for Israel' (Joshua x. 13, 14). Isaiah tells us that the Lord 'will gather together the dispersed of Judah from *the four corners of the earth*' (Isaiah xi. 12); and St. John the Divine assures us that he 'saw four angels standing on the *four corners* of the earth, holding the four winds of the earth, that the wind should not blow on the earth, nor on the sea, nor on any tree' (vii. 1). Now, these historic details do not war against a *theory*, or *theories*, of any kind, but taken literally they are misrepresentations of existing things, and could not, therefore, be received by me as the inspired utterances of the Almighty, but merely the figurative expressions or poetic descriptions of the respective writers. It has been established beyond all cavil that the sun does *not* move round the earth in twenty-four hours, and that it is the earth which revolves around the sun. It is only a few monomaniacs who think that the earth is a square plain, having 'four corners,' and therefore I say that the above utterances are the statements of fallible men like unto Herodotus or Livy. Moses describes the coney, or rabbit, and also the hare, as 'unclean . . . because he cheweth the cud, but divideth not the hoof' (Leviticus xi. 5, 6). So in reference to another department of natural history, in the third chapter of the first book of Moses, called 'Genesis,' it is written of the serpent, 'and dust shalt thou eat all the days of thy life.' At the present time, naturalists know that the serpent does not '*eat dust*' in the strict sense of the words, or swallow it, to a greater extent than many other creatures. It is narrated as a portion of the curse, and decreed also as a punishment 'upon thy belly shalt thou go.' Bible commentators like unto Scott inform us, that previous to '*the fall*,' the stature of the serpent was (probably) erect, his appearance beautiful, and his habits innoxious, but because of his participation in the primal sin, because of his disobedience, '*because* thou hast done this, thou art cursed above all cattle, and above every beast of the field; upon thy belly shalt thou go; and dust shalt thou eat all the days of thy life' (Genesis iii. 14). D'Oyly and Mant, in their Bible, published under the sanction of the Society for the Propagation of Christian Knowledge, tell us that the curse of the serpent consisted in bringing down his stature, which was probably in great measure erect before this time; and in the meanness of its provision, 'and dust thou shalt eat,' inasmuch as creeping upon the ground it cannot but lick up much dust together with its food." All this comment is contrary to fact. No creature living is more exquisitely organized for its habits and sphere of life than is the serpent. One of the greatest of European naturalists, Professor Richard Owen, thus eloquently describes the form and character of the serpent :—' It is true that the serpent has no limbs, yet it can outclimb the monkey, outswim the fish, outleap the zebra, and suddenly loosing the close coils of its crouching spiral, it can spring so high in the air as to seize the bird upon the wing; thus all these creatures fall its prey. The serpent has neither hands nor claws, yet it can wrestle with the athlete, and crush the tiger in the embrace of its overlapping folds. Far from licking up its food as it glides along, the serpent lifts up its crushed prey, and presents it grasped in the death coil as in a hand to the gaping mouth. It is truly wonderful to see the work of hands, feet, fins performed by a mere modification of the vertebral column. But the vertebræ are especially modified to compensate by the strength of their individual articulations for the weakness of their manifold repetitions, and the consequent elongation of the slender column.' [*Lecture to Young Men's Christian Association*, 1864.] As Joshua and Moses and David erred in all these statements, so St. Paul has erred in his strong expression, in his sublime epistle, where he writes, 'Thou fool, that which thou sowest is not quickened *except it die.*' All these statements are contrary to *fact*. The hare does not chew the cud; the sun does *not* go round the earth; the serpent does not live upon dust; the seed which reappears as grain does *not* die; the outer *wrappers* of the germ die, but the germ, the essential *seed*, remains alive, and develops, first the blade, then the ear, after that the full corn in the ear. Now, as I *know* from the evidence of my senses, corrected by my reason, that the sun does not sensibly move along the heavens, that the earth is *not* a square plain with 'four corners,' that the hare does *not* 'chew the cud,' and that a corn seed does *not* die before it becomes fruitful, I say that the writers of these statements—Moses, Isaiah, St. John the Divine, and Paul of Tarsus— were not *divinely inspired* to write them, but wrote them simply as truthful men anxious to convey the truth to their hearers or readers, and that they *did* convey a truth, but associated with so much error as to demonstate that 'plenary inspiration' did not belong to them; their language was truthful so far, as they, fallible men possessing only the knowledge of their age and race, *could* make it; their words were not false words; they were *intended* to convey, and *did* convey, the convictions of the speakers. As good men unaided by *special* Divine power, they could not have done otherwise than they did; they dealt honestly with the semblances of things: for the sun *does appear* to move, the earth *does appear* to have four corners—North, East, West, and South—the hare *does* move his jaws like unto a ruminating animal, and the grain *does appear* to *die;* yet, notwithstanding, and nevertheless, this confusion of appearance and reality proves that for us to reverence the Bible as an organic whole, to receive each and every statement of every writer therein as the immediate *inspired* Word of God, is to commit the same error in respect to the words of these men—to the *words* of Paul, for instance—as did the men of Lycaonia in respect to the *persons* of Paul and Barnabas when they 'lifted up their voices, and said, The gods are come down to us in the likeness of men' (Acts xiv. 11). Individually, I cannot perceive the necessity of a man being 'inspired' to narrate truthfully a fact within his own cognizance: the fact, if reported by several eye-witnesses, may be reported in varying forms, with more or less lucid detail, according to the observing power and narrative skill of the respective writers; but, as the reports of honest men, each report, for the purpose it was given, would be substantially true; and the very difference of statement would tend to confirm, in judicial minds, the substantial truth of the narrative. But all this becomes changed, when direct, Divine Inspiration is claimed for the narrator—for then, verbal error, or discrepancy in detail, would justify a doubt as to the Divine character of the narrated statement;—would become, in fact, the test of the Inspiration both of the Writer and the writing; inasmuch as the all-wise and omniscient God could not err in word or fact. To illustrate what I mean, I will name the varying verbal differences in the narratives of St. Matthew, Mark and Luke, as to the Gadarese Demoniac. Viewed simply as an historical narrative by ordinary 'uninspired' men, there is no difference which may not be explained by the respective knowledge and the degree of education in the individual narrator. Thus, St. Matthew and St. Mark tell us that the swine rushed down into the *sea* '$\epsilon\iota\sigma\tau\eta\nu\ \theta\alpha\lambda\lambda\alpha\sigma\sigma\alpha\nu$'—whereas St. Luke, the most educated man of the three narrators, tells us that 'the herd rushed down the steep into the lake' $\epsilon\iota\sigma\tau\eta\nu\ \lambda\iota\mu\nu\eta\nu$. The water in question is undoubtedly a lake. You may, perhaps, call it a trifling difference; but I deem it a *crucial distinction*, when plenary inspiration, *i.e.* verbal and actual, is claimed for the narrative, for it shows that the respective narrators described the incidents much in the same manner as they would have been described, at this hour, by reporters as varying in their antecedents and circumstances as did Mark and Luke. If all the three narrators had been under the guidance and control of *one Divine* illuminating Power, a lake would not have been called a sea, neither would a sea have been called a lake. In the meantime, I have no desire to retract my statements as to 'Inspiration,' its nature and its continuity; for I believe that all men are alike inspired who have clothed pure thoughts in noble language; like unto the Grecian peasant Cleanthes, who, three hundred years before the Christian Era, could address

Him whom he believed to be the Divine Power:

> Hail! for to bow salute to Thee,
>   To every man is holy.
> For we, from Thee an offspring are,
>   To whom, alone of mortals
> That live and move along the Earth,
>   The mimic voice is granted;
> *Therefore*, to Thee I hymns will sing,
>   And always shout thy greatness.

* * * *

> Nor upon Earth is any work
>   Done without Thee, O Spirit!
> Not at the æther's utmost height
>   Divine, nor in the Ocean,
> Save whatsoever the infatuate
>   Work out from hearts of evil.
> Thou orderest disorder, and
>   The unlovely lovely makest.

* * * *

> But, Jove all bounteous! Who in clouds
>   Enwrapt, the lightning wieldest;
> May'st thou from baneful Ignorance
>   The race of men deliver!
> This Father! scatter from the soul
>   And grant that we the wisdom
> May reach, in confidence of which
>   Thou justly guidest all things;
> That we, by thee in honour set,
>   With honour may repay Thee,
> Raising to all thy works a hymn
>   Perpetual; as beseemeth
> A mortal soul; since neither man
>   Nor God his higher glory,
> Then rightfully to celebrate
>   Eternal Law, all ruling.

In that prayerful hymn, I humbly opine, are thoughts as tender, and more pure than many which are recorded in the *canonical* book, called 'The Song of Solomon.' Rawlinson, in his work on ancient Egypt, records devotional hymns of the most lyric beauty and pathos; and Max Müller gives us, from the 'Rig-Vedas' of India, prayers breathed by mortals some three thousand years ago, as touching and as 'inspired,' as tender and prayerful in thought and expression, as some of the exquisite Psalms of David. Here is one of many—'If I move along trembling like a cloud driven by the wind; have mercy, Almighty, have mercy! Through want of strength, thou strong and bright God, have I gone astray; have mercy, Almighty, have mercy! Whenever we men, O Varuna, commit an offence before the heavenly host, whenever we break the law through thoughtlessness, punish us not, O God, for that offence' (Rig-Veda viii. 89). From Egypt, we hear a voice, of which some verses in the 118th Psalm seem like an echo—'Let no prince be my defender in my troubles; let not my memorial be placed before men. My Lord is my defender: I know his power: He is a strong defender: there is none mighty beside him. Strong is Ammon and knoweth how to make answer. He fulfilleth the desire of all those who pray to him' (*Records of the Past*, Vol. VI. pp. 99, 100). How like to the words—'It is better to trust in the Lord, than to put confidence in man : it is better to trust in the Lord than to put confidence in princes.' All these plaintive records tell us that, instinctively, the human heart turns to the great God, and breathes the language of prayer — of prayer like unto that which in the Bible we call inspired ! The Zeus of Cleanthes—the Varuna of the Hindoo—the Ammon of the Egyptian, are names of the same significance to those respective individuals, as is that of Jehovah to the Hebrew, or of God to ourselves. They are, respectively, the names of a Power —the very highest Power which the mind and the heart of each individual is able to conceive ; the Power in which he 'lives and moves and has his being,' and by whom his destiny is determined. It is a shallow, a very shallow philosophy—nay culpable ignorance — which would brand such persons as Idolators. Each individual practically worships the same Great Being under a different name. Imperfect intelligence has assigned absurd attributes to Zeus, or Jupiter, to Varuna and Ammon ; and alas ! has not the same cause ascribed an unholy character, and malignant acts, to the all Holy One whom we call God ? Yes. I must return to the direct thread of my observations, and repeat, that 'Inspiration' has come to all who have clothed pure thoughts in noble language, or who have been prompted to self-sacrificing and noble deeds — as Paul before Felix, Festus, and Agrippa on Mars Hill, and in the dungeon at Rome; Servetus at Geneva; Huss at Constance; Luther at Erfurt, and before the Diet at Worms; Howard in the prison dens of England and Europe, and the plague-smitten regions of Tartary; Clarkson as he sat on a stone-heap on the road-side in Cambridgeshire, and vowing a vow to grapple to the death with slavery; Latimer in the Star Chamber, and on the burning pile at Oxford; Ambrose as he confronted the bloodthirsty Emperor Theodosius; John Wesley among the miners in Cornwall; Henry Martyn translating the Scriptures into Oriental languages under the burning sun of Persia; John Williams at Rarotonga and Erromanga; and Moffat and Livingstone in the far-off barbarous regions of Southern Africa.

Vicar. Really these are bold statements from one who so positively stated his great reverence for Scripture and was so emphatic in his appeals 'to the law and the testimony' in support of his arguments. Therefore I must remind you that the *prophets* could not have been otherwise than Divinely inspired; the future which they portrayed was hidden from mere mortal vision or mental foresight. Moreover, we have the direct authority of Scripture itself on this point, for Peter tells us: 'The prophecy came not in the old time by the will of man: but holy men of

God spake as they were moved by the Holy Ghost' (2 Peter i. 21); and so all-important to the sustenance of the faith is this word of prophecy, that St. Peter calls it 'a more sure word' even than his own personal testimony as to the voice of recognition, which from heaven proclaimed Jesus as God's beloved Son, in whom he was well pleased, and which he and his companions, James and John, 'heard when we were with him in the Holy Mount.' This very statement shows that the words of prophets, inspired thus, transcend all *human* testimony; for assuredly no higher human testimony could hardly be asked for—or if asked for, obtained—than that of three men of moral worth testifying to a fact seen and heard by all three of them simultaneously.

Parishioner. This is the second or third time you have been somewhat satirical as to my varying estimate of the Scriptures; but I fail to recognize any inconsistency on my part. As I have already said, I rely wholly on their teaching as to the Nicene and Athanasian Creeds, and shall yet revert to them in connection with these; although to do so *further* seems superfluous iteration, for the texts already quoted render my position scripturally unassailable. To quote more texts certainly entitles me to the satire, 'And thrice he routed all his foes, and *thrice he slew the slain.*' Yet, to show to you what a wealth of evidence sustains my conclusions, more scriptural proofs shall be forthcoming. I have no desire (for it is no part of my present purpose) to controvert the powerful passage you have given as to the 'sure word of prophecy,' although it is taken from an Epistle which has been more discussed, perhaps, than any other in the Canon, and that Eusebius, Didymus of Alexandria, and St. Jerome regarded it with more than distrust. Whether Peter, at the time of stating the words, if he did state them, began to feel that his experience in the Mount may have been illusory, I cannot say; but of all the stupendous illustrations of human weakness I have ever heard, none approaches this alleged fact in the life of Peter: that he, who had seen with his bodily eyes Jesus transfigured before him, so that 'his face did shine as the sun and his raiment was white as the light'— saw and heard Moses and Elias (who had been dead for centuries) talking with Jesus—that this very Peter who so appreciated the celestial manifestation as to exclaim to Jesus, 'LORD, it is good for us to be here'! and to propose the building of three tabernacles, 'one for thee, one for Moses, and one for Elias'; and heard, moreover, 'a voice out of a bright cloud, which said, "This is my beloved Son, in whom I am well pleased; *hear ye him*"' (Matt. xvii. 1-4)—that alone, of all the disciples of Jesus, this very Peter, *after this* august experience and *celestial demonstration*, should 'curse and swear, saying, I know not this man of whom ye speak,' is the most marvellous fact recorded in the annals of history. Your narration of the circumstance, however, is hardly accurate, for we have not *three men* testifying to a fact which *they saw simultaneously;* for it is most astonishing that neither John in his Gospel nor James in his Epistle alludes to this miraculous manifestation of Divine power, this stupendous attestation of the relation in which Christ stood to the SUPREME.

Vicar. It is painfully evident to me that, however much, for the end you have in view, you may quote the Bible, there is a large portion of the 'Canonical' Scriptures which you have ceased to accept as authentic. You state that you have no desire to controvert the powerful passage I gave as 'to the sure word of prophecy'; but you immediately hinted that it was obtained from a doubtful source, or a source more doubtful than other portions of the Scripture. But even if it came from a solely secular source, it recites *a fact* which is historically true, for most assuredly men in 'the old time' *did* prophesy; and that they *were* moved by the Holy Ghost is *proved* by the circumstance that their 'prophecies' forestalled history by many centuries, and yet were they verbally accurate and true. Thus, Jacob, in his dying moments, more than sixteen hundred years before the coming of Christ as the Messiah, distinctly assured his sons that 'the *sceptre* shall not depart from Judah . . . until Shiloh come' (Genesis xlix. 10); and as respects the history of the Transfiguration, if neither James nor John refer to this sublime incident, it is most fully recorded by *all* of the synoptic writers—Matthew, Mark, and Luke; so that the event has three historians, besides that of one of those immediately at the scene.

Parishioner. My views on inspiration have been expressed already; and if the Church had adopted centuries ago the opinions which are *now* published by some of her most advanced theologians, the unbelief which now pervades the minds of the vast majority of the intellectual classes and the mechanics and artisans of Europe would never have sprung up. If irrational and absurd theories, and equally absurd facts, had not been pressed upon them by authority; if the 'Bible' had not been represented to them as the 'Koran' is to myriads of Mohammedans—as Divine and sacred to its *minutest syllable*—they would never have turned upon it with the disdain and contempt they now do. If its *true character* had been taught them they would have accepted the good and rejected the evil; but as *all* is proclaimed as the infallible 'Word of God,' they turn with disdain from the 'Word,' and, alas! even dispute the existence of its alleged Author. But to revert to your statement as to the literal fulfilment of Jacob's prophecy after the lapse of so many centuries, even this prophecy, which has for ages been quoted by divines as a most illustrative proof of 'the sure word of prophecy,' is melting away under the advanced and advancing knowledge of the present day. It happened to me individually that nearly thirty years ago I was acquainted with a most intelligent Jew, and I asked him whether he had ever read the 'Old Testament' in the English language, and in the version generally accepted by the Protestants of this country. He said he had read it most carefully. I then asked him whether it accorded with the *Hebrew* Scriptures as he read them. He replied, 'For the most part, but there *is one most momentous misstatement* as to what Jacob said respecting the coming of Shiloh. If our Hebrew records contained it we could *not be* as now, hoping that a Messiah would yet come to the redemption of the Jews from their long wanderings, and their restoration to power, prosperity, and greatness in Palestine; for most assuredly hath "the sceptre departed from Judah," and there is no "gathering of the people," and they are now as much as ever scattered and dispersed over every nation of Europe and Asia, although not now treated as they once were, except perhaps in the dominions of Russia.

Many individual Jews are very wealthy and most influential in various countries; but as a *nation* we are kingless and without a sceptre, and yet the Messiah has *not* come to us.' Since this conversation, I have been informed by good Hebrew scholars that the verse, properly translated from the Hebrew into English, would give to 'Shiloh' the meaning of a *place*, and not a person. The very oldest version of the Old Testament, the Septuagint, gives the verse as follows: 'A prince shall not fail from Judah, nor a captain out of his loins, until the things come that are laid up for him.' This is by no means so definite a prophecy of the realized Messiah. But on this subject, as on several others, I am waiting patiently for the revision of the 'Old Testament' by those learned Hebrew scholars and critics who are now engaged upon this most important and most serious labour.*

Vicar. Looking at the ripe scholars and sound divines who have been so long labouring at this important task, there is not the slightest proba-

* More than eighteen months have passed since the above was written, and the new revision of the Old Testament has since appeared, and the words 'until Shiloh come' remain as in the old, but in a marginal note the following words are given: 'till he come to Shiloh'; and for the sentence 'Unto him shall the *gathering* of the people be,' the revised Bible gives 'Unto him shall the *obedience* of the people be,' while a marginal note reads 'having the obedience of the peoples.' Moreover, as a matter of historical fact, the 'sceptre' *had* departed from Judah many years before the birth of Jesus of Nazareth.

bility of the general text being so altered as to harmonize with your statements.

Parishioner. It may not be so altered in its general statements, but I shall certainly be surprised if the individual text to which I have referred be not altered in the manner I have indicated. The days of 'bibliolatry' are, however, numbered. The manner in which even clergymen abstain from reading in their families the *whole* Bible: the fact that, instead of being as formerly the *chief book read in schools*, it is now, by statute, made exceptionable in Board schools, and indeed optional with each individual scholar: the dread which many intelligent mothers have of their daughters reading many of the chapters of the Old Testament: the fact that dignitaries of the Church, such as a prebend of a cathedral and a chaplain in ordinary to the Queen, have felt it prudent to publish 'A School and Children's *Bible*,' '*shorter*, and at the same time better adapted for the use of children or *young persons*': all show that the superstitious reverence of the past is fading away, and that the most thoughtful and pious Christians are recognizing the truth written by Professor Jowett, the Regius Professor of Greek in Oxford University, more than twenty years ago (which *then* roused indignation), namely, that 'the Bible *should be interpreted like any other book.*' Because it has not been so, it has, to use the words of that profound scholar, come to pass that 'the Book in which we believe all religious truth to be contained is the most uncertain of all books, because interpreted by arbitrary and uncertain methods.' I am firmly convinced, from the observations and reflections of forty years, that the unbelief, the 'agnosticism' which now pervades the intellectual professions, and the 'upper' and 'lower' classes of society, is due almost exclusively to the teaching and practice of the 'Evangelical' or 'Low' Church parties during the first half of the present century. The extravagant notions they held respecting the Bible; the bitterness with which they attacked all who questioned the accuracy of *any* of its statements, now almost surpass belief. Trained under these constricting influences, I have listened with apathy to pulpit utterances, which would now fill me with pain and disgust. One of the most eloquent pulpit orators I have ever known, and to hear whom I have walked several miles, Sunday after Sunday, preached from the pulpit at Camden Chapel, Camberwell, in the January of 1836, as follows (and not only did this, but assented to its publication), 'There is so much of comfort and so much of innocent delight derived from the Bible *to all* who *take it as God's Word*, that to attempt to disseminate scepticism is worthy of nothing but the fiend; and that the man who devotes himself to this endeavour, even if *he had truth on his side*, should be driven out by acclamation as a pest to society, as the monster who would strip his followers of a consolatory and harmless possession, and give nothing in exchange but the most dreary and blighting forebodings' (*Sermons*, by H. Melville, B.D. London, 1838, p. 228). This fanatical reverence for the Bible by the 'Evangelicals,' the superstitious exaltation of it in the place of Papal Infallibility, and the cruel intolerance and persecuting spirit which they manifested toward those who honestly pointed out the errors and untrue statements which were found within the pages of the 'authorized English Bible'; this their conduct, together with their fanatical perversion of St. Paul's teachings, were the germs of the present widely diffused scepticism. The scornful indifference with which they treated deeds of beneficence and moral excellence, through their dogma 'that works done by unregenerate men, although they *may be things which God commends, and of good use to themselves and others*, yet because they proceed not from a heart *purified by faith* (*i.e.*, by the acceptance of their theory) *they are therefore sinful*, and cannot please God, *or* make a man meet to receive grace from God ': *this* conduct, coupled with the more audaciously presumptive statements that 'they who, having *never heard* the Gospel, know not Jesus Christ, *cannot be saved*, be they never so diligent to frame their lives according to the light of nature or the laws of that religion they profess,' and not being saved they are cast out 'from the comfortable presence of God,' to endure 'most grievous torments in soul and body, without intermission, in hell-fire *for ever.*' *For ever!* as a popular preacher of this School in our day has said, 'When the doomed jingle the burning irons of their torment, they shall say, "For ever!" While they howl, echo cries, "For ever"—

> '"For ever" is written on their racks,
> "For ever" on their chains:
> "For ever" burneth in the fire,
> "For ever" ever reigns.'

It is difficult to suppose that Mr. Charles H. Spurgeon (or any other man) can believe such horrible statements in the same sense as he believes that if he put his finger into a fire he would suffer excruciating pain. 'Church-going,' 'chapel-going,' and the listening for a special time to 'a sermon,' have become habits of routine, so that men speak of and listen to things the full meaning of which they do not realize, when spoken at a special time, on a special occasion, and in a special place. The words spoken, as a rule, from a pulpit on a Sunday, to a 'Sunday congregation,' have not the same influence as if they had been spoken by a 'layman' on a week-day from a public platform. That is, speaking

generally, although such teachings have aroused
the virtuous indignation of a few individuals, and
these again have aroused the attention of others
beyond the pale of the Church, and hence the
result I have stated. Such statements as those
of Melville and Spurgeon have aroused the
virtuous indignation of hundreds, nay thousands
of honest men, and have led to the consequences
I have described. It was this kind of teaching
that made the intelligent *Mill* (according to his
own statement) an Atheist. And I doubt not
that it was through such perverse teaching that
one so gifted, so amiable, and so philosophic as
the late Professor Clifford, could have been
induced deliberately to describe Christianity as
'that awful plague which has destroyed two
civilizations and but barely failed to slay such
promise of good as is now struggling to live
amongst men.'

Vicar. I have long mourned over the fact that
the teachings of the 'Low Church' party well-
nigh deprived the Church of England of her
highest gifts—the apostolic succession and the
sacramental graces involved therein, the regeneration by baptism, absolution of sins, and the
blessed efficacy of the Holy Eucharist—but I
have not credited them with the fearful consequences to which you refer. I know their
doctrine was exclusive and selfish, and their
worship cold and negative, preaching being

considered of more importance than prayers or praise. But where do you obtain the dogmas you ascribe to them?

Parishioner. Already have I given you some appalling ones from the sermons of Melville and Spurgeon, from church and from chapel; statements which would have filled you and me with indignation had we heard them now for the first time. No adult human heart, untrained in such horrors, could dilate with satisfaction on such grievous torments besetting soul and body without intermission, 'in hell-fire for ever.' No African savage, except under the fierce feelings of revenge, could thus dilate on his doomed fellow-creatures 'jingling the burning irons of their torments *for ever*'! The transforming influence of habit (as I have before shown) alone enables men to utter and to hear such things without deep emotion, but *this* enables them to do both with no more feeling than an ordinary Chinese would watch the gyrations of a praying-wheel. I have illustrated it before by facts in natural history described by Darwin, but I will narrate more direct human testimony, showing how passive, or rather apathetic, the trained mind becomes while listening to statements which fill the young and unsophisticated with dismay. Mr. Brooke Herford tells us that when Mr. Ellery Channing was a little boy his father took him in the chaise for a drive, when he himself was going some distance to hear a famous preacher. The lad had heard the preacher much spoken of at home, and really felt, young as he was, an interest in the forthcoming sermon. It was what is called 'a fine sermon' of its kind. It described in very flowing language the lost state of man, his utter abandonment to evil, the eternal doom that hangs over him, his helplessness to avert it, and the method of salvation held out in Christ to those who would wish to escape the everlasting torments of hell. The youth was terrified, for he naturally accepted every word as true, and thought that all around him would henceforth give up all amusements and business, and give their entire thoughts and devote all their energies to escape 'from the wrath to come.' When he and his father went out of the church some neighbour inquired of his father what he thought of the sermon, to which he replied, in an emphatic manner, 'Sound doctrine, sir.' This remark from his own father increased his awe, because it seemed to stamp its truth with increased vividness. He thought his father would speak to him, but when he (the child) got into the carriage he was so full of awe that he did not speak a word to his father, who also remained silent for a time, but presently he began to whistle. When he reached home even the father did not impart the appalling intelligence to his family, but sat down at the fire, took off his boots, put his feet on the mantelpiece and began to read a newspaper as if nothing was the matter. At first William was surprised, but not being given to talking, he asked no explanation. Soon, however, the question rose, 'Could what he had heard be true'? He answered himself, No. His father did not believe it, other people did not believe it, it was not true. And the lad felt he had been trifled with and deceived. What appalled the child, in that 'sound doctrine,' had become of 'none effect' to the man, and the effect of such statements diminishes by transmission from parents to whom such phrases have become habitual, although they have ceased to call up any feeling in correspondence with their own education. Hence the present generation are not thrilled by them as was the past. To the last generation they were a reality, and, therefore, a power. Such dogmas as I have given you specimens of are to be found in the writings or preachings of all the Evangelical divines at the beginning of this century, and were an arousing and transforming power under the preachings of Wesley, of Whitfield, of John Newton, Simeon, Venn, and others. I have been familiar with their doctrines and sermons, as I have so often said, from my childhood; I was nurtured in that creed, and, just as the animal taste for some special kind of food in early childhood rarely, if ever, forsakes the adult, however changed his circumstances may be, so in early manhood, and long after, I advocated them by pen and word, in the page and on the platform. Such things cleave to you with almost the tenacity of your bodily skin. These national and hereditary beliefs are seldom set aside; never, I believe, after the age of fifty years. The changes which do ensue are the results of a general intelligence acting on the minds of a rising generation. Harvey said no physiologist over the age of forty years accepted his theory of the circulation of the blood, demonstrated as it was to the very senses of men; and the testimony of our fathers and our own experience have shown that the universal belief in witches was not overthrown by the arguments of any individual, but has disappeared (except in remote villages among the very ignorant) as the minds of men have become enlightened on the general laws of nature and of life. It is in this manner that 'Evangelicalism' and many other 'isms' are fading from the minds of men; it is by the operation of this law that Paul is receding before Christ, or rather, I ought to say, that the teachings *imputed* to Paul are fast disappearing and the true meanings of that brave and ardent apostle are becoming understood and accepted. The great and eternal truths which Paul, in common with his Lord and Master, taught—namely, that 'God is not mocked,' and that 'whatsoever a *man soweth*, that shall he also *reap*'; that 'love is the fulfilling of the law'; that 'blessed are the merciful, for they shall obtain mercy'; that 'now abideth *faith*, hope, love, *these three; but the greatest of these is love*'—are rapidly becoming the simple creed of the intelligent and good in all nations.

Vicar. What do you mean by Paul receding before Christ?

Parishioner. I have already told my meaning. If I must be more explicit, I say that in all the more powerful or popular pulpits of the time to which I have referred, the *life and teachings* of Christ were seldom referred to, although His name was constantly on the lips, yea, uttered with a frequency—I had almost said flippancy—which deprived it of all reverence; His words, His teachings were ignored, and the theory of 'justification by faith' was interminably dwelt upon, and carried to such an excess that deeds, acts, services, were practically despised, nay, regarded as *hindrances* to salvation, and the reprobate and openly profane were pronounced to be in a safer position than the known moral man or philanthropist. *Doctrine* was placed first in the category of requirements, instead of in the second; as Jesus said, 'If ye *do my will* ye shall *know of the doctrine.*' Clergymen regarded *preaching* as their first and highest duty. In truth their views were precisely those expressed by the Presbyterians in their 'Catechism' to the following question, 'What are the outward means whereby Christ communicates to us the benefits of his meditation?—The outward and ordinary means are all Christ's ordinances, especially the Word, sacraments, and prayer; all which are made effectual *to the elect* for their salvation. The Spirit of God maketh the reading, but *especially the preaching of the Word* an *effectual means of enlightening.*' The keeping of the 'Lord's day' in a super-Jewish manner, and especially by listening to long gloomy sermons, and by introducing into ordinary speech a number of set phrases linked to the holy name of 'Jesus,' were considered the chief characteristics of 'a child of God,' the mark of 'one of the elect' who had been 'saved by grace.' To expatiate on the parables of the Samaritan and the Good Shepherd; to tell 'of ninety and nine just persons which need no repentance,' and of those in the Judgment hour who professed ignorance of Jesus and yet were rewarded for their 'good deeds,' while those who had cried 'Lord, Lord,' who had prophesied 'in his name,' and in His 'name had cast out devils,' and 'in his name done many wonderful works,' were *not accepted*—was to be reproached by the popular clergy of that day as 'unsound,' 'self-righteous,' and 'without the pale of the covenanted mercies of God.'

Vicar. You have given me a very gloomy

picture, but as a young priest I am glad to hear of the experience of one who felt an interest in religious things before the great 'Tractarian' movement in Oxford, to which the Church and the nation owe so much. Will you tell me something further of the broad distinctions which marked the conduct of the parochial clergy and the more serious or religious members of the Church of England prior to that event?

Parishioner. The change is so great, the distinctions are so vast and so numerous, that I seem to be living in another age or in another country. From 1830 to 1845, for instance, the sermons that I heard occupied from forty minutes to an hour in their delivery, instead of, as now, from fifteen to thirty minutes. Although I rarely missed a morning service I never once heard any illusion to passing events or national incidents, except occasionally to the death-scene of some parishioner. I never once heard the love of money denounced, or the importance of any special social virtue, except the support of 'Missions to the Heathen' may be considered such. The utter depravity of man, the glorious privileges of the elect, the all-sufficiency of faith, and the eternity and torments of hell for the 'unregenerate,' were the staple and almost unvarying themes. Sunday after Sunday these subjects were given in long dull discourses, seldom varied even in their sentences, and never in their illustrations. Then the *name* of Jesus formed a portion of every third or fourth paragraph ; *now* I frequently hear sermons in which the name is not uttered, although the *spirit* of His teaching is *always apparent:* *then* a greater portion of the hour's essay consisted in the quotation of isolated texts of Scripture ; *now* I seldom hear these profusely introduced, except by some young and timid curate preaching soon after his ordination : *then* the Devil as a personality and the physical torments of hell were preached with ' much unction ' ; whereas for the past five years I have not heard one or the other minutely and specifically described : *then* the *eternity* and *never-ending torments of the* ' damned ' was a frequent theme ; *now* it is seldom or only incidentally referred to, and not once during five years have I known it used as an *inducement* to repentance and newness of life : *then* the ' fierce anger' and the 'wrath of God' were continuously preached ; *now* the 'love of God ' and the 'mercy which endureth for ever' are the most frequent themes from the pulpit : *then*, as I have already said, the national, political, and social incidents of life were not used to inculcate lessons of warning or encouragement ; *now* they are frequently brought forward, and efforts are made to convince the hearers that the spirit of Christianity should pervade and influence all the transactions of the senate, the mart, the counting-house, and the family life : *then* the terrors of Sinai were brought forward and enforced with all the passionate rhetoric the preacher could command ; *now* the Beatitudes of the Mount are dwelt upon with all the tenderness and persuasive eloquence which a loving father might employ in addressing his own children : *then* the hymns were seldom exultant and grateful, often simply doctrinal, and frequently painful and ghastly in their rhythmical descriptions and contrasts of God's wrath and Christ's love, of the Judgment-day and the torments of the damned ; *now*, happily, they are often sweetly prayerful and loving, like unto Newman's 'Lead, kindly light,' Mrs. Adam's 'Nearer, my God, to Thee,' and Bishop Heber's 'Thou art gone to the grave,' and Mr. Lyte's 'Abide with me.' The three first-named hymns, moreover, imply and *predicate* the *coming* of *even a better time*, inasmuch *as they are used in all Churches*, although they are written respectively by a 'Roman Catholic,' a 'Unitarian,' and a bishop of the 'Church of England.' As I have said before, the wish of my life has been to see a *National Church*, in which all could pray and worship in a spirit of catholic unity ; that some form or system could be adopted which all God-fearing men could accept as readily as they now accept the same hymns for praise — notably, 'Lead, kindly light' and 'Nearer, my God, to Thee,' whose authors are separated as 'far as the poles asunder' by their respective Churches at the present moment.

Vicar. This is what our Church continually prays for in accordance with the teachings and prayers of her Divine Head; her litany breathes it, as I have already pointed out to you; and if I may use such a phrase, she pours out a very diapason of prayer for this result in her noble Collect on Good Friday, where she says, 'Have mercy upon all Jews, Turks, infidels, and heretics, and take from them all ignorance, hardness of heart, and contempt for thy Word; and so fetch them home, blessed Lord, to thy flock, that they may be saved among the remnants of the true Israelites, and be made one fold, under one Shepherd, Jesus Christ our Lord.'

Parishioner. Yes, the Church prays for this desirable result, or I ought to have said the *Churches*, for each one, of the seventy or eighty, offers to the Great Eternal some such prayer; but in each case it is meant that the 'one fold' is their *own special sect, Church*, or *conventicle*, and the condition of entrance is the adoption of their especial 'shibboleth' or creed. The '*great* Western Church' will exclude the '*great* Eastern Church' so long as it refuses to add the word 'Filioque' to its elaborate creed; the 'Church of England' and the 'Independent Church' stand aloof on the question of 'elder,' 'presbyter,' or 'bishop'; and the 'Baptist' shudders with horror at the idea of 'suffering little children' to be baptized; and so on through the whole series of sects and Churches. The Roman soldiers cast lots as to which of them should possess the seamless robe of Christ, rather than tear it into parts and each take a share; but modern 'Christians,' less respectful of Christ's 'seamless' doctrine than the Pagans of His seamless robe, have torn it into many fragments, each taking a part, and then holding up his little fragment as the *whole garment*, or the most essential part of it; and '*to put on Christ*' *is* to accept *this scrap of theirs* as the whole garment of truth, wholly regardless of the other fragments which are to be found elsewhere, and which are cherished with equal fanaticism by *their* possessors. I have heard of sailors who are fearless in every storm because they possess a 'bit of the true Cross,' and 'that never goes down in the most troublous ocean.' And so it is with the sects: each one has 'a bit of the truth' (many who have only a fragment look at it through so magnifying an illusion as to consider it the whole), which they regard as so potent as to enable them above all others to sail in safety amid all the storms and tempests of life to the Land of Eternal Peace.

Vicar. These are painful delusions. There can be but *one* faith, *one* hope, *one* baptism;

there can be but one Church of Christ. It may admit possibly of some controversy as to whether the Anglican or the Roman be the Church; but the question is limited to that postulate. But I have no desire to discuss this matter now, as I so much wish to hear of your past experiences in the practice and teachings of our Church. I especially wish you to give me some illustration of what you have yourself heard from a pulpit in the Church of England as to 'original sin' and the 'eternity of torment.'

Parishioner. Of the first I have heard nothing inconsistent with the Ninth Article of your Church; and all that now appears to me erroneous, viewed in the light of Christ's teaching, was in *perfect accord* with the ninth, tenth, and thirteenth Articles of your Church. In truth, preachers were *consistent* in their theories; and although I believe the effects of their sermons were ultimately mischievous, as, being opposed to the great principles of justice and mercy, and the innate sense of these qualities in the rightly cultured mind, *they have led* to the present widespread apostacy throughout Europe, yet were they most logically consistent with the '*Articles of Religion*' to which they had pledged themselves, with, perhaps, the exception of the manner in which they dealt with the punishment of the unconverted and unregenerate, for neither the 'Articles' nor the 'Catechism' of the Church of England pronounce on this awful subject except *inferentially*. It is unfortunately true that such preachers *could* quote the Eighth Article of their Church as authorizing them to pronounce an eternity of punishment to the misbelieving, for it asserts that the Athanasian Creed 'ought thoroughly to be received and believed,' and this Creed affirms that those who do not believe it 'shall *without doubt* perish everlastingly.'

Vicar. 'To *perish* everlastingly' does not necessarily include an *eternity of torment;* and the sacrament of baptism is the antidote to the consequences of original sin. But I should like you to avoid discussion and to give me an *illustration* from your own experience of the manner in which the awful subject of a never-ending personal torment was treated in the pulpit of the Church of England more than a quarter of a century ago.

Parishioner. 'To perish everlastingly' may admit of two interpretations, but I question whether *you* would accept the doctrine of personal annihilation. I feel assured that the Church meant by these words those horrible and never-ending tortures so graphically described by Tertullian, and depicted with such force by the pencil and brush of Orcagna on the walls of Santa Maria Novella in Florence. As for the merciful qualification you suggest for many; through the sacrament of baptism, the clergymen under 'whose ministry I sat' did not admit of the sacramental grace of baptism as applicable to *all* who were baptized : one of them published a book on the subject, from which I have already quoted. He was a sincere and earnest man. He declared 'all my prejudices both by nature and education were in favour of baptismal regeneration; and I used earnestly to contend for that which I now believe *to be* a *theory of man's inventing.*' In few things is there a greater revulsion of opinion in the Church than on the subject of '*sacramental*' grace. In my humble judgment it is a retrograde action. Materialism appears to be gaining an ascendency over the spiritual life—a reaction like unto that which Paul feared in the Church at Galatia when he wrote, 'After that ye have known God, or rather are known of God, how turn ye again to the weak and beggarly elements, whereunto ye desire again to be in bondage'? (Gal. iv. 9). However, we are not dealing with this now, or, I must declare that there was more of *personal piety*, more of the *deep sense of spiritual things*, a more *vivid* realization of the *presence and power of the Most Holy Spirit*, than is *now* recognizable in many of the so-called 'priests' of the Church of England, with whom forms and ceremonies and 'beggarly elements' seem to be the aim and the end. To return to your question, and to be a faithful chronicler of my experience.

I must say that although the clergy of my earlier days shrunk from calling themselves 'priests,' yet was the term 'a preacher of the Gospel' a misnomer. It was no *euangelion*, no 'good tidings of great joy which shall be to *all people*,' that they preached. 'Does he *preach the Gospel*'? became a cant question. A 'sound man' and a 'Gospel minister' became cant phrases to describe the clergymen who preached in all their bold unmitigated form 'original sin,' 'entire depravity,' 'predestination,' 'election,' 'sovereign grace,' and, to the many, 'reprobation' and an 'eternal hell.'. The Gospel (*euangelion*, the good message), the 'good tidings of great joy which shall be to *all people*,' as proclaimed by angel voices over the fields of Bethlehem, was seldom preached in its integrity and fulness. As I have already said, 'gospel' became a cant word, and signified the very opposite of its original meaning, as completely as in common parlance the word 'prevent' now differs and has become degraded from its primitive meaning of 'going before'—to aid, assist, and further. That beautiful word 'gospel' had ceased to mean 'good news' or 'tidings of *great joy to all people*.' 'Preaching the Gospel' meant, in the 'vernacular' of the 'Evangelical' party, the 'Clapham Sect' (which became for some years the most influential 'section' of the Church of England), the preaching of all those 'horrors' which I have already described, and which may be epitomized by stating that it implied that the Great Creator of all men had created many millions of souls which would 'without doubt perish everlastingly'—no, not '*perish*,' but suffer, and shriek, and writhe with the most excruciating agonies for ever and for ever—while He had also created a comparative few (of whom the preacher was invariably one) whom He had 'predestined' and 'elected' 'to be saved' 'through the precious Blood of Christ'; further, that the more heinous and criminal the lives of the 'elect,' the 'greater glory to God'; further, that the bulk of mankind had not, and could not have, the *will* or the *power* to turn to God. But I cannot trust myself to speak on this subject; but happily I have here the exact answer given categorically on this question by a great 'Evangelic' authority : 'What is effectual calling? Effectual calling is the work of God's almighty power and grace, whereby (out of his free and special love to his elect, and from *nothing in them* moving him thereunto) he *doth* in his accepted time invite and draw them to Jesus Christ, by his word and spirit savingly enlightening their minds, renewing and *powerfully determining their wills*, so as they (although in themselves dead in sin) are hereby *made willing and able* freely to answer his call, and to accept and embrace the grace offered and conveyed therein. *All the elect*, AND THEY ONLY, are *effectually* called, although others may be, and often are, outwardly called by the ministry of the Word.' As I have already said, there is really nothing in this fearful statement which is not embodied in the Seventeenth and Eighteenth Articles of the Church of England. The 'Articles' in the present day are practically buried in the pages of the Prayer Book; but these men made them a living power. I heard a lady—a most diligent attendant at her parish church—say, the other day, that she had *never seen* or *heard of* 'the Articles'! I am glad that this is so. In my early manhood it was far otherwise. Yet still the fact remains that these 'Articles,' and these Articles only, are the *legal tests* of orthodoxy in our law courts whenever the question of doctrine becomes the subject of judicial inquiry. It is one of the many logical inconsistencies of practical life that hundreds—nay thousands—call themselves, or are called by others without contradiction, 'members' of a Church of whose doctrines they are in absolute ignorance. This *fact* leads me to hope that as thousands thus 'worship' in 'the Church,' without any knowledge of 'the Articles,' and with little conception of the meanings of the words of the 'Creeds,' the time may come when neither creeds nor articles will be demanded of priest or people beyond the simple confession, 'I believe that Jesus Christ is the Son of God,' upon which

Philip the Apostle, when under the special guidance of 'the Spirit,' baptized the treasurer of Candace, the Queen of the Ethiopians.

Vicar. You have spoken at great length, but have hardly complied with my request. I wished you to tell me how the subject of eternal torment was dealt with by Anglican preachers of your earlier day, and you have dwelt long upon subjects which the more influential and, I may add, the more cultured of our priesthood have agreed as far as possible to ignore and never refer to. I think the doctrine on which you have spoken a very fearful one when separated from the sacramentarian system, which is the antidote of the many evils which afflicted the Church during the latter parts of the Georgian period. I have not read the 'Articles' since my ordination, and *then* only for 'pass' purposes; but I cannot think they state in any distinctive form the doctrines which you quoted as a categorical reply to the questions of 'election' and 'predestination'; but as they belong to the misnamed 'Reformation' period of our Church they never attracted and rivetted my attention as did our glorious liturgy, and thus I have largely forgotten them. But do you seriously mean that the doctrines which you have delineated can be fairly drawn from them?

Parishioner. Yes, and no others. The 'Prayer Book,' if its appendix, the Articles (and, as I have said, these are the *title deeds* of your office and its rights), is a part of it, is as twofold and as antagonistic the one to the other as are the 'High' and 'Low' Church clergy whose duty it is to read it. The Church is nobly consistent in her catechism, her liturgy, and all her formularies. The priest who accepts her 'catechism' can perform all her rites and ceremonies with heartiness and probity, without the 'mental reservation' and word-torture which others resort to to justify their inconsistency. From the moment he takes the infant in his arms to bless it with the holy rite of baptism and thereby make it 'a member of Christ, a child of God, and an inheritor of the kingdom of heaven,' to the day when he in his official capacity proclaims that 'it hath pleased Almighty God of his great mercy to take unto himself the soul of our dear brother here departed,' and gives hearty thanks 'that it *hath* thus pleased HIM to deliver this our brother out of the miseries of this sinful world,' all his acts are consistent and harmonious. The liturgical offices of the Church are a beauteous unity, full of brightness, of hope, of calm contentment and peace. But her 'Articles of Religion,' so dear to the 'Evangelists' as being 'according to the Word of God,' are not so tranquillizing by reason of their espousing in all its fierceness the doctrines of 'predestination,' 'election,' and 'grace' to which I have referred. The Eighteenth Article, for instance, embodies the spirit of every phrase which I quoted, and which seems to be so very repulsive to your feelings. All the myriads of human beings who follow Brahma, Buddha, Confucius, and Mahomet, all the tens of thousands in Africa and elsewhere who have never heard the name of Jesus, are left in a hopeless condition; nay further, the Article hurls its anathema against those who, remembering the words of Paul, should presume to say that 'there is no respect of persons with God'; that those 'who have sinned without law shall also perish without law'; that 'when the Gentiles, which have not the law, *do by nature* the things contained in the law, these, having not the law, are a law unto themselves.' This 'Article,' like to the 'Westminster Confession,' pours contempt on such a notion. It has, however, the great merit of clearness and plain speech; it is not 'jesuitic,' equivocal, or beset with that vile philosophy which gives to words a 'non-natural' sense and an 'inner meaning.' Moreover, it has this merit: it is not written 'in a tongue not understood of the people,' but all is clear, terse, and forcible—as follows: 'They also are *to be had accursed* that *presume* to say that every man shall be saved by the law or sect which he professeth, so that he be diligent to frame his life according to that law and the light of nature.'

Vicar. Really this appears very repellent. I am glad that I have never from the pulpit—or, indeed, anywhere else—enunciated such views. I think they are calculated, as you say, to cause people to distrust and to disbelieve, when opinions so at variance with the natural sense of justice (to say nothing of mercy) are taught by persons in authority.

Parishioner. Alas! my dear friend, we can all of us see the minute mote in our brother's eye more readily than we can behold the beam which is in our own eye. Candour compels me to say, in the words of your favourite classic, Horace,

>   Mutato nomine de te
>   Fabula narratur.

As I have already said, the doctrines of predestination, and election, and 'sovereign grace' have led to fearful statements. For instance, I have known an 'Evangelical' preacher say that 'there were infants in hell not a span long.' But *your* doctrine on the all-importance of *baptism* has produced exactly the *same* results. The emphatic statement of the Nicene Creed which thousands of 'Church people' utter every Sunday, 'I believe in *one baptism* for the *remission of sins*,' and which faith has been the faith of centuries, has produced results as tragic as any which have arisen *practically* from the theory which has excited your displeasure. The 'Evangelical' theory has never in England been aided in its tyranny by the civil power, and all its preachings have had reference solely to the *spiritual* or *eternal* state; whereas this creed respecting baptism to this hour inflicts on the unbaptized babe the same ignominy which falls to the lot of the murderer or suicide, namely, to be interred without any religious rites, and, in fact, to be buried, to say the least, as a pet dog. In fact, the history of infant baptism teems with ridiculous as well as tragic stories. I know few things which so blend the laughable and the horrible as the teachings of 'the Fathers' in this matter; and it has, as I have said, exerted its influence for ages. As a student I once had to read Wall's *History of Infant Baptism*, in which he states that with the exception of Vincentius, who speedily retracted his 'heresy,' he was unable to discover any *orthodox* divine during the first eight centuries of the Christian faith who *believed otherwise* than that unbaptized infants never entered heaven. Indeed, *Saint* Fulgentius (happily his work is in Latin), in his treatise *De Fide*, preceded by many centuries my Evangelical friend in his notions of the baby habitants of the infernal world, for he says, 'Be assured, and doubt not, that not only men who have obtained the use of their reason, but also little children who have *begun* to live in their mother's womb, and *have there died*, or who, having just been born, have passed away from the world without the sacrament of holy baptism, *must be punished by the eternal torture of undying fire.*' Can it be wondered at that the Hindoos and Mohammedans shrink aghast from a 'religion' which teaches such things? or that English philosophers like Mill and Clifford turn from it with disdain? I said that some ridiculous results ensued from this 'dogma,' and assuredly they did; but the horror which springs up in my own soul from this theory of 'baptism' prevents my enumerating them. The mental anguish which a mother nurtured in such a faith must have felt when 'her hour was come' (more especially if it had come prematurely), and she far away from priests, passes the power of words to describe. No, my dear Mr. Hierous, you are not in a position to cast a stone at your 'Evangelical' brother on the cruel consequences of your respective beliefs. But I cheerfully admit that it has not occurred *to you*, as it did not occur *to them*, to realize in full the absolute horror which such theories inspire in unsophisticated minds. They ask you to believe the respective doctrines to be the teachings of Holy Writ—believe that they are the ordinances of the Most High God—and teach them accordingly; the *result* being that intellectual men whose plastic childhood has not been moulded into such dogmas, and also hundreds of other *reflecting* minds who *have been reared* under such theories, but who have by natural, intellectual, and moral force emerged from the thraldom of hereditary ideas, turn alike from the Church and from the Book which inculcate, or are supposed to inculcate, such ideas. They *know* them to be at variance with the intuitions of a sound mind and a sound heart, and with the courage that appertains to rectitude they denounce them as false, and say with emphasis, '*Fiat justitia, ruat cœlum.*'

Vicar. Your notions are very painful to me, and I ought not to listen to such implied heresy. The creeds which have come down to us through so many centuries, hallowed as they have been by the acceptance of some of the most wise and most holy of men, cannot be otherwise than true, from that very circumstance. Had they been false and untrue they would long since have come to an end. Are you aware that Dr. Pusey, one of the most pious and most learned theologians of the present day, has written a profound and elaborate volume sustaining and enforcing those very views which you say have produced such dangerous results? and, further, that the saintly poet of *The Christian Year* recognized the transforming power of the most holy rite of baptism? I can never forget his expressive lines—

> A few calm words of faith and prayer,
> A *few bright drops of holy dew,*
> Shall *work a wonder there*
> Earth's charmers never knew.

> What sparkles in that lucid flood
> Is water, *by gross mortals ey'd;*
> But, seen by *Faith, 'tis blood*
> *Out of a dear Friend's side.*

And then, as if he were well-nigh transported with the transforming and transfiguring influence of this rite upon the babe visible before him, he sings—

> O tender gem, and full of Heaven!
> Not in the twilight stars on high,
> Not in moist flowers at even,
> *See we our God so nigh.*

Parishioner. The writings of these men are not unknown to me, nor the men themselves. Neither possessed a *judicial* mind. Each was incapable of weighing evidence—nay, would not listen to, much less accept, evidence which seemed to militate against their preconceived notions. Although kindly in their family and social relations, both would have persecuted as bravely as Bonner himself had the civil laws permitted them. Witness their conduct towards Hampden, the late Bishop of Hereford, and towards others. As I have already said, I lived in the same town as Keble, and *know* that he avoided, as he would avoid a poisonous snake, some of the clergymen in the district who held views on baptism and 'sacramental grace' different from his own. I *know* that it would be 'as a voice crying in the wilderness' to say anything which implied that the 'saintly Keble' could be sullen and morose, and it would serve no useful purpose to proclaim it. In truth, I rejoice in the great results which his widespread fame produced after his death, and that tens of thousands of pounds were lavishly poured in by *partisans* and others to found and sustain a memorial college to his perpetual honour. He possessed great qualities of mind and heart, but certainly not so great as the reverence felt towards him by Cardinal Newman and others would seem to indicate. But he was peculiarly deficient in the cool mental qualities which would have fitted him for the judicial bench or have enabled him to attain rank as a 'scientist.' By living a life of seclusion from his earliest childhood, under the constant hourly supervision of an affectionate and learned father, by incessant application and study under the same father's guidance, through natural reserve and shyness shunning the companionship of boys of his own age and the sports of boys, he gave himself wholly up to reading. I rarely saw him without a book in his hand, whether riding on horseback or walking; and by these unusual circumstances he attained, as might have been expected, a large amount of learning of a special kind at a very early age; he had, in fact, been 'coached' from his infancy for that particular 'scholarship' which he gained before he had quite completed his fifteenth year. His father had himself been a successful competitor for the same 'scholarship' in his own youth ; and, moreover, to arrive at a strictly accurate conclusion as to the precise merit of the attainment, it must not be forgotten that 'Corpus' was a small college ; that in awarding the 'scholarship' there was always a strong bias on the part of the examiners in favour of *youth* in the candidates ; that these circumstances, together with the special studies and special conduct likely to attain success, were known thoroughly to the youthful Keble's preceptor, his own father, who had always kept up his intimacy with 'Corpus' and its 'heads.' The father personally accompanied his highly-trained son to Oxford when he went up for the examination. So excellent a 'coach' was Mr. Keble for this particular 'scholarship,' that both John Keble and his brother Thomas were successful competitors for it. These exceptional and peculiar advantages do not, of course, deprive the 'boy-Fellow' of a great honour, but they go far to intimate that there was no 'prodigious' marvel about it, requiring an intellect of exceptional power or genius to achieve it. His great attainments afterwards, such as winning 'double first class' in his university, were such as few men reach ; and few there are who have been so early, so exclusively, and so persistently trained for a given end. However, to have achieved in his university the same distinction which shed honour on the illustrious statesman Sir Robert

Peel entitles Keble to a high niche in the temple of fame, and will 'keep his memory green' in the hearts of English 'Churchmen.' His friendly biographer, Sir J. T. Coleridge, writes that Keble's fame 'must rest upon his sacred poetry.' This is probably true; yet any impartial critic must admit that the 'sacred poetry' owes much of its popularity, and its writer his extensive influence, to the same causes which made the hymns of John Wesley so popular, and John Wesley the power he was, and is, among teeming thousands of his countrymen—namely, the poetry of Keble and of the Wesleys was popular because it ministered to the feelings, the desires, and opinions of large 'religious' bodies holding special religious theories, which they rejoiced to see championed in melodious verse. In poetic power, *per se*, *The Christian Year* is not equal to *many* poems which have not attained the half of its popularity; and even as '*sacred poetry*,' were it not linked to a large and enthusiastic section of the Church of England, it would not be regarded as superior to the poems of James Montgomery, the modest poet of Sheffield.

Vicar. Really your views of poetry are as heretical as your opinions on other subjects. Surely you do not mean seriously to state that John Keble was not distinguished for his extreme humility and modesty? And may I ask you to take an early opportunity to read his beautiful hymn for 'St. Mark's Day' (which, by-the-bye, was his own birthday), and you will then see what a. fine spirit of Christian sympathy and catholic tolerance he possessed. Moreover, when you allege that his was not a judicial mind, I think you ought to have given some fact or facts in illustration of this; and as you yourself claim to be liberal and tolerant, may I be allowed to remind you of the just sentiment, *'De mortuis nil nisi bonum'*?

Parishioner. I have great admiration for the life and some of the writings of the author of *The Christian Year.* What I wished to convey is, that he was no Colossus, either in intellectual power, moral attainments, or administrative capacity, as the lavish honours which have been paid to his memory would imply. His fame is the fame of a party chieftain, and will wane as the opinions of the party recede before the advancing intelligence of the age. As for his humility, I have no desire to question it. He was, constitutionally, the most shy man I have ever known—so shy that it was embarrassing to him even to write in the presence of strangers —so much so that he has been known to say, 'I hate any one to see how I hold my pen'; and this congenital shyness, timidity, or diffidence— by whatever name you call it—helped to swell the chorus of praise which was bestowed upon him for his 'Christian humility' and modesty.

Moreover, all persons—princes, potentates, or pigmies—gain immeasurably in renown by privacy and seclusion. The Latins inculcate this in the proverb '*Omne ignotum pro magnifico,*' as the English do by saying of its opposite, 'Familiarity breeds contempt.' We learn from various biographies that John Keble was less frequently in the 'common room' at Oriel than was any of the very distinguished Fellows of his time, and a Fellow of the same college, in his charming *Reminiscences*, has pertinently observed that ' the slightest word he dropped was all the more remembered from there being *so little of it*, and from it seeming to come from a different and holier sphere.' This retiring habit enabled him to sustain unimpaired the great reputation which his 'youthful Fellowship' had procured. Fortune favoured him. The 'Tractarian movement' at Oxford welded a chain which linked him to the esteem of a powerful party. *The Christian Year* and the Prayer Book speedily became twin companions in the esteem and reverence of hundreds, both in the sanctuary and the home. The two books became as symbolic of the 'Puseyite' and 'High Church' parties as the unctuous phrases of the 'Blessed Gospel,' 'sovereign grace,' 'the Lord's Day,' and the like were of the Evangelical, or 'Low Church,' party. At a time when the 'Evangelical' party excluded everything ornamental — music, painting, and sculpture—and held the material 'cross' in special dislike as symbolic of Popery, excluding it from their churches, and when possible from the graveyards, the covers of *The Christian Year* became ornamented with a gilt cross, or with some other symbolic monogram device, and its pages were duly adorned with 'church red lines,' and the like; thus enhancing its sale by thus becoming more expressive of party zeal and purpose. Such ornaments are common to religious books now, but it was very different fifty years ago. The white surplice in the pulpit and the 'cross' on the altar-cloth or book-cover were as *'war-paint'* to an Indian savage, exciting the warmest emotions, and thus enhanced the sale of *The Christian Year* and the popularity of its author. As party zeal toned down, the book, from its attractive appearance, and the tranquil nature of its themes, came to be adopted as a 'gift book' among 'Church people' generally, who, without strong 'views' of any kind, were still desirous that such books as they *did* give to their young friends should be religious and 'proper,' and consistent with their own position as 'Church-going people.' In addition to these circumstances, the 'Christian renaissance,' so to speak, which has diffused itself among all classes of society in reference to symbolic ornament, has had its influence in inducing *such* purchasers to select a 'religious' book which at the same time had the 'nicest-looking covers.' From all these causes *The Christian Year* attained a circulation which is unparalleled in the annals of poetry; but, I repeat, it is not its 'poetry,' but its character as a *'Church book'* and a party-poem, that has kept it alive and maintained its sale.

Vicar. You deal with the beautiful poem of *The Christian Year* in the same daring manner, and explain its popularity and that of its Author on the same principles, as Gibbon had the audacity to do in reference to the spread of Christianity itself; that is, you explain it by secondary causes rather than from its own inherent excellence and diffusive power. This must be prejudice on your part. You have not, however, ventured to dispute the Christian, catholic, tender, and tolerant spirit of Keble for which I reverence him, and which breathes so holy a fragrance from every line of his beautiful hymn on St. Mark's Day. I observe also that you have evaded my remonstrance in respect to the opinion you have given as to Keble's not possessing that honest and robust mind which would enable him to be strictly judicial in his conclusions. For my own part, I believe him to have been so God-fearing a man as to prefer truth before all things, and that, like unto his beloved Master, his 'zeal' for his Father's house made him wish to purge the Church of 'all them that sold and bought in the temple,' and of all other polluting things; that self-advancement and 'love of money' were things which *he* never coveted after; that he fled 'these things and followed after righteousness, godliness, *faith, love, patience*, and meekness.'

Parishioner. You have formed no inaccurate opinion of Keble as to his zeal for his Father's house, and of his desire to purge his beloved Church from all polluting things. He was ordinarily as meek as was becoming in a man; he was tender as a child in all his family relations; he was very benevolent to his parishioners at Coln St. Aldwin's. Although his father was *legally* 'vicar,' yet, for all practical purposes, the poet was the vicar and pastor of the place all the time that I knew him. His family means enabled him to be a liberal almoner of blankets and coals at Christmas, and he was therefore held in great reverence and esteem by the humble villagers in that place; yet his excessive shyness often caused him to be awkward, distant, and reserved in his *personal* intercourse with them, and many even of his charities were performed by deputy. He had real sympathy for the suffering and respect for the lowly, but the great seclusion in which he had been nurtured from earliest childhood, his practical inexperience of 'life' in its various phases, his ignorance of its necessities and business requirements often made him confused and embarrassed in conversation and in his private ministerial addresses. He was frequently glad under such circumstances to fall back upon the Book of Common Prayer and to 'read the Offices.' This excessive shyness—and it was almost morbid—even so late as 1833 caused him to be very little at Oxford, where his distinction as the 'boy-Fellow' and 'Professor of Poetry' had been deservedly gained. He preferred the seclusion of his most secluded home at Fairford, and when compelled by duty to be in Oxford he sought not rooms in far-famed Oriel, but in a private house in the city. I am quite sure that this excessive 'nervousness,' as it is miscalled, served to heighten his reputed humility and modesty, humble and modest as he certainly was. In respect to my seeking for secondary causes to explain many of Keble's qualities, I avow at once my full belief in the formative influences of a man's environments. No nunnery was more secluded from observation or more shut off from the power of observing incidents external to itself than was John Keble's birth-place and home at Fairford. I knew it well, having lived in it for several years, and spent many hours of reading in the little room in which a great portion of *The Christian Year* was written. The house was shut in by a lofty wall from the high road which passed in front of it. At the outer side of the western boundary of the patrimonial property there were four or five cottages, but these were scarcely visible from the grounds, and their occupants could not, even from the upper windows, catch a glimpse of the garden opposite, because of the lofty wall, high elms, and other trees. In other directions were fields and gardens only, and Mr. Keble's 'paddock,' which joined his garden, was rendered quite 'private' by walls and lofty trees, which formed an oblong embowered parade very dear to the musing poet. The approach to the residence was at one end of it, and from its own grounds, and no one approaching the house could see its inmates, except by the rarest chance, as only one window at the corner of the dining-room was visible in this direction. The town itself afforded few, if any, visitors, for the Vicar of Fairford and his parishioner Mr. Keble were not on cordial terms of friendship. There were very few young men of his own status in society in the neighbourhood with whom he desired to associate; hence the shyness, reserve, and love of solitude which marked his after-career. When this shyness was surmounted by personal intimacy, he became genial, pleasant, and, as is frequently the case with shy people, even demonstratively exuberant with fun. In the family of a dear friend of my own, I am told that, when he was young and frequently visited them, after the reserve of the few first hours had been melted away by their geniality, welcome, and kindness, he could, and did, become very merry and exultant; that before he was 'ordained' he enjoyed a dance with their daughters very much; and afterwards he often displayed much merriment, was fond of giving them grotesque riddles to solve, and was otherwise very diverting. His letters at that period—about 1820-21, I think—were much appreciated by them, as they abounded in humour, quaint descriptions, and scraps of poetry; while over all was diffused, as it were, a spirit of purity; and the peroration of each letter, if one may so describe it, almost invariably referred to high and holy matters. His pathetic nature and reserve were, I think, intensified very much after the death of his father, although he had reached his ninetieth year; and among the other influences which helped to mould his character were the frequent illnesses of his sisters, to whom he was warmly attached: one, Sarah, he lost early from consumption; Mary Ann, his favourite sister, the most cheerful, bright, and sparkling of the three sisters, died in 1826. So fond, indeed, was he both of Mary Ann and Elizabeth that in writing to my friend Mrs. P. purposing to introduce Mary Ann to her, he said, 'Not my *wife* Elizabeth, but my *sweetheart* Mary Ann.' It was with her that he walked and rode most, and she was (to use his playful words) his 'sweetheart'; but in Elizabeth also he had a 'wife who sympathized with him in all reverence of holy things, and in loving care of the humble, the sick, and the needy.' She lived long—yea, even to three-score years and ten. Although in comparatively early life she had to undergo the amputation of a leg, and was in other respects an invalid, yet was she habitually cheerful and serene, ever reflecting the purity and goodness of her Divine Lord. She passed away in peace—so peacefully that her loving brother, who was, in his hoary age, reading to her a psalm, was unconscious that her spirit had fled until the attendant nurse informed him that Miss Keble had been dead some minutes. He buried her at his dear village of Horsley. Sarah and Mary Ann sleep beneath the shadow of the beautiful church at Fairford, whose 'storied windows' are a pictorial illustration of the life of Jesus whom they loved so well. Not the house of Bethany, when Mary and Martha and Lazarus lovingly ministered to their gracious benefactor, was the home of purer and more Christian affection than was the home of Keble at Fairford, when in 1823 he gave up the office of tutor in Oxford and returned flushed with honours to his aged father and beloved sisters—'his sweetheart and his wife,' as he so happily and affectionately described them.

Vicar. You have interested me intensely in your later remarks, as they seem to me an apologetic recantation of your previous deprecatory remarks on *The Christian Year*, and of its sainted author. Your tone then was such as to suggest that you must have been smarting under some personal feeling which excited prejudice and caused you to take a harsh, and therefore an unjust, view of the poetry, as also a very exaggerated view of the spiritual defects of the writer. Your reference to the home of Bethany and its inmates whom Jesus loved prompts the thought that, after all, you regarded the Keble family as peculiarly and especially Christ-like, with an abiding, steadfast, even joyous sense of the immediate presence of their Lord.

Parishioner. I repeat I have no bias. I strive to hold the balance steadily and uprightly. If it did oscillate it would be in the direction of undue praise. A man would be indeed crass, stupid, and unjust were he to deny merit to a book which has found hundreds of thousands of purchasers, and which continues to be in demand in the households of pious Churchmen. As to the writer, I personally know that he was kind, pious, generous, and sympathetic; and further, zealous in the extreme for the honour and the power of the Church of which he was a priest; but I know, also, that the very ardour of his piety and the positiveness of his convictions made him harsh, morose, nay severely unjust towards those who held other views, and were, like himself, positive in their convictions, and eager to impress them upon others. I have never heard, and have never read of, more than one man who could be *just* and *tender* and *true* under *all* circumstances of conflict of opinion and personal wrong, and, alas!

> Now he is dead! Far hence he lies
>   In the lorn Syrian town;
> And on his grave, with shining eyes,
>   The Syrian stars look down.

Vicar. You should give some facts illustrative of Keble's aversion to others, more especially of the priesthood, which you think at variance with my opinion of his very large-hearted, Christian catholicity—that spirit of love which is greater than faith and hope—the spirit which prompted and gave utterance to these beautiful lines in his poem on 'St. Mark's Day':

> And sometimes e'en beneath the moon
> The Saviour gives a gracious boon,
>   When reconcilèd Christians meet,
> And face to face, and heart to heart,
> High thoughts of holy love impart
>   In silence meek or converse sweet.
>
> O then the glory and the bliss,
> When all that pain'd or seem'd amiss
>   Shall melt with earth and sin away!
> When saints beneath their Saviour's eye,
> Fill'd with each other's company,
>   Shall spend in love th' eternal day!

Here, as it seems to me, is the true spirit of Christian love and of catholic unity, the foretaste and joyful recognition of the 'communion of saints,' far removed from that jealous and invidious spirit to which you have so often referred. What can be further apart in spirit than these lines and the conduct of John, who forbad one from casting out devils in Jesus's name 'because he followeth not with us,' and what more in harmony with HIM who said, 'Forbid him not: for he that is not against us is for us'? I wish also to remind you that you have not given me any fact corroborative of your idea that Keble was too timid—in other words, not robust enough—honestly and judicially to investigate *facts*, and to *accept the consequences*, whatever they may be, as 'scientists' or the great investigators into natural phenomena claim to do.

Parishioner. I could give some which have fallen under my own immediate observation, and which would prove that, in 1835, it was not only the fault of the then Vicar of Fairford that there was no realization of the beautiful lines you have quoted—the

> gracious boon,
> When reconcilèd Christians meet,
> And face to face, and heart to heart,
> High thoughts of holy love impart
> In silence meek or converse sweet.

The said Vicar believed and published that the views on baptism promulgated by Dr. Pusey and espoused by Keble were unscriptural; and this proceeding excited in the latter an 'aversion' or repulsion of the kind which I have stated. Sir J. T. Coleridge, in his biography of Keble, refers to it as a 'discomfort which would have decided him now, *of itself*, against choosing Fairford as his residence when his choice was free.' The 'discomfort' must have been considerable, when it is remembered that Fairford was the 'birth-place' and the 'burial-place' of his family, and the 'home' his own personal property or that of his brother. But you seem to forget that I *have* instanced his conduct towards Hampden and also to Arnold, with whom he was at one time friendly; from both of these men he became estranged because they chose to think differently on 'Church matters.' But, as bearing on this particular, I might quote Newman, who in his *Apologia*, writing of John Keble, for whom he once had a reverence almost idolatrous, says, 'He was shy of me *for years* in consequence of the marks which I bore upon me of the *Evangelical* and Liberal schools; at least, so I have ever thought' (p. 18). In fact, like too many saints of whom history tells, Keble was too apt to associate intellectual difficulties, and the conscientious scruples and inquiries springing out of them, with a sinful heart and 'the pride of reason,' and was by no means so quick to perceive that 'intolerance' and a lack of charity *sometimes* spring from 'spiritual pride.' In fact, as even his all-too-partial biographer states, 'those with whom he lived and of whom he saw most had such a reverence for him, that his opinions were seldom canvassed *with that freedom in conversation with himself which is good for the wisest of men'*; and again the writer thinks that the *querulous* and *severe* spirit which he sometimes manifested would have been kept in abeyance, and that it would 'have conduced to the *holding of opinions with more charity*, if honours had been offered to and accepted by him.' In short, what I may have said which appears to you unfair to the reputation of Keble, and which I *know* to be the shade necessary to make the picture lifelike and true, can be substantiated by two or three little incidents: for simple circumstances occur sometimes which lift the veil and reveal the true character of a man. In a letter to a friend he writes, 'I don't care to read *Ecce Homo*, but it will be a very agreeable disappointment if the writer turns out *a Christian* at last, and I will pull off my hat to him and beg his pardon.' Here is an illustration of a conclusion, not altogether charitable, drawn of a man (however right it may accidentally have proved) because of the writing of a book he deemed heretical, although he had not *cared to read it.* Again, here is a statement, written by the son of Keble's most friendly biographer, of an interview he had enjoyed with the poet and divine: 'I was telling him how much I had been impressed with the difficulties as to the inspiration of Holy Scripture, which were growing stronger and spreading more widely day by day; and that it seemed to me this would shortly become (this was in the year 1851) the great religious question of the time. I added that there was not, so far as I knew, any theory or statement on the subject which even attempted to be philosophical, except Coleridge's, in his *Confessions of an Inquiring Spirit*, and that I wished Mr. Keble, or some one as competent as he, would take up the subject and deal with it intellectually and thoroughly. He showed great dislike to the discussion and put it aside several times, and on my pressing it upon him, he answered shortly *that most of the men who had difficulties on this subject were too wicked to be reasoned with.*' Surely, here was the spirit of Torquemada ; here the idea and the principle upon which the Spanish Inquisition was founded, through which the *auto-da-fé* was lighted up, and by which the Massacres of Bartholomew were perpetrated and justified. One sees not in this speech the Christian love which 'hopeth all things,' but rather the mischievous zeal and sectarian discipleship which prompted James and John to go to their Divine Master and to implore from HIM permission to ' command fire to come down from heaven and consume ' those who did not further their wishes, and which called forth from the Holy One the severe rebuke, 'Ye know not what manner of spirit ye are of.'

Vicar. You have, indeed, come to startling

conclusions respecting the holy man whom the Church, at least a large section of it, has honoured for these twenty years as pre-eminently distinguished for tenderness and humility. It would excite the indignation of tens of thousands had they heard, as I have been pained to hear, the name of the sainted Keble associated with the blood-stained name of Torquemada. I must ask you to withdraw the comparison for your own sake, if you desire to be thought truthful and just, and to escape the strong censure of the religious world.

Parishioner. There is one Tribunal before which I am anxious to appear truthful and just, because before *that* Tribunal appearances and realities are one and the same thing. Other tribunals are influenced almost exclusively by appearances, and they may misjudge me, and they *would do so* if they thought, as you appear to do, that I placed the popular poet of *The Christian Year* on the same plane of moral worth as the notorious Torquemada. As to the indignant 'censure of the religious world,' this is one of the inflictions which the truth-seeker and the truth-lover must expect. For example, were he to say in Cairo, or Constantinople, or within the precincts of the Grand Mosque of the Omar, or even in Jerusalem itself, that 'Mahomet was an impostor,' he would possibly be stoned to death or trampled under foot by 'the religious world.' 'The chief priests and the scribes' of every religion have been, in every country and in every age, prone to the cry of 'Crucify him' against all 'who have difficulties on the subject' of their dogmas. 'They are too wicked to be reasoned with' is their general feeling ; and if these 'too wicked' ones cannot now be beheaded or burnt in London, Oxford, or Gloucester, as were More, Latimer, and Hooper, and scores of others in other places, yet are they 'ostracized' by such 'priests,' and 'boycotted' from all social intercourse with 'the religious world.' Yea, even now in the nineteenth century such truth-seekers 'are too *wicked to be reasoned with*' by the 'unco' gude' of all sects; and hence their doctrines spread among the majority of the laity; and thence it has come to pass that in this country that which in 1851 was 'a little cloud out of the sea like unto a man's hand' has now spread far and wide, and pervades the highest literary reviews and journals of the time, and dominates powerfully the minds of some of the highest officials in the State. It is very sad, but it *is the fact*, that some of the kindest and most tender men in their family circles have from religious zeal become great persecutors ; yea, in persecuting the lowly followers of the Prince of Peace they have thought 'they were doing God service.' Some of the most benevolent men I have known in private life have been the most strenuous upholders of the doctrine of eternal torment; yea, Keble himself was one of these; and I have heard the gentle Wriothesley Baptist Noel dilate upon this theme with a zeal which has sent a thrill of anguish through my soul. These are the men who unconsciously spread 'agnosticism' and atheism over our land. Dr. Pusey even, tender as he was in his domestic relations, *did*, *by* this very idea—by mistaking 'difficulties' for 'wickedness' (like his friend Keble)—exercise a priestly sternness and reproof which hurried one agitated soul into the public avowal of atheism. As Polonius said of Hamlet's madness, so say I of this priestly intolerance—

> 'Tis true; 'tis true 'tis pity;
> And pity 'tis 'tis true.'

Vicar. As followers of Him who said it was 'better to pluck out an offending eye or to cut off an offending hand rather than the whole body should be cast into hell,' they could not do otherwise than thus speak and act towards those who disturb faith and are given to change, and with whom you sympathize too much. Your reference to Dr. Pusey seems to me pointedly precise. Are you at liberty to name the special instance of a person who was led to the public avowal of atheism, or, to use your words, was 'hurried' on to its 'avowal' through want of tender sympathy and Christ-like love on the part of that venerable and venerated man you named?

Parishioner. It has not very much astonished me that even you, habitually kind as you are, should so readily acquiesce in, and even espouse, this stern and cruel conduct; although I did not quite expect that your thoughts would so quickly rush to the extreme of 'casting into hell' those who, having 'difficulties' on the subject of the 'inspiration of Holy Scripture,' and who, consequently, ' were too wicked to be reasoned with.' It would seem as if there were something special in the studies and training for the priesthood which disposes men to become intolerant and punitive in respect to speculative thought; and further, to associate and link together sin and punishment, to regard all suffering as the direct penal result of sin in a punitive sense, as did the early disciples of Jesus when they asked Him 'who did sin, this man, or his parents, that he was born blind?' Jesus answered, 'Neither hath this man sinned, nor his parents: but that the works of God should be made manifest in him' (John ix. 2, 3). The feelings of 'Caiaphas' seem to be indigenous to the priestly mind: as a class, they are quick to discern when a man 'hath spoken blasphemy,' to become intensely excited—if not, as Caiaphas, so as to 'rend their clothes,' yet, like him, to be disposed to say to those who resort to advice and persuasive argument, 'Ye know nothing at all, nor consider that it *is expedient for us, that one man should die* for the people, and that the whole nation perish not.' General experience has shown that not even in the cruelty and shame of slavery did the ecclesiastic mind perceive anything hostile to the spirit and teaching of Jesus. The large-hearted American poet, John Greenleaf Whittier, tells us that in the report of a pro-slavery meeting at Charleston on the fourth of the ninth month, 1835, in *The Courier* paper it is stated, 'The clergy of *all denominations* attended in a body tending their sanction to the proceedings, and adding by their presence to the impressive character of the scene.' This sad fact stirred his soul deeply, and he wrote some scathing lines on the circumstance. I remember two verses :—

> Pilate and Herod friends !
> Chief Priests and Rulers as of old combine !
> Just God and Holy ! is that church which lends
> Strength to the spoiler, thine ?

> Woe to the Priesthood ! woe
> To those whose hire is with the price of blood —
> Perverting, darkening, changing as they go
> The searching truths of God !

I must say, also, that in our own country neither the harsh penal code of our forefathers, nor in the severity and unwholesomeness of our prisons, nor in the ignorant barbarities of our lunatic asylums, did the clerical mind so quickly and clearly recognize iniquity as it did in a speculative 'dogma'; nor did they protest against them until Clarkson, and Romilly, and Howard, and Conolly raised their voices and wielded their pens, and devoted their lives to their removal or reform. Indeed, that distinguished philanthropist Dr. Conolly, who stripped every strap, manacle, and chain off every lunatic in 'Hanwell,' and never once permitted one to be placed on the many hundreds who were under his care, has again and again told me that he never knew a clergyman who, when in official capacity, did not uphold the idea of physical force and punishment. He had known many who in their private capacities were kind and beneficent, but never one who as member of a committee, or in any administrative capacity, did not advocate 'restraint' in all its material forms, and 'chastisement' as the most efficient corrective of evil. My own experience, which has not been slight, confirms his so far as it relates to the treatment of the insane. The idea that 'this man had sinned'—that the malady differed in essence from other diseases, and was moral rather than physical—seemed generally present to them when going through the wards of a lunatic hospital. Consequently they always favoured the repressive system in all its varied forms. 'Demoniac possession' seemed to be present to their minds, and they appeared unable to detach the demonized from the 'demon.' Often have clergymen reminded me by their inquiries and by their conduct of the vigorous monk Luther, who is reported to have said, 'Idiots are men in whom devils have established themselves; and all the physicians who heal those infirmities as though they proceeded from natural causes are ignorant blockheads, who know nothing about the power of the demon. Eight years ago, I myself saw, and touched, at Dessau, a child of this sort which had no human parents, but had proceeded from the Devil. He was twelve years old, and in outward form exactly resembled ordinary children. He did nothing but eat, consuming as much every day as four hearty labourers or threshers could. In most external respects he was, as I mentioned, just like other children; but if anyone touched him he yelled out like a mad creature, and with a peculiar sort of scream. I said to the Princes of Anhalt, with whom I was at the time, "If I had the ordering of things here I would have that child thrown into the Moldau at the risk of being held its murderer." But the Elector of Saxony and the Princes were not of my opinion in the matter.' Fortunately for the poor child, the 'lay' Elector of Saxony and the Princes of Anhalt had not had their minds and their hearts hardened by 'dogmatic' training in their childhood, and were therefore unwilling, I presume, to believe that the child 'had no human parents,' or that it could claim direct descent from his Satanic

Majesty. My experience has probably been 'unfortunate' in respect to the clergymen and the Dissenting ministers I have known; but certainly the greater proportion of them were very intolerant of opinions adverse to their own, and, like Keble, were prone to regard their opponents as 'too wicked to be reasoned with.' You may be sure that I intend no personal discourtesy if I say that this strong theological bias so often perverts the judgment, that it has become a proverb that in secular things the clergy generally give a wrong decision. The satirical jokes of the hour illustrate this statement. It has been said that a distinguished professor, when lecturing at South Kensington, told his pupils that in his early days he was often perplexed as to the precise position of the 'mitral valve' in the human heart, until the happy idea occurred to him that 'mitral' was an adjective formed from 'mitre,' which was the crowning ornament of a bishop, and as bishops were usually on the wrong side, he had henceforth no difficulty in remembering that the 'mitral' valve was on the left side of the heart. But all this raillery apart, it is a sad historic fact that ecclesiastics have been the opponents of progress and of reform on almost all occasions. While ready 'to compass heaven and earth' to retain, or make 'proselytes,' ecclesiastics of all kinds have been comparatively indifferent to conduct, so long as their friends were 'sound in their faith' and strict observers of the forms, ceremonies, and sacraments of their respective Churches. They were always ready to *believe* good of those who were 'of the household of faith,' but not so ready to believe in the good motives and pure conduct of those 'of the contrary part,' not so ready implicitly to accept the teaching of the Great Master—' A good tree cannot bring forth evil fruit, neither can a *corrupt* tree bring forth *good fruit*. . . . Wherefore, by their *fruits shall ye know them.*'

Vicar. There is a covert satire in your remarks which I shall not endeavour to imitate. Neither lay nor clerical finds it easy to act up to the sublime doctrine which you have quoted from the Gospel of St. Matthew, and I will admit that it is the highest attainment in the Christian life. But just now I am wishful to hear of the incident you referred to in the conduct of that holy man Pusey, whose teachings and whose conduct I reverence only short of the teachings and conduct of our blessed Lord and His immediate apostles.

Parishioner. It is no secret now; it has been published to the world. Mrs. Besant, the wife of a clergyman, was beset with difficulties in respect to the deity of Christ. She had in past years great reverence for Pusey, who had wielded a great influence over her, and whose writings had taught and guided her for many years. She corresponded with him, receiving many letters, and subsequently received a kindly invitation to a personal interview, which she joyfully accepted. I need not recite all the details, but will give the closing part of the interview in her own words, as given in the journal she *now* edits, entitled *Our Corner*. 'He had no conception of the feelings of the sceptical spirit; his own faith was solid as a rock, firm, satisfied, unshakable; he would as soon have committed suicide as have doubted of the infallibility of the "Universal Church." "It is not your duty to *ascertain the truth*," *he told me sternly*. "It is your duty to accept and to believe the truth as laid down by the Church; at your peril you reject it: the responsibility is not yours so long as you dutifully accept that which the Church has laid down for your acceptance. Did not the Lord promise that the presence of the Spirit should be ever with his Church to guide her into all truth?" "But *the fact* of the *promise*, and its value, are *the very points* on which I am doubtful," I answered. He shuddered. "Pray, pray," he said; "Father, forgive her, for she knows not what she says." It was in vain I urged that I had everything to gain and nothing to lose by following his directions, but that it *seemed to me that fidelity to truth forbade a pretended acceptance of that which was not believed*. "Everything to lose? Yes, indeed. You will be lost for time and lost for eternity." "Lost or not," I rejoined, "I must, and *will, try to find out what is true*, and I will not believe until I am sure." "You have no right to make terms with God," he answered, "as to what you will believe and what you will not believe. You are full of intellectual pride." I sighed hopelessly. Little feeling of pride was there in me just then, and I felt that in this rigid unyielding dogmatism there was no *comprehension* of my difficulties, no *help for me in my strugglings*. I rose, and thanking him for his courtesy, said that I would not waste his time further, that I must go home and just face the difficulties out, openly leaving the Church and taking the consequences. Then for the first time his serenity was ruffled. "I forbid you to *speak* of your *disbelief*," he cried. "I forbid you to lead into your own lost state the souls for whom Christ died." *Slowly and sadly I* took my way back to the station, *knowing that my last chance of escape had failed me.*'

The emphases are my own. To me this scene appears like to some poor creature sinking into the wave and clinging to a person on the shore, who, failing to wring from her a specific promise, shakes her off from him with horror and leaves her to perish. Well might Mrs. Besant add, 'I recognized in this famous divine the spirit of the priest which could be tender and pitiful to the sinner repentant, humble, submissive, craving only for pardon and guidance, but which was *iron to the doubter*, to the heretic, and *would crush out all questionings* of "revealed truth," *silencing by force, not* by argument, all *challenge of the traditions* of the Church.' That opinion of Mrs. Besant respecting the character of Dr. Pusey is precisely the opinion which personal knowledge, information derived from friends who knew him intimately, and the perusal of his writings have compelled me to form of the author of *The Christian Year*, and which I have endeavoured to convey in our long and rambling 'parley' respecting him.

Vicar. I recognize nothing in the conduct of the saintly Pusey towards Mrs. Besant as described by you which derogates from his high character. As a priest of the Most High God, pledged by solemn vows to be ready with all faithful diligence *to banish and drive away all erroneous and strange doctrines* contrary to God's Word, he could not have acted otherwise than he did. You seem to forget that the divine Paul, when he ordained Timothy to the priesthood, commanded him to *reprove* and to *rebuke*, and to Titus also he emphatically said, 'Speak, and exhort, and *rebuke with all authority*. Let no man despise thee.' It is evident that some strong, unhappy bias influences your judgment, when the acts of my clerical brethren are in question. You must perceive, by my reference to the instructions which Paul gave to Timothy and to Titus, that the conduct which you have condemned in them was simply the discharge of a solemn duty; the earnest appeal of a responsible person trembling for the destiny of those committed to his care. Discharging this high duty by 'exhortation,' and if failing in this, by 'rebuke,' Dr. Pusey's conduct in the case of Mrs. Besant calls for my esteem, rather than my disapproval. 'Strange doctrines' lead to wicked acts, and, therefore, especially demand 'rebuke,' that such acts may be prevented. The aforesaid case was a very extreme one, for, if her views became generally accepted, the entire hopes of all Christendom would have been destroyed. Your opinions must totter and fall, if based solely on the conduct of Dr. Pusey towards Mrs. Besant. What other evidence are you able to give as to the sensitiveness and cruel intolerance of the clergy in matters of opinion, as compared with their conduct in reference to moral habits and customs?

Parishioner. The evidence is embarrassing because of its redundancy. I feel that I have been redundant in illustrations already, and if that which I have already given does not suffice to confirm my statement and influence your judgment, no further facts will, I fear, suffice to do so. I have shown already, by broad facts from the history of progress, from the history of the slave trade, Political Reform, the Penal Code, the treatment of the insane, and from the history of the acceptance and appliances of scientific discoveries, how 'clericalism' has blocked the way, until vanquished by numbers. As, however, you ask for further evidence, I would name the outcry against and the persecution which followed the scholarly Essays of Professor Jowett, Temple, Rowland Williams, Baden Powell and others, in 1860. Their clerical brethren stigmatized the seven writers as the 'Septem *versus* Christum'—and every available means of persecution were then resorted to; although, in accordance with the changeless law, 'Truth is great and will prevail'—the clamour has died away, and one of the seven alleged opponents of Christ now holds the distinguished position of Bishop of London. From this high pre-eminence, Dr. Temple must often smile at the futile, frantic efforts made by the 'High Church' clergy to prevent his ordination to the See of Exeter, in 1869, under the administration of Mr. Gladstone, because of his essay in the said *Essays and Reviews;* and the smile might justly mount to laughter, as he calls to remembrance the opposition of the burly Archdeacon of Taunton, and his farcical mimicry of papal power in the parish church of East Brent, when on the fourth Sunday in Advent in 1869 [to use his own words] he made 'public protest at Morning and Evening Prayer against the consecration of Dr. Temple to the office and work of a bishop in the Church of God.' The most lynx-eyed hunters of heresy would have to exercise ingenuity to find heresy in the essay *On the Education of the World*—unless it be heresy to write that 'Life, indeed, is higher than all else ; and no service that man can render to his fellows is to be compared with the heavenly power of a life of holiness. But next to that must be ranked, whatever tends to *make men think clearly and judge correctly*'—and yet, for writing this pure and moral essay, the doctor excited the bitter hostility of the archdeacon, who with five or six intolerant bishops, protested, as aforesaid, against his consecration. Another instance of clerical malevolence and the tendency of ecclesiastics to overlook great public services in the presence of 'unsound opinion,' or 'heresy, was the case of Colenso, Bishop of Natal. Instead of relying on their own scholarship and knowledge, and showing, by facts and arguments, that his statements in respect to the Pentateuch, and his deductions from the writings of Paul were erroneous, his clerical brethren at the Cape, and subsequently in England, did all they possibly could [but happily in vain], by legal procedure, to deprive him of his bishopric. Dr. Colenso was first arraigned before the Bishop of Cape Town—it was a long and dreary affair, for although the learned Colenso wisely declined to accept as an authority the tribunal before which he was summoned, and appeared only by proxy to protest against the whole proceeding; yet, does the account of his clerical inquisition occupy some four hundred pages of close print, as published in a book at the time. 'The very Reverend the Dean of Cape Town' was the chief accuser—and one reads with amazement, at the present day, that any man should attempt to deprive another of his priestly office, because the other, 'taking his stand upon the doctrine of the Divine Fatherhood, sees all doctrines and examines all theories only in the light of God's love' (*Trial of Dr. Colenso, Bishop of Natal.* London. P. 44). In 1880 the Church 'Society for the Propagation of the Gospel' met in full conclave; and the pious soul which sees 'God in history,' must rejoice that it was so; because the proceedings of that body called forth the holy courage of Dean Stanley, one of the noble spirits which constitute the 'salt' of the Church, by whose 'active savour' it is preserved from entire corruption. The example and the words of this pure-minded Christian will shine as a beacon light to guide many meek and lowly spirits into the way of truth. The Dean stood almost alone, amid the frowning conclave, but with a saintly courage, like to that displayed by Paul before Festus, he upheld the great principle of liberty, 'the liberty wherewith Christ has made us free,' and vindicated the oppressed. 'I am ashamed,' he said, 'that these questions should occupy your attention, relating as they do to one, who, as a propagator of the Gospel, will be remembered long after you are all dead and buried. I know that everything I say will be received with ridicule and contumely; nevertheless, I say, that long after we are dead and buried, his memory will be treasured, as that of the one missionary-bishop in South Africa who translated the Scriptures into the language of the tribes to which he was sent to minister; the one bishop who, assailed by scurrilous and unscrupulous invective unexampled in the controversy of this country, and almost in the history, miserable as it is, of religious controversy itself—continued his researches in a manner in which he stood quite alone, and never returned one word of harshness to his accusers; the one bishop that was revered by the natives, who asked him to intercede for them with the Government, and that without reference to any other bishop of South Africa; the one bishop to whom the natives came long distances to place themselves under his protection, or even to have the pleasure to look upon his face. You need not call "order"! I will not be restrained by this mockery, these jeers, this ridicule, these gibes! I say, there will be one bishop who, when his own interests were on one side, and the interests of a poor savage chief on the other, did not hesitate to sacrifice his own, and with a manly generosity, for which this society has not a word of sympathy, did his best to protect the suppliant; did not hesitate to come over from Africa to England to plead the cause of the poor unfriended savage, and when he had secured the support of the Colonial Office, unlike other colonial bishops, he immediately went back to his diocese. For all these things "The Society for the Propagation of the Gospel" appears to have no sympathy; but, you may depend upon it, outside these walls, in the world at large, whenever Natal is mentioned, they will win admiration; and posterity will say that, among the propagators of the Gospel in the nineteenth century, the Bishop of Natal was not the least efficient' (*Edinburgh Review*, October 1881, p. 318). I have now, I think, in the history of *The Essays and Reviews*, and in the noble episode of Colenso and Stanley, shown how disposed theological sectaries are to persecute 'opinions' and how ready to overlook great services in the persons of those whose 'opinions,' are different from their own, and, therefore, 'heretical'—placing doctrine before practice—reversing the order of Christ, who said, if ye 'do my will ye shall know of the doctrine.' In vindication of your position I must say you did well to quote Paul, for in his early career he was a good type of the Puseys, the Denisons, the Capetown Greys, the Kebles, and other good men, who were, or 'who seemed to be, Pillars of their Church,' and yet never reached (so far as we know) that virtue which St. Paul in his later days called the greatest of all the Christian virtues —namely, love—'ἀγάπη.' The Pharisee of Pharisees: the zealous Saul, the man who 'made havoc of the Church, entering into every house, and taking men and women, committed them to prison': the man who, 'breathing out threatenings and slaughter against the disciples of the Lord, went' [most wisely for his purpose] 'unto the *high priest*, and desired of him letters to Damascus to the synagogues, that if he found any of *this way, whether* they were men or *women*, he might bring them *bound* unto Jerusalem': the man who, after being struck to the earth as a '*persecutor*,' rose again with *new ideas*, but with the *old, ardent*, zealous, persecuting, self-confident *spirit*, so that he could as confidently and as heartily 'breathe out' threatenings against the co-believers of his former 'faith' as heretofore against the Christians; and exclaim, 'If an *angel from heaven*, or if *any man* preach any other gospel than that which *we have preached, let him be accursed*': is a fair representative of the divine who was 'iron to the doubter,' and would crush out all questioning of revealed truth, '*silencing by force, not* by argument,' all who opposed him. Paul should have remembered his own sincerity and honesty of purpose when he 'profited in the Jew's religion,' and was 'exceedingly zealous of the traditions of his fathers,' and not have been so ready to pour out anathemas on others; should have remembered that his Divine Master looked upon and loved the young ruler who had sought of Him the way to inherit eternal life, although he was unable or unwilling to obey Jesus and to sell all he had and give to the poor, 'and come, take up the cross, and follow me.' I have said, in my haste, that Paul should have remembered the conduct of his Lord; but Paul was human, and in him, as in others, Christianity is a principle of growth, and has its stages of perfection, which no man has more fully described than himself. I had, in my warmth, forgotten for the moment that a time did come when Paul nobly recognized the rights of the individual conscience, and placed on record rules and principles which will ultimately crush all religious intolerance and establish the reign of equity and love. All I have said is apposite and true, but for the moment his great after-growth in holiness and spiritual insight had been forgotten, and I sketched his defects and errors as one might have spoken of Peter only in his hour of cowardice, falsehood, and denial, instead of remembering him in later years when penning his noble epistles. Paul's persecuting zeal was fiery and wrong, but it belonged to those weaker moments when 'the law in his members warring against the law of his mind' was temporarily triumphant. Never may it be forgotten of him that, 'although he *knew* and was *persuaded* by the Lord Jesus that there is *nothing unclean of itself*,' yet could he bear with the weaker brother who *did* regard a thing as unclean (Rom. xiv. 14). Here was an inspired man, inspired as to this very subject, bearing with an erring and ignorant brother. It is an unparalleled example among Christian teachers, for even the 'Pilgrim Fathers' who left our shores to find a land where they could escape tyranny, and, like Paul, 'worship the God of their fathers' after the way 'which they call heresy,' became in their turn intolerant, despotic, and cruel, exceeding in their bitterness — towards the 'Quakers,' for instance—all the 'persecutions for Christ's sake' which they themselves had received at the hands either of Queen Elizabeth, King James, or Charles the First. Irrational zeal too often blinds the intellect and hardens the heart, and causes a poor purblind mortal to usurp the authority of the Most High, and *practically* to say to HIM, Be it mine

>thy bolts to throw
>And deal damnation round the land
>On each I deem thy foe.

Vicar. I fear that the latitudinarianism of your views has destroyed in you that reverence and zeal for *God's law* which are necessarily entertained by all good men. The awfulness of violating any law of God is with them so intense that they feel that the wrongdoer must be punished for his sin, otherwise the sovereignty of God is impugned, the distinction between sin and holiness is dimmed, and the kingdom of Satan is made to throw its pernicious shadow over the kingdom of God. All demarcations are confused, and right and wrong become interchangeable words. You seem wholly to forget that there never was a time in the whole range of Bible history when the disobedience and infraction of any Divine law went *unçensured* and *unpunished*. Each sin had its penalty: the Sabbath-breaker was stoned to death, nor less so those—whether son, daughter, brother, 'or the wife of thy bosom, or thy friend, which is as thine own soul'—who endeavoured *to entice others to a worship* other than that which had been prescribed to them by Moses. To spare, to conceal, to pity such an one became a sin of the deepest dye. The language of the Divine command is clear, explicit, and stern as to how the faithful Israelites are to act under such circumstances: 'Thou shalt surely kill him ; *thine hand shall be first upon him* to put him to death, and afterwards the hand of all the people. And thou shalt stone him with stones, that he die; because he hath sought to thrust thee away from the Lord thy God, which brought thee out of Egypt, from the house of bondage.' And the explicit reason for this condign punishment is fully and distinctly given, namely, that *'all Israel shall hear, and fear*, and *shall do no more any such wickedness as this is among you'* (Deut. xii. 9-11). 'Moses was very meek, above all the men which were upon the face of the earth,' yet he displayed a holy zeal in carrying out these commands; and Pusey was following in his footsteps by the conduct which has called forth your condemnation. It is good not to be wise above that which is written. Strict and literal obedience to God's command is the best sacrifice that man can offer, as Saul had to learn when he spared the best of the sheep and of the oxen of the Amalekites, even though they were reserved 'to sacrifice unto the Lord God' (1 Sam. xv. 15). To crush one's own feelings, even though they appear to be right and tender and just, as did Abraham when he climbed the mountain of Moriah in obedience to the command, 'Take now thy *son, thine only son Isaac, whom thou lovest*, and get thee into the land of Moriah; and offer him there for a burnt-offering upon one of the mountains which I will tell thee of' (Genesis xxii. 2), is the becoming conduct of man. Abraham did not stop to inquire of the proud reason whether it was right to be cruel, nay, whether it might not be *murder* which he was about to commit. The acts and words you have censured in Keble and Pusey became them as saints of God, and the impulse which swayed their souls was precisely the same feeling which prompted David, the 'man after God's own heart,' to sing 'Do not I hate them, O Lord, that hate thee? and am not I grieved with those that rise up against thee? I hate them with perfect hatred: I count them mine enemies' (Psalm cxxxix. 21, 22). You seem to have forgotten that the humble and the meek can be heroic and judicially severe, and who it was that made 'a scourge of cords,' 'overthrew the tables,' 'poured out the changers' money,' and drove the 'money-changers' out of the temple pell-mell with 'sheep, and oxen, and those that sold doves.' And, remember that, paradoxical as it may seem, it was not from the wrath of the lion, but from the *wrath of the Lamb*, that 'the *kings* of the earth and the great men, and the *rich* men, and the *chief captains*, and *the mighty* men' hid themselves in dens and in the rocks of the mountains, when the prophetic seer described the awful vision of the opening of the sixth seal. It was because of 'the wrath *of the Lamb*' that the 'chief captains' and the 'mighty men' implored the mountains and the rocks to fall upon and hide them, 'for the great day of his wrath is come; and who shall be able to stand?' (Rev. vi. 15-17).

Parishioner. I have listened patiently to your justificatory plea for persecution; although, notwithstanding your somewhat bitter remark on my latitudinarianism, there was nothing new in it, and very little from which I should dissent, *provided* the *conditions*, or rather the circumstances, were always as clear and indisputable as in the cases to which you have referred. The 'good' and 'gentle' persecutors to whom you have alluded, wished to persecute because of the *opinions* held by certain individuals; whereas nearly every scriptural incident that you have brought forward in support of your theory had to do with *deeds*, not *ideas*, with facts and overt deeds, and is thus altogether in another category from the cases condemned by me. The Sabbath-breaker, the picker-up of wood, violated the *law* of his tribe by an overt act, and thus became amenable to the punishment which the special law prescribed. The case might have been approximatively parallel to the cases of uncharitable judgment to which I have alluded if the wood-gatherer had been punished—*not* for *gathering* up the wood, but for disputing with his tribe whether such a Sabbath law had *ever been* promulgated by *Jehovah*. The 'enticing' to a strange worship approaches somewhat nearer, but is still removed or separated by an immense distance, and by the huge contrast in value, *as evidence*, between the testimony of a man who is an *eye-* or *ear-witness of a fact* and the man who receives something as an alleged fact centuries after its occurrence, and after it has been transmitted through two or three distinct and separate languages. The enticer and enticed were contemporaneous with the miraculous events by which they were brought 'out of Egypt and from the house of bondage'; and certainly, if not contemporaneous, they were the offspring of those who were so, and their great leader Moses was still with them. Gratitude, reverence, and parental obedience all indicated and urged obedience, and the 'enticer' was committing *treason* against God, their immediate ruler, and despite also to his human parents and to the appointed ruler of the people. Of course in the long ages this condition of things would have changed; but, in any way, all my reasoning has been to the effect that full, absolute, immediate obedience to a command of God *is* the imperative *duty* of all mankind. The subject respecting which we are at issue *is*, What *has* been, what *is*, the *conduct* demanded of us *by the Most High?* We are at one in all that you have said respecting Abraham and the conduct of Saul. I do not see what bearing they have on our discussion. I have not consciously once argued *against* persons making *justice* precede mercy, or that any *feeling*, however benevolent in itself, should cause us to forego a clear and unequivocal command of our

Maker. I battle for freedom of thought and opinion as to *what constitutes* such a command. The command being known—*known* to have emanated from the source of all wisdom in the *form* which it is presented *now* to the individual— *then* obedience — absolute, unconditional obedience—becomes us, and this only. If you will do me the favour to recall my earlier statements you will perceive how sincerely I have upheld this principle : that it is the very basis on which I have proceeded, and for which I contend ; it is not only the foundation-stone, but the foundation itself, upon which all my arguments have rested.

Vicar. Your tone in reference to the sainted champions of our Church, Dr. Pusey and the gentle Keble, justified me in my remarks, because you certainly more than implied that they were wrong in their deportment towards unbelievers, and it was needful for me, in justice to their memories, to show that they were acting as holy men of old had acted under similar circumstances. I was jealous of their reputation. I was unwilling that they should be charged with imperfections so gross as those which you implied, and I found it easy to show that *kind-* and *tender*-hearted men could keep those feelings in check under their high sense of duty to God. I wished to assert, and most emphatically to assert, that both were truly Christian men, thoroughly anxious to know the truth, and to value it above all things.

Parishioner. And I was equally anxious to show that, good in a sense as each of them was, they fell far short of that high standard of Christian excellence to which you thought they had attained. Both were self-confident. Each of them partook somewhat of the spirit of the Pharisee who thanked God that he was not as other men, or even as *that publican.* In their priestly arrogance they could treat others who took intellectually a different view of the requirements of the Christian life with harshness and personal dislike. Under such circumstances they became too quickly indignant; too ready, if need be, to 'rend their robes' in furious protest against 'the blasphemy' which their imaginations had conjured up; and in other respects to show an unmistakable 'sacerdotal succession' from the high priest Caiaphas to whom I have referred. As I have said, and cannot refrain from repeating, it is the sense of 'expediency'—the 'necessity' to destroy the individual to 'save the nation,' to 'put out of the synagogues' those that bow not to their authority, to kill 'heretics' and 'think that he doeth God's service'—which cause vain men who 'have a zeal for God, but not according to knowledge,' to become 'persecutors of the Church of God.' Hence the feeling towards the Huguenots, which made Alva exclaim, 'Kill them all : God will know his own,' and induced Pope Gregory the Thirteenth, in his confidence, self-glorification, and blind zeal, to have a medal cast as a triumphant commemoration of the ' Massacre of St. Bartholomew'—that 'glorious victory' when at least 70,000 persons were murdered in the name of Jesus!! But to revert again to our immediate subject, to return to our estimate of the character of John Keble. I am compelled to say that he had not the courage to grapple personally with arguments adverse to his own creed. He loved the placid calm which comes from an unquestioning faith; it was so even in secular matters. He was once travelling with the brother of an acquaintance of my own. When they came in sight of Lichfield Cathedral, Keble was charmed with the west front of that beautiful structure, and expatiated on its excellence, on the devotion and skill which it indicated on the part of the designers and builders of churches and cathedrals in the past; and then, as if mourning over the degeneracy of the present time, and exulting in the 'ages of faith,' he exclaimed, ' They do nothing like that in these days.' When his companion assured him that he *had seen the entire front chopped away* and ' sheets of copper laid on the rough wall, big nails driven in, tarred cords stretched from nail to nail, and all the niches, saints, and angels of the old work *reproduced* in Roman cement upon this artificial banking,' so far from being grateful for the information, as a man 'thoroughly anxious *to know the truth*' and 'to value it above all things' would have been, and as you say Keble was, he became annoyed, and rebuked his companion sharply 'for not letting him *remain under an illusion.*' 'What good could it do to him *to know* how the thing was done?' '*Ex uno disce omnes.*' This incident reveals fully, entirely, completely the *innate* character of the man. In that fact any observer and reflecting psychologist would find the key to all his conduct as a 'Churchman,' and a rational exposition of his theological tenets.

Vicar. Are you quite sure that the incident is authentic? I may, perhaps, have to take your own line of argument and be exceedingly desirous for clear *proof* for every statement. Still it is not improbable that the poet of *The Christian Year* would form a very different estimate of the inquisitive spirit than you do. He knew well that it was the craving for the '*knowledge* of good and evil'—the desire to 'be as gods, knowing good and evil'—that led to

> man's first disobedience, and the fruit
> Of that forbidden tree, whose mortal taste
> Brought death into the world, and all our woe.

Every poem he wrote breathes of faith, of humility, of trust, and reverence. I regard him with love and honour because of this dislike of questioning, and the child-like spirit of acceptance of the teachings of the Church which he everywhere, at least indirectly, inculcates. 'In quietness and confidence shall be your strength' was the 'motto' of his banner—was the special 'sword of the spirit' which he loved to wield in moments of distrust or difficulty. He would, I am sure, have asked in the words of Job, 'Canst thou by searching find out God? canst thou find out the Almighty unto perfection? It is as high as heaven; what canst thou do? deeper than hell; what canst thou know?' (Job xi. 7, 8). Yes, Keble had heard and obeyed the voice of Him who said, 'Come unto me . . . for I am meek and lowly in heart, and ye shall find rest unto your souls.' Thrice happy in this well-founded faith himself, he wished others to find it also. Like Andrew of old, he was anxious to tell all, 'We have found the Christ' and 'to bring them to Jesus.' From his own spiritual experience he could write, as in his exquisite poem for Christmas Day—

> Thee, on the bosom laid
> Of a pure virgin mind,
> In quiet ever and in shade
> Shepherd and sage may find—
> They who have bowed untaught to Nature's sway,
> And they who follow truth along her star-paved way.
> The *pastoral* spirits first
> Approach thee, Babe divine,
> For *they in lowly thoughts are nurs'd*
> *Meet for thy lowly shrine:*
> Sooner than they should miss where Thou dost dwell,
> Angels from heaven will stoop to guide them to thy cell.

His was the spirit of those blessed ones who 'have not seen and yet have believed,' and his dislike, if he had it, to ratiocination was from *the consequences it led to* by disquieting the minds and hearts of many.

Parishioner. I admit and admire all that you say respecting the actual *desires* of Keble. Doubtless he wished that all should possess his own serene belief and his own theological theories. His intentions were pure, and the spirit inculcated in the sweet poem you quoted is Christ-like and captivating. What I deplored, and deplore, was the bitter, narrow, persecuting feeling which sprung up when others were unable to see *mentally* as he saw, or to accept the doctrines which he believed to be essential to salvation. He could not rise to that philosophic spirit which breathes in the fourteenth chapter of St. Paul's Epistle to the Romans; he was too apt to forget that each individual soul had its own perceptions of right and wrong, and that 'to his own master,' and to his 'own master' alone, 'he standeth or falleth'; 'yea, he shall be holden up, for God is able to make him stand.' Perhaps all may have been different—I need not say perhaps, for his conduct *would have* been different—had he been trained under scientific rather than ecclesiastical influences; for, as I have before intimated, with the first *doubt* is a stimulus to inquiry, with the latter it is regarded as a 'sin.' The first accepts no 'authority' as final apart from facts; and as for 'reverence of the past,' he thinks with Lord Verulam that 'we have a mistaken apprehension of antiquity, calling that so which in truth is the world's nonage—"*Antiquitas sæculi est juventus mundi.*"' Ecclesiastical training, as I have already said, is the opposite of all this; obedience to authority is here a virtue, and the ironical sarcasm of Juvenal—'*Marcus dixit. Ita est*'—reads to them like a truism. Some of Keble's earlier college associates had not this slavish respect for 'authority' and disdain of 'rationalism'—notably Arnold of Rugby; and, singularly, the 'judicious Hooker,' whose works Keble so lovingly edited, could write, 'For men to be tied and led by authority, as it were with a kind of captivity of judgment, and though there be reason to the contrary not to listen unto it, that to follow like beasts the first in the herd—they know not, nor care not, *whither*—this were brutish.' Again: 'That authority of men should prevail with men either against or above reason is no part of our belief'; and further: 'Companies of learned men, be they ever so great or reverend, are to yield unto reason.' Moreover, with all his powerful pleadings for the authority of the Church, Hooker can yet write, 'Be it in matter of the one kind or the other' [doctrine or order], 'what Scripture doth plainly deliver, to that the first place both of credit and obedience is due; the next whereunto is whatsoever any man can necessarily conclude by force of reason; after these the voice of the Church succeedeth' (Vol. I. p. 446). In these sentences are to be found the 'potentiality and the power' of developing all I wish in respect to the rights of the individual 'Churchman' as in opposition to the practical conduct of Keble towards the doubting and inquiring minds about him.

Vicar. You somewhat surprise me by these quotations; but still, no honest man can read Hooker carefully without being impressed with the power, the lucidity, and the earnestness with which he upheld the 'ecclesiastical policy' of our Church, and defended that policy as against the Papacy on the one hand and Puritanism on the other. While Jewel wrote apologetically for his Church, Hooker established a basis for it, on the broad principles of universal law, which showed that the Church of England needed no apology inasmuch as she was 'built upon the foundation of the apostles and prophets, Jesus Christ himself being the chief corner-stone.'

Parishioner. Perhaps so. I do not feel that I am in a position to discuss the point further than to reiterate my belief that the quotations I have given would not have been endorsed by your hero. In those phrases of Hooker are the germs of that 'freedom of faith' for which I contend. It is possible that, like other men of profound wisdom before him, Hooker uttered truths of which he himself was not fully conscious of the greatness and ultimate fruition. Men of thoughtful and philosophic minds have, indeed, often done so. They have been the unconscious prophets of the science of the future. Long before the now-accepted facts of psychology were known, Parmenides said the 'highest degree of *organization* gives the highest degree of thought'—a fact which has since widened the whole domain of scientific research, and which at this moment is the basis of the philosophy of Darwin, Spencer, Huxley and others. Parmenides' statement was like gold hidden in a mass of ore, which concealed it, and thus a long age of bewildering metaphysics occupied the study and thoughts of mankind. It has been so even in the regions of physics and material things. Centuries before Watt utilized the powers of steam, its power had been indicated by Hero of Alexandria (200 years B.C.); and in our own country the Marquess of Worcester, in the seventeenth century, had detailed experiments which are now seen to contain the elements of all that has since been achieved by Papin, Savory, Newcomen, and Watt. The progress of knowledge is slow although sure, and even the greatest minds cannot wholly emerge from their 'environments.' Even Newton thought and wrote foolishly on some topics; and Sir Thomas Browne, perhaps the most learned physician of his age, Sir Matthew Hale, and even William Shakespeare, thought, spoke, and acted on the subject of *witches* in a manner which would now create a smile on the face of a boy in the 'sixth standard' of a charity school. Thus

> All throughout the ages an increasing purpose runs,
> And the thoughts of men are widened by progress of the suns.

Vicar. And what has been the practical result of this widespread knowledge of material things? An increase of irreverence, self-confidence, and irreligion; a willingness to rest wholly in a knowledge of secondary causes; a substitution of nature for God, of a blind, impelling, impersonal force in lieu of a creative and upholding will. Even in its least repellent form—I mean that which one of Her Majesty's inspectors of schools (who is the distinguished son of an illustrious divine) calls 'the eternal power, not ourselves, that makes for righteousness'—it is a frightful dream, of which one might almost say, as of Ezekiel's roll, that it is replete 'with mourning, lamentation and woe.' A frightful dream, because the 'eternal power' which this literary athlete has so misnamed is described by himself as a power which does not 'think, or will, or love,' and essentially, therefore, is the same blind 'necessity' of which Lucretius wrote some nineteen hundred years ago—

> Since too of its own nature the vast mass
> Sprang forth spontaneous, rousing every power
> To every mode of motion, rashly oft,
> Oft vain and fruitless, till at length it formed
> Th' unchanging rudiments of things sublime,
> And heaven and earth, and main and mortals rose.
>
> * * * * * * *
>
> These truths avowed, all Nature shines at once,
> Free in her acts, no tyrant to control,
> *Self-potent*, and *uninfluenced* by the gods.
>
> (Book 2.)

The cold blighting materialism, the godless universe, which seem generally to be the offshoot 'of science, falsely so called,' were an ample apology for Keble's dislike to it. I think more is lost than gained when the rainbow, for instance, is simply looked upon as the necessary prismatic result of light shining through water, and nothing more. I sympathize from my soul with Campbell in the lines:

> Triumphal Arch, that fillest the sky
>   When storms prepare to part,
> I ask not proud Philosophy
>   To teach me what thou art.
>
> * * * * *
>
> *When Science from Creation's face*
>   *Enchantment's veil withdraws,*
> *What lovely visions yield their place*
>   *To cold material laws!*
>
> And yet, fair bow, no fabling dreams,
>   But words of the Most High,
> Have told why first thy robe of beams
>   Was woven in the sky.

> When o'er the green undeluged earth,
>   Heaven's covenant, thou didst shine,
> How came the world's grey fathers forth
>   To watch the sacred sign!
>
> *   *   *   *   *
>
> How glorious is thy girdle, cast
>   O'er mountain, tower, and town;
> Or mirror'd in the ocean vast,
>   A thousand fathoms down!
>
> *   *   *   *   *
>
> As fresh in yon horizon dark,
>   As young thy beauties seem,
> As when the eagle from the ark
>   First sported in thy beam:
>
> For, faithful to its sacred page,
>   Heaven still rebuilds thy span,
> *Nor lets the type grow pale with age*
> *That first spoke peace to man.*

Parishioner. I sympathize no less than yourself with those exquisite lines. They are very beautiful, even if not true in all their details. They were true to the writer, and poetry does not cease to be poetry in every case, even

> When Science from Creation's face
> Enchautment's veil withdraws.

For my part, I consider Shakespeare's lines on adversity, in the play of *As You Like It*, very poetical, although I know that the simile he uses is no longer accepted by naturalists. When Shakespeare wrote it was fully believed; and if 'Science has withdrawn the veil of enchantment,' and the alleged fact is fact no longer, yet has

Shakespeare wedded it to a moral in such consummate language that the wand of his genius restores the glamour of 'enchantment'—

> Sweet are the uses of adversity;
> Which, *like the toad, ugly and venomous,*
> *Wears yet a precious jewel in his head.*

And so with the image in that exquisite comfort-giving Psalm of David's, in which he sings, 'Who redeemeth thy life from destruction; who crowneth thee with lovingkindness and tender mercies; who satisfieth thy mouth with good things; so that *thy youth is renewed like the eagle's.*' We feel the illustrative force of the simile, although a scientific experience may tell us that the youth of the eagle is simply like the youth of other creatures—a 'golden age' of sunshine, happiness, and power; an evanescent season of love and joy; never to 'be renewed,' although in a subdued form it may, when past, linger for awhile in the memory as a sweet remembrance, as the after-glow of an autumn eve may brighten the horizon for a time with the gorgeous hues and reflections of a sun that has set with a golden glory, to be followed speedily by the darkness of a night of *never-more.* Science may tell us all this, but Hope will whisper of a 'life saved from destruction,' and the soul will cling to the image 'of a youth renewed like the eagle's,' to the fond dream of a Psyche emerging from the chrysalis of death, clothed with immortal youth, and dowered with every capacity for rapture and love.

Vicar. I have listened with a pleasant surprise to this outburst of emotion on your part, so far removed from all your previous pleadings for knowledge, so different from your strong wish that the clear cool light of science should be thrown upon the mists of theology to dispel their 'mirage' and to open up the realities of life and experience. The 'increasing purpose' and the 'widening thoughts' which come 'with the progress of the suns' do not, then, it appears, meet every want of the human soul: *there are* requirements and needs which neither the scales and the tests of the chemist, the scalpel of the anatomist, the microscope and researches and experiments of the biologist, nor the batteries, the cells, and the coils of the physicist can supply! I hope, even yet, that increased and increasing reflection, joined with that honesty of purpose which you claim, may show you that divines have not been wrong in resisting in every possible way the assumptions of science and the 'dogmatism' (for *dogmatism* is not *confined* to clerical circles) of too many of its professors. I believe that not only has the teaching of the modern school of biologists and physicists tended to dry up the sources of poetry, but that it is also, as I have said before, the main cause of the irreverence and irreligion which characterize alike the 'club circles' and the workshops and factories of our large and flourishing towns at the present moment.

Parishioner. That oratory and poetry alike flourish best in the earlier stages of civilization, as do the singing of birds and the fragrance of flowers in the spring-time and early summer, I will not dispute. Knowledge has certainly a tendency to diminish wonder and to check the exuberance of fancy; and the songs of the syrens and the dances of Pan and the dryads and nereids disappear from our shores and our forests when the geologists and the botanists explore their recesses. Still, poetry is not likely to leave the earth so long as the human heart beats with the emotions of passion, of hope, of fear, and of ambition; and the very discoveries and expositions of science will furnish their own marvels and their own attractions and beauties. One of our very greatest poets has, in sooth, sung of philosophy itself in the following lines :—

> How charming is divine philosophy!
> Not harsh and crabbed as dull fools suppose,
> But musical as is Apollo's lute,
> And a perpetual feast of nectar'd sweets,
> Where no crude surfeit reigns.

It becomes, therefore, a man of prose to be silent on this topic after so poetic a defence from such a source; but I demur wholly to your statement as to the advance of scientific knowledge being the *primary* cause of the irreverence and irreligion to which you refer. We have already spoken on these topics, and I shall not open them up further than to state that advancing knowledge, and the rigid, impartial, and fearless research which science enjoins, did cause thoughtful and reflecting minds to *question* some of the dogmatic statements of divines; and these statements, having been fiercely defended and upheld by theologians as all-important, and among the very essential truths of revelation, led to an investigation which caused their overthrow and abandonment. In brief, the injustice and general wrongfulness of some of the leading tenets of what is accepted as *orthodox* Christianity, and a belief in which is 'necessary to salvation,' have led to a very considerable revolt from the ranks of popular Christianity; but I do not consider that the progress of science is to be blamed for this disturbance. Ahab, in his mental blindness and self-complacency, could say to Elijah, 'Art thou he that troubleth Israel?' overlooking that the true and primary source of the trouble was the conduct of his father and himself; as Elijah said, 'in that ye have forsaken the commandments of the Lord, and hast followed Baalim' (1 Kings xviii. 17, 18). So advancing science has tried, as by fire, every dogmatic tenet; 'of what sort it is,' and the wood, and the hay, and the stubble *have* suffered loss.' *Their* disappearance has caused too many to think that other constituents of the foundation will disappear, overlooking the fact that the 'gold and the silver' admit of purification 'by fire,' and are made more resplendent by the very agency which has destroyed the 'hay and the stubble.' We are living in a state of transition, of doubt, and of agitation; but good men should remember *Who is* the refiner, Who it is that, in the language of Malachi, 'sits as a refiner and purifier of silver,' who shall purge even the gold and silver from dross, and thus restore a condition of things when 'the offering of Judah and Jerusalem shall be pleasant unto the Lord,' as in the days of old, and as in former years. Yes, when the 'wood,' and the 'hay,' and the 'stubble,' so dear to persons of mere routine and habit, shall 'have suffered loss,' shall, in fact, have disappeared in the act of purification; the 'gold and silver,' as I have said, will have become more resplendent by the process. Science has been a handmaiden to purify, but she has not been, as you think, the chief agent in disseminating the sad scepticism, which we both deplore, and which has become so general among the educated classes of society, and which is even to be found in some of the most eloquent and popular preachers in the Church of England. The views you deem so erroneous are held by some good men, ordained members of the

Church 'Establishment,' who are anxious to rid her formularies of tenets which they know to be false, and which, *practically*, are causing many of the laity to accept of her services, as a form useful in a police sense among the 'masses' of the people in the present state of education, but by no means conducive to that high and pure worship which St. Paul inculcateth on the Church at Corinth, when he wrote 'I will pray with the spirits, and I will pray with the *understanding* also.' As I have said repeatedly, the chief cause of the evils you deplore have been the monstrous doctrines I have described to you, aided by the persecuting spirit of the clergy as represented by Convocation. My faith, however, in the future remains firm. Dark as is the present hour, light must come, inasmuch as the word and the works of the Almighty cannot contradict each other. Science and religion must ever be the handmaidens of God. Wherever there is direct contradiction between these respective principles, there *must* be error, either as to the alleged word, or the supposed fact, and time will determine to which factor the error appertains. Reconciliation is inevitable. As the Psalmist, in his day, sang 'Mercy and truth are met together, righteousness and peace have kissed each other'—so do I now believe that there 'shall be light at eventide,' and that 'divines' and 'scientists' will alike perceive that there is no antagonism between their respective pursuits, and alike rejoice in the fulfilment of the prophecy which informs us, 'Truth shall spring out of the earth, and righteousness shall look down from heaven' (Psalm lxxxv. 11).

Vicar. It grieves me to find that you still regard the Athanasian and Nicene Creeds, which are the holiest expressions of the true faith, as co-equal causes in developing distrust and disbelief in many minds, with the appalling doctrines of which you have given specimens from earnest preachers in various schools of thought; and, as alike contributory to the irreverence in respect to holy men and holy things of which I complain. I do not think it can be so, or that these combined causes have acted, even to a tenth degree, with the scientific writings to which we have so often referred in our protracted parleys. The doctrine of 'Evolution,' so widely accepted, depriving man, as it does, of his divine origin—tracing his source from a slimy mollusk—and placing him in the same category as apes and monkeys, is the clear and palpable cause of the godless feeling of the 'masses' in the metropolis and elsewhere. So long as science enunciates such things as facts, it must have the condemnation of the ministers of. God, and Convocation would be faithless to its highest duty if it did not by tongue and pen denounce such fatal falsehoods. However much the intolerance and injustice of clerical bodies in the long past may be deplored, all recent transactions of Convocation must be commended, for, while pointing out and rebuking erroneous doctrines, they have been studiously considerate of the rights of individuals, ever reverencing the moral law, even at the cost of being deemed too lenient to the special heresy condemned.

Parishioner. All will be well! Sad as it is to know that even learned men, even an upright and distinguished judge can write, and publish in a widespread Journal, 'The world seems to me a very good world, if it would only last. It is full of pleasant people and curious things, and I think that most men find no great difficulty in turning their minds away from its transient character. Love, friendship, ambition, science, literature, art, politics, commerce, trade and a thousand other matters will go on equally well, as far as I can see, whether there is or is not a God, or a future state.' The present stage of thought is transient, and is, as I have so frequently said, the revulsion of feeling, the result of disgust excited by the description of God, as given in the impassioned harangues of preachers and the writings of 'theologians.' The intellect enlightened ' by the progress of the suns ' could not accept, as God, a being endowed with attributes repellent to every sense of justice, and of humanity ; and, in the recoil, doubted the existence of a God at all. Atheism is unnatural to man; his tendency is to be, 'in all things too superstitious,' and to have Gods many and lords many. Neither his reason nor his feelings will long accept such wild chimeras as to his origin, as you have sketched from pseudo-scientific writers. Some of our best men of science, the Owens, the Spottiswoodes, Mivarts, Carpenters, and other distinguished Members of 'The Royal Society,' have shunned such a theory; and I have given you before the words of the great High Priest of Biology, Darwin himself, as to creation. In all the minute microscopic phases of his embryonic life, and even through the whole of his fœtal existence, Man may in all the organs appertaining to mere animal life exhibit 'homologues' of lower creatures, and of the ape; but no sooner does he breathe the air of heaven than he becomes endowed with 'potentialities' which no known animal possesses, or can possess. Man standing erect, self-conscious, and speaking his thoughts in articulate language is enthroned in a sphere, which no other known creature has attained to. When, in some far-off future, an ape struggling with self-consciousness, and with the thought of the 'Ego,' shall exclaim spontaneously, in articulate words, Whence? What? Whither? then and not until then, the doctrine of human 'Evolution' will cease to be a mere hypothesis. To repeat a former expression, there is the widest possible distinction between theory and established science; and the lovers of true science are slow to accept even plausible 'theories,' testing them soberly and seriously by all known methods of experiment before they remove them from the region of plausible conjecture or 'hypothesis.' Therefore have I said, 'All will be well,' so far as the deductions of science may affect a true theology. I wish I could endorse your opinion as to the conduct of 'Convocation' in recent times. I see in it still the old spirit which, as I have before said, prompted Caiaphas to say, 'Ye know nothing at all, nor consider that *it is expedient for us*, that one man should die for the people, and that the whole nation perish not' (John xi. 49, 50). You seem to have forgotten the painful episode of Colenso, but, in its essence, the whole thing was repeated years after in respect of the Revisers of the New Testament; with a like gratifying evidence in the person of Dean Stanley that the spirit of a Micaiah, an Elijah, a Paul, may still dwell in the heart of the true sons of God. When the Convocation had deliberately determined that 'the Revisionists of the New Testament should be chosen on grounds of special learning or scholarship, to whatever nation or religious body they may belong,' it was, of course, opposed by George Anthony Denison, the Archdeacon of Taunton (*who* was opposed to all revision), proposing as an amendment the words, 'save only and except such as deny the divinity of Christ.' This amendment was lost by a majority of twenty-three against seven: this majority being secured in the idea, that the aid of learned Jews might in some directions prove useful. Some months afterwards, when it was discovered that under this clause a learned Unitarian had been elected into the Committee of Revisers, the indignation of many of the bishops became very great. Some, even of those who had formed a part of the majority, were greatly perplexed and eager for the exclusion of Mr. Vance Smith, the scholar elected. 'I am sorry,' 'I regret,' 'I retreat,' 'I have passed a perpetual Lent,' exclaimed Dr. Harold Browne, since Mr. Vance Smith has been admitted to Communion at Westminster. Bishop after bishop wished all their pledged action to be rescinded, and the learned critic elected to be expelled. 'Good faith and pledged faith,' shouted one, which was echoed by many others, must be thrown overboard 'to make reparation to the injured honour of our Lord and Saviour.' The Bishop of Chichester added not only 'good faith, but logic and consistency,' and that in the renunciation of these things, his brother bishops had done 'a noble act of self-sacrifice.' Thus, my dear Sir, the Convocation overlooked a 'moral law,' and then arose once again, like inspired

Elijah in the presence of King Ahab, the high-souled Dean Stanley, and in burning words exclaimed, 'Alas! and has it come to this, that our boasted orthodoxy has landed us in this hideous heresy! Is it possible that it should be supposed that we can consent for a moment to degrade the Divine attributes of our Lord Jesus Christ to the level of a mere capricious heathen deity? Can we believe that anything but dishonour can be conferred on him by making his name a pretext for inconsistency, for vacillation, for a breach of faith between two contending parties? I have read in that sacred book, the meaning of which it was the object of this revision to bring out more clearly to the people of England,—I have read in that sacred book that one of the characteristics of those who dwell on God's holy hill is "whoso sweareth to his neighbour and disappointeth him not, though it be to his own hindrance." I have also found in the other part of the sacred book it is declared, "Not every one that saith unto me Lord, Lord, but he that doeth the will of my Father," and we know that the will of the Father is—judgment, justice, and truth "shall enter into the kingdom of heaven." I for one lift up my voice against any such detestable doctrine, and that our Lord and Saviour can be honoured in any way but by a strict adherence to the laws of honour, integrity, and truth. I repudiate the notion that anything but dishonour can be brought on his sacred name, by that which from every recorded word, and every act of his sacred life, we must be certain he would have entirely opposed.' (*Contemporary Essays in Theology*, by Rev. J. Hunt, p. 119). As is usual, fanaticism for a time triumphed; notwithstanding this impassioned utterance of Divine remonstrance on the part of the Dean, the resolution was carried by ten bishops as against four, but the four were Mackarness, Hervey, Temple, and Cannop Thirlwall, Bishops of Oxford, Bath and Wells, Exeter, and Llandaff. It is a matter for thanksgiving that neither in the case of Colenso, nor in the more recent case of Mr. Vance Smith, did fanaticism ultimately gain its object: and in the latter instance the intellectual power and judicial qualities of these four dignitaries give great moral force to the minority, but the immediate actual result testifies to the unchanged spirit of 'Convocation' as a corporate body, justifies my statement in reference thereto, and is my response to the latter part of your question.

Vicar. I am gratified by your remarks on the 'Evolution' hypothesis, and by the broad lines of demarcation which you have drawn between Man and the animal world generally, and also that you recognize so distinct an epoch in his life history, at which this vast change takes place, because it accords so fully with the belief of a purer age, and regulated the practice of its divines in the rite of the Holy Sacrament of Baptism. I still consider the popular writings on Biology and Geology to be the great causes of the widespread distrust in religious matters; and of that irreverent spirit which you admit prevails in respect to holy men and holy things: a spirit in sad contrast to that reverential, humble, and child-like spirit displayed by Keble, and by other distinguished sons of our venerable Church.

Parishioner. I am not aware that I said much about 'holy men' and 'holy things,' or 'reverence' and 'irreverence,' for it grieves me to observe that our noble language is, as it were, being defaced, if not degraded, by fashionable slang on the one hand and the cant terms of religious sects on the other. Words of the gravest import are foolishly travestied, and effeminate men and masculine women toss them about incessantly in their glib and jejune utterances. The young school-girl thinks it indicates womanly wisdom and *haut ton* to talk to her brothers and others of being 'awfully jolly,' of an 'awful swell,' or a 'jolly boss,' and the like; and in your own ranks the words 'holy' and 'reverence' in various combinations have become well-nigh as marked a *shibboleth* of your party as were the words 'the Gospel,' 'the Lord's day,' 'the grace of God,' and 'the blessed Jesus'—pronounced with a special nasal unction —the characteristics of the Evangelical section when, some thirty or forty years ago, it was a power in the State. I wish that all this mischief to our literature and language could be prevented; for sublime words lose their sublimity and their meaning when so long made the vehicle of brainless folly, and their place can never be filled up. The linguistic cant I have named repelled many persons of culture and taste from the Evangelical party who had no special dislike to their theory of salvation; and the fine adjective 'holy' is becoming tarnished by its too frequent use among the 'guilds' and 'fraternities' of your section or regiment of the Church militant.

Vicar. Without discussing this matter, it is everywhere felt that the reverential spirit is fading from our midst; it is perceptible even in the family circle, and, as in other spheres, a mischievous slang is its exponent, and, as I believe, often its instigation. We are in accord as to the infinite importance of words. The solemn utterance of our Divine Master on this topic seems to be wholly forgotten by society. In presence of the universal flippancy of speech, it is a fearful thought to remember that 'for every idle word that men shall speak, they shall give an account thereof in the day of judgment.' Habit or custom may, perhaps, mitigate its irreverence: but it is difficult to believe that a son who habitually speaks of *his father* as 'the governor' or 'the boss' possesses that filial piety or reverence which he ought to have; or think otherwise than that the fifth commandment is forgotten, and therefore disregarded and violated. As I have said, you may see this want of reverence even in families; it is still more conspicuous in the deportment of children towards their seniors; still more so in the deportment of labourers, mechanics, and others towards their superiors who are not their immediate employers. The Catechism, learnt and acted upon by a past generation, is shamefully forgotten in the present day. Keble, when at Horsley, was indefatigable in instructing the rising generation in this, the Church's noble epitome of religon; and as he was himself pre-eminently distinguished for his reverence and humility, I should hope that in *that* district the peasantry are exceptions to the denizens of our large towns, who seem never to have known what is their duty to their neighbour. How few, if asked the question, would individually and cheerfully say, ' To love, honour, and succour my father and mother; to honour and obey the Queen, and all that are put in authority under her; to *submit* myself to all my governors, teachers, *spiritual pastors* and masters; to order myself *lowly and reverently* to all my betters.' Irreverence and a disregard of 'authority' (which, by-the-bye, you seem to regard as a virtue) are the earlier outcomes of that teaching (not immediately by our schools) in our papers and reviews to which I have so frequently referred : the ultimate fruit of which will be agnosticism, atheism, and anarchy.

Parishioner. The outlook *is* most serious, as I have already said. We are for some time likely to suffer from the consequences of the past. Erroneous teachings, the love of mammon, the wealth and luxury which that love has created, the huge and hideous contrasts which exist among us of enormous wealth and extreme indigence, of voluptuous magnificence and unutterable squalor and wretchedness, grovelling superstitions and brazen-faced atheism, make up a condition of things at which the stoutest heart might tremble. I cannot, and I do not, wish to disguise from my view the facts of irreverence and insubordination to which you have referred. But the case is far from hopeless. We may rest in the assurance that God is supreme ; and though 'the earth may be removed, and the mountains be carried into the midst of the sea,' all humble and trusting souls may safely say, ' The Lord of Hosts is with us ; the God of Jacob is our refuge.' But apart from these personal considerations, there is a line of conduct to be pursued which may avert the national calamity which seems impending. There *is* such a thing as a *grovelling* reverence and a blind submission to authority, which is a stupendous evil ; and these two evils have, I repeat, been largely contributary to the calamity which now threatens us. I maintain that your views are too constricted, and, if I may say so without offence, too clerical or priestly. There is no reason why we should dash against Scylla merely to avoid Charybdis, for our duty is to steer between them. Their position is well known. Virgil tells us:

> Dextrum Scylla latus, lævum implacata Charybdis
> Obsidet;

and, as Ovid properly says:

> Medio tutissimus ibis.

One divine at least in our own day has clearly and wisely described the limits of that 'reverence' on which you so fondly expatiate. Arnold of Rugby, in his *Lectures on Modern History*, said: 'Reverence shown for that which does not deserve it is no virtue; no, nor even an amiable weakness, but a plain folly and sin. But if it be meant that he is wanting in proper reverence, not respecting what is really to be respected, *that* is assuming the whole question at issue; *because what we call divine* he calls an idol; and, as, supposing that we are in the right, we are bound to fall down and worship, so, supposing him to be in the right, *he is no less bound* to pull it to the ground and destroy it' (*Modern History*, pp. 210, 211). That is the sentence of a wise man and a just man. The blind reverence, or rather the slavish reverence, ' to authority' inculcated by the Church of Rome, and by her admirers and secret disciples in the Church of England, will never be accepted by the present generation ; and our prospects would now be brighter if it had never been accepted in the past. There are some minds prone to reverence, and it is a beautiful quality when under the control of the intelligence ; otherwise it degenerates rapidly into slavish and abject awe. Gall, Spurzheim, and Combe have all published 'casts' and portraits of men distinguished for this feeling ; they called the 'organ' 'veneration,' and placed it high up on the head. The portrait of John Frederic Oberlin, the good and benevolent pastor of the Ban de la Roche, was, I well remember, selected as a 'fine example' of this configuration ; and the handsome head of Cardinal Newman meets all the requirements of the *late* phrenologists in this particular. If Spurzheim were now living he would like a cast of it, and he would tell his followers to observe how large was the organ of 'veneration,' and he would then ask them to listen to the following facts in the Cardinal's autobiography as demonstrative that the material configuration and the mental attribute associated with it were in accord : ' The first time that I was in a room with him ' [Keble] ' was on the occasion of my election to a Fellowship in Oriel, when I was sent for into the Tower, to shake hands with the Provost and Fellows. How is that hour fixed on my memory after the changes of forty-two years—forty-two this very day on which I write! I have lately had a letter in my hands, which I sent at the time to my great friend John William Bowden, with whom I passed almost exclusively my undergraduate years. "I had to hasten to the Tower," I say to him, "to receive the congratulations of all the Fellows. I bore it till Keble took my hand, and then felt so abashed and unworthy of the honour done to me, that I seemed *desirous* of *quite sinking into the ground.*" ... When one day I was walking in High Street with my dear earliest friend just mentioned, with what eagerness did he cry out "There's Keble!" and with *what awe did I look at him!*' (*Apologia pro Vitâ*). These incidents reveal the essential character of the man as clearly and truly as a chemical test, or tests, reveal the constituents of a fluid. This anecdote is as expository of Newman's character as was the Lichfield incident that of Keble's. Newman was profoundly reverential, and, as I have already said, his *feelings* are the *same* now as heretofore; *differently directed*, but in themselves unchanged, as the zeal of 'Saul of Tarsus' differed only in direction from the zeal of 'Paul called to be an apostle of Jesus Christ.'

Vicar. I have been waiting for you to describe the tenets which you think have conduced or contributed to the widespread infidelity of the present time, and my incidental praise of the reverential spirit has caused you unduly to expatiate upon it, and has ultimately brought you round again to your too favourite theory of the interdependence of cerebral organization and mental attributes—a theory which I have censured as destroying free will and being otherwise most mischievous to the spiritual interests of mankind.

Parishioner. As to the matter of 'free will,' I must leave you to discuss it when you have occasion to deal with the ninth of the Articles of your religion; or if you are desirous of combating it, I can refer you to a combatant worthy of your steel in Martin Luther, and his commentary on St. Paul's Epistle to the Galatians. And speaking of Martin Luther, it may be an interesting exercise to you some day to compare an authentic portrait of that pugnacious polemic with one of Melancthon. As a preliminary study, I would suggest that you look also at the portrait of some prominent pugilist, like to Sayers, or, as a true transcript from nature, at the head of Charles the Wrestler in Maclise's fine picture from Shakespeare's play of *As You Like It*, and then, recalling the life, the 'table talk,' and general conduct of Luther to your mind, contrast the *form* of *his* head with the large, full-fronted, well-domed, lofty head of Melancthon, and see whether there is not *something in that contrast of form* and *contrast of character* which will justify a further research on your part as to the relation between 'matter and spirit,' between 'mind and organization.' I shall feel personally very grateful to you whenever you will show to me a person distinguished for his religious toleration, his benevolence, his great intelligence and reverent spirit—men, I mean, like unto Melancthon, Oberlin, Heber, Dean Stanley, and the late Frederick Robertson, of Brighton—in whom the anterior and superior portion of the head is not large, handsome, and smoothly arched; it whom, that is, a perpendicular line, carried upwards from the opening of the ear to the top of the head, and an horizontal line taken from the same spot to a point corresponding with the anterior termination of the forehead, would, by having a third annexing-line drawn from a level with the second at the middle of the anterior base of the forehead, form a smooth convex outline, thus, ⌒; or—what would be an equivalent fact—show me a person possessing a like character to Melancthon, to Stanley, or to Robertson, having a *low* and *narrow* forehead—low and narrow as compared with the large and protuberant mass of skull *behind* a line drawn vertically from the apex of the head to the opening of the ear; and I will abandon immediately my present firm conviction 'that the highest degree of organization gives the highest degree of thought'; yes, will abandon it for ever as a mischievous heresy, and will endeavour to believe that when Paul wrote to the Romans respecting the potter having the 'power *over the clay, of the same lump* to make one vessel *unto honour*, and another to dishonour'; and again to Timothy, concerning the vessels in a great house 'of gold and silver, but *also* of wood, and of earth, and some to honour and some to dishonour,' he did not mean to imply any material or physical distinction, or any insuperable obstacle to the formed lump making itself into some other vessel, or that the 'wood and the earth,' the 'gold and the silver' were permanent forms having fixed and unchangeable qualities; but, *until then*—until you, or someone else has shown me an individual in whom very high qualities have been associated with the low configuration I have described—I shall continue to accept the lessons which nature and observation have hitherto taught me; viz., that there are men, as there are vessels, of whom some *are made* 'unto honour,' and others 'unto dishonour.' Perhaps I ought to apologise for having dwelt so much upon this theory, because *in it*, and in it alone, I find a solution for what is otherwise a deep and insoluble mystery, namely, the different conclusions to which men come from the *same facts*. We find it so in all matters, whether they relate to conduct, to sermons, books, speeches, works of art, or any other thing to which their attention is drawn. This difference of opinion has existed through all time. In the classic ages, Terence tells us, 'Quot homines, tot sententiæ'; and Horace, in the second book of his Epistles, writes :

> Denique non omnes eadem mirantur amantque :
> Carmine tu gaudes ; hic delectatur iambis ;
> Ille Bioneis sermonibus et sale nigro.

And only a few days ago a most striking illustration—perhaps the most instructive that could be possibly given—occurred in the great judicial Court of Appeal (where, alas ! it was no rare thing), where men of the highest attainments, and with minds perfectly unbiassed and of the most honourable purpose, were in *absolute agreement* as *to the facts*, but came to *opposite* conclusions respecting them. A daily paper states as follows : 'Lord Coleridge, in giving judgment on Saturday in the case of Regina *versus* Powell, said the case exhibited a very serious instance of the different conclusions which educated minds could come to on *one state of facts*. The question to be decided was whether on the facts of the case, there was a false pretence. He and his brothers Huddleston and Mathew were strongly of opinion that *there was*, while his brothers Grove and Manisty *were as strongly of opinion* that there was not. *Neither party could understand the decision arrived at by the other.*' These Judges are differently organized, and hence the above condition of things. This being so with contemporaneous *facts*, with facts which *all accepted as facts,* does it not become us to be absolutely tolerant one of another in respect to conclusions on religious matters? Does it not become a crime—yea, a murder—to destroy a fellow-creature because he draws 'conclusions' from *ancient history* which we choose to brand as 'heresy'? If two judges, equally able, equally just, draw different conclusions and give a different decision on the facts (the *same facts respecting which all are agreed*) from the decision of three other judges, and 'neither party *could understand the decision of the other*,' how absurd, how mad is it to expect uniformity of opinion on the conflicting facts and conflicting statements of a history transacted centuries ago! If the constitution of human nature precludes unanimity on earthly matters, how can it be in perfect accord on 'heavenly things'? Well might the great 'teacher come from God' say, 'If I have told you earthly things, and ye believe not, how shall you believe if I tell you of heavenly things?' A generous toleration of religious opinion ought to be—yea, I will venture to say, even to atheism—the most universal of sentiments, instead of being the most rare. It is sad to think that even John Locke, in writing his noble work on 'Toleration,' could not 'rise to the height of his great argument,' but must needs except the Papist for political, and the Atheist for moral reasons.

Vicar. Such a universal toleration can only co-exist with a universal indifference to religion and an utter disregard of the glory and honour of God. Very different was the spirit of Hezekiah, and Josiah, and Jehosaphat, who broke down the altars, burnt the groves, and destroyed the sepulchres of those who had held in honour the ' gods of the heathen.' Moreover, it is directly antagonistic to the commands of the Most High as given in ' Exodus ' and ' Deuteronomy,' where the command to the Israelites is imperative to ' destroy their altars, break their images, and cut down their groves : for thou shalt worship no other god : for the Lord, whose name is Jealous, is a jealous God' (Exodus xxxiv. 14).

Parishioner. If we were now under a theocracy as the Israelites were at that time, I should not have said anything respecting toleration ; but all the circumstances are altered—so changed that the true worshippers of God are not always distinguishable ; so changed, indeed, that centuries ago the very high priest of the temple of God could charge Jesus Himself with blasphemy, while the common people shouted, 'We found this fellow perverting the nation. . . . Away with him. . . . Crucify him, crucify him '; while later on, priests and people alike, under the same frenzy, shouted against the holiest man of the time, Stephen, 'Away with such a fellow from the earth ; for it is not fit that he should live.'

From that unhappy hour, through long ages, the blind, infatuated zeal of theologians has caused them to act on a like principle and to shout the same cry. The ascendency of the secular power has during the past century controlled this zeal, and rendered it civilly impotent as regards inflicting penalties on life or property: yet many pious men and thousands of pious women still regard themselves as exclusively right, and others who differ from them as *wickedly* wrong. There are few lives known to me so religious, so holy in its general career, as that of Cardinal Newman, and yet how painful it is to read some of his addresses and essays, and to observe how an ecclesiastical system and theory have steeled a heart naturally susceptible and kind. In his essay on *Anglican Difficulties*, he gives us most touching details of the sayings of many good men in their dying hour—sayings which would have demonstrated to any impartial observer how great was their faith, their trust in and love for God. The dying words of such men as Bunyan, Harvey, Whitefield, Walker, Arnold, and Scott, have been gleaned from their respective biographies to show their futility. There is scarcely a word of sympathy; they are given to show how delusive such expressions and feelings are apart from the belief in a special ecclesiastical system of 'sacramental grace.' He depicts the end of one well known to him—one who was beloved by such men as Whately and Max Müller—one whose whole life was a life of self-sacrifice to what *he believed* to be the truth (and Newman has done no more)—one who breathed thoroughly and truly in all his actions the prayerful spirit of the hymn composed by Newman himself—

> Lead, kindly light, amid the encircling gloom,
>   Lead thou me on ;
> The night is dark, and I am far from home,
>   Lead thou me on.
> Keep thou my feet ; I do not ask to see
> The distant scene ; one step enough for me.
>
>   *   *   *   *   *
>
> So long thy power hath blest me, sure it still
>   Will lead me on
> O'er *moor* and *fen*, o'er crag and torrent, till
>   The night is gone,
> And with the morn those angel-faces smile
> Which I have loved long since, and lost awhile.

Yes, of the good Blanco White, whose bodily sufferings were most intense and prolonged, the Cardinal wrote thus : 'Alas ; there was another, who for three months " lingered," as he said, " in the face of death." " O my God," he cried, " I know thus dost not overlook any of thy creatures. Thou dost not overlook me. So much torture. . . . to kill a worm ! Have mercy on me ! I cry to thee, knowing I cannot alter thy ways. I cannot if I would, and I would not if I could. If a word would remove these sufferings I would not utter it." "Just life enough to suffer," he continued, "but I submit, and not only submit, but rejoice." One morning he woke up, and, with firm voice and great sobriety of manner, spoke only these words : " Now I die !" He *sat as one in the attitude of expectation*, and about *two hours* afterwards *it was as he had said*. And he was a professed infidel, and *worse than an infidel, an apostate priest*' (*Anglican Difficulties*). Such is the point of callousness to which ecclesiastical training can reach ! It can so operate on the mind and the heart of a naturally kind man as to enable him to pen such sentences as those I have related, and 'to think that he is doing God service.' It certainly wrung from his instinctive natural conscience the words, ' Of course, we think as tenderly of them as we can ' [but, alas ! then came the awful ' but '], '*but* the claim in their behalf is unreasonable and exorbitant if it is to the effect that their state of mind is to be taken in evidence, not only of promise in the individual, but of truth in his creed. . . . The *Catholic*, and HE ALONE, has *within him* that union of external with internal notes of God's favour which sheds the light of conviction over his soul, and makes him both fearless in his faith and calm and thankful in his hope ' (*Anglican Difficulties*, p. 70). Newman would be startled and pained, grievously pained, if he were charged with falsehood ; and yet, practically, the most wilful fictionist could not more falsify truth than the Cardinal has done in the above passages of his essay. His casuistry may, perhaps, enable him to defend himself successfully in a conclave of cardinals or in a 'convocation' of York or Canterbury, but certainly not before a jury of twelve men trained to weigh and balance evidence and to sift the alleged facts upon which the evidence is based. His own narrated facts, given for a different purpose, *prove* to the extreme point of demonstration that others beside 'the Catholic' possess every grace which 'can shed the *light* of *conviction* over their souls, and make them *fearless* in their faith and *calm* and *thankful* in their *hope*.' He records of Bunyan that his *last* words to his friends, sorrowing around him, were, 'Weep not for me' [as if he had been a saint !], 'but for yourselves. I go to the Father of our Lord Jesus Christ, who, doubtless, through the mediation of his Son, will receive me, though a sinner, when we shall ere long meet, to sing the new song and be happy for ever.' 'Mr. Whitefield rose at four o'clock on the Sabbath day, went to his closet, and was unusually long in private ; laid himself on his bed for about ten minutes, then went on his knees and prayed most fervently he might that day finish his Master's work.' Then he sent for a clergyman, 'and, before he could reach him, closed his eyes on this world, without a sigh or a groan, and commenced a sabbath of everlasting rest' (Sidney's *Life of Hill*). What 'notes,' internal or external, are wanting in the above instances? Where did the '*light of conviction*' shine brighter on the soul, where was ever a more 'fearless faith,' where a more 'calm and thankful hope,' than the conviction, than the faith and the hope displayed by Bunyan and Whitefield? My soul writhes with the mingled feelings of pain and indignation as I reflect on the cold, scathing words of Newman over the memory of Blanco White—'*worse than an* infidel, an apostate priest!' Terrible words to be uttered of one who had displayed such sublime submission to the will of his Father and his God'—a submission reminding one again of the tender words of Job: 'Though he slay me, yet will I trust in him!' More terrible still that they should have been written by one who, if not 'an apostate priest' himself, *had* 'apostatized' from the Church to which he had bound himself by sacred vows; who had 'apostatized' from the 'order and ministry of priesthood of the Church of England' —by the man and priest who, to use the words of the historian Carlyle, had 'apostatized from *his old faith in facts, and took to believing in semblances.*' All this is most sad and most mischievous, provokes a bitter spirit, and urges to an unchristian-like retaliation. When I read these cold and cruel words of Newman over

Blanco White, whose spirit had undergone like conflicts with the soul of Newman, although they led to a more manly issue, the words of Hamlet came rushing to my lips, and I could have said to him :

> I tell thee, churlish priest,
> A minist'ring angel shall (this man) be
> When thou liest howling.

Vicar. It certainly seems a sad thing thus to speak, more especially of one who, like himself, had foregone the most solemn vows in obedience to strong convictions and the irresistible voice of conscience. Still, as the Cardinal maintains, there *is a standard of truth* wholly apart from the convictions and the feelings of individuals ; and it would be a most dangerous principle to accept what you imply—that so long as a man is in earnest and personally truthful, it would matter little what his creed may be. Such a system would abolish order and lead directly to anarchy and chaos. You should not forget that tender and loving and charitable as was our Divine Lord, His utterances towards the Pharisees were scathing and terrible, and exceeded in their condemnation all the phrases that you have reported as bitter and wrong in the pious Cardinal.

Parishioner. I accept your statements as regards the procedure of our Divine Lord.

They are veritable history, and if the Cardinal possessed the same power of reading the heart, and the same Divine intuition of knowing what *was* truth, as did Jesus of Nazareth, I should recall my statements. Moreover, could it be shown that in drifting from 'Evangelicalism' to 'Anglicanism,' and from 'Anglicanism' to the most gross tenets of Popery, he had sought guidance with greater humility and with a more intense desire to reach the truth than did Blanco White under corresponding conditions of spiritual perplexity: or could it be proved that Blanco White sought guidance from any other source than from the great God who made him : I should at once acknowledge that your defence is just and irrefutable ; but as the case stands, I reiterate my statements that the Cardinal's remarks are severe, yea, presumptuous. The sentences which he has given us as proceeding from Blanco White in his bodily anguish indicate a sublime submission and a noble faith. They remind one, as I have said, of the grand utterance of Job in his affliction : 'Though HE slay me, yet will I trust in him.' The same pious thought—that seeming loss may prove great gain, that the withholding or withdrawal of light may lead to still higher revelations of God's love—breathes in one of White's sonnets—as grand a sonnet as human poet ever penned, called

Night and Death.

Mysterious night! when our first parent knew
   Thee from report divine, and heard thy name,
   Did he not tremble for this lovely frame,
This glorious canopy of light and blue!
Yet, 'neath a curtain of translucent dew,
   Bathed in the rays of the great setting flame,
   Hesperus with the host of heaven came,
And lo! creation widened in man's view.
Who could have thought such darkness lay concealed
   Within thy beams, O sun! or who could find
Whilst *fly* and *leaf* and *insect* stood revealed,
   That to such countless orbs thou mad'st us blind!
Why do we then shun death with anxious strife?
If light can thus deceive, wherefore not life?

Vicar. Certainly, that is a highly poetic sonnet, full of philosophic thought; and, with the author's unsettled yet conscientious mental history, and his great and long-continued bodily suffering, can hardly fail to make all kindly hearts sympathize with him—that is, so far as to compassionate and to be sorry for him. To use Newman's words, 'Of course, we think of him as tenderly as we can'; but there remains the excruciating thought that he died without the pale of the Church, with no direct acknowledgment of the sole ransom for guilt which has been provided against the consequences of the primæval sin, and no sacramental grace for the blotting out of the numerous sins which he had committed subsequent to his baptismal regeneration. But this sad episode is carrying us somewhat beyond our subject; and, moreover, I am anxious again to enter my solemn protest against your materialistic theory, which links mind inseparably with matter, and intrudes into the spiritual kingdom by limiting the capacities of individuals for spiritual attainments in this life, and thus inferentially their enjoyment of celestial happiness and bliss.

Parishioner. Pardon me, for my warmth compels me to say that it matters little what measure of 'tenderness' you and the Cardinal 'can think' of that struggling, heroic, yet submissive man of whom we have been speaking: his spirit has gone up to the Tribunal of 'his Father, and your Father; of his God, and your God,' and, even in this life, not Paul himself could say more heartily than he, 'With me it is a very small thing that I should be judged of you, or of man's judgment: yea, I judge not mine own self'; and had he made direct verbal prayers to the Great Ransom you refer to, it would not have 'lightened' his darkness in the estimation of the Cardinal, who places in the same category of doubtful conditions some who died uttering tones of triumphal trust in the 'Redeemer.' The authority of 'the Church,' with all the attributes annexed to it, has no firmer basis than the 'faith of those men whose testimony to their creed is so worthless' in the estimation of a presumptuous priesthood which arrogates for itself an apostolic descent.

The enlightened *reason* of men must necessarily be the final test of any 'religious tenet,' whether it be discussed in Councils, in the closet of the Pope, the Westminster Assembly, or the Privy Council of Her Majesty. Butler and Hooker are, I think, in accord on this matter. My 'materialistic theory,' as you are pleased to define it, has no further limitations to the spiritual capacities of individuals, or to their celestial enjoyments, than have the metaphors of Paul to which I have referred, and find its prototype in these words of Jeremiah: 'Then I went down to the potter's house, and, behold, he wrought a work on the wheels. And the vessel that he made of clay was marred in the hand of the potter: so he made it again another vessel, as seemed good to the potter to make it. Then the word of the Lord came to me, saying, O house of Israel, cannot I do with you as this potter? saith the Lord. Behold, as *the clay is in the potter's hand*, so are ye in mine hand, O house of Israel' (xviii.). It is because each individual has been thus especially moulded—some 'marred' in the moulding, some remoulded 'again into another vessel,' 'some to honour and some to dishonour,' while another shall be 'a vessel unto honour, sanctified and meet for the Master's use '—that the *same facts* and the *same arguments* from the *same facts* produce such *different convictions* on *different minds*, and lead to all the varieties in the forms and tenets of religion which are scattered through Christendom. This has already been sufficiently dwelt upon; but I must remind you, in passing, that the 'vessels of wood and of earth' have their respective uses in the 'great house'; that they are under the same roof and the same guardian or ownership as are the 'vessels of gold and silver.' And as to limitation of 'celestial happiness,' I cannot think of a more apt illustration of the joys of heaven in relation to individuals than one used by Samuel Johnson: 'People of varying capacity reach heaven, where *all* will be *full* of happiness, but, like great and little bottles, some will contain much more than others.' Surely, to be full is all-sufficing; as 'limitless' as heart could wish so far as measure or quantity is concerned. 'Materialist' and 'materialism' have been made to signify opprobrious terms; but there is nothing inherently base in matter, and its indestructibility is complete, inasmuch as it takes the same Almighty Power to destroy as it did to create it. No reverential mind need shrink from it as a base or unworthy thing, for the Almighty Being can clothe it with whatever attributes it may please HIM. It was an act of *reverential faith*, entailing salvation from suffering *and death*, in the time of Moses to look upon a *brazen* serpent; seven hundred years later, in the days of Hezekiah, it became an act of righteousness well pleasing in the sight of God *to break it into pieces*, inasmuch as in 'those days the children of Israel did burn incense to it.' Legend, tradition, credulity, superstition, had in the course of ages, then as now, perverted what was once a proper and religious act into gross idolatry. The image had for centuries ceased to fulfil a good purpose; it had become what King Hezekiah called 'Nehushtan,' a piece of brass; and 'he did right in the sight of the Lord' 'to break it into pieces,' although it *was once* 'the brazen serpent *that Moses* had made.' 'Relics' like unto this, and like unto those which the Cardinal extols—the nails of the Cross, the crib at Bethlehem, the winding-sheet at Turin, and 'pieces of our Lady's habit to be seen at the Escurial,' near to which the poor dupes see 'incense burnt,' and of which they are told 'each particle of each has in it at least a dormant, perhaps an energetic, virtue of supernatural operation'—should always be broken to pieces when they have become simply 'Nehushtan,' for who other than a 'materialist' in its worst sense could now attach 'a supernatural operation' to 'relics' so legendary, so widespread, and so numerous as those which the priestly imagination of the Cardinal has described with such glowing eloquence as among the 'paraphernalia' of the Church he has so warmly espoused—paraphernalia none the less precious to him although despised by the 'Spouse' to whom he (the Cardinal) pledged his earliest love and his earliest vows, from whom he has divorced himself in order to espouse another of whom he once deliberately said, and *swore*, that she ought not to have any 'authority, ecclesiastical or spiritual, within this realm. '*So help me, God.*' When the mighty thus fall, how tolerant ought we to be one to another, how slow to brand as 'worse than an infidel, an apostate priest,' a fellow-priest or layman who has seceded from our creed. How ready ought we to be to deal with 'such an one in the spirit of meekness, considering thyself, lest thou also be tempted.' I have nothing further to say as to the efficiency of direct spiritual guidance to each inquiring soul : 'the quietness and the confidence' which come down upon a soul so blessed ; the 'doctrine' and the 'speech,' 'which drop as the rain and distil as the dew'—'as the small rain upon the tender herb, and as the showers upon the grass'—upon the heart and intelligence of one in whom the Spirit of Christ dwells.

Vicar. You appear to me, my dear friend, quite unconscious of the heresy you have imbibed. It seems to me that you are in ignorance of the sole scheme of religion which God has provided for the redemption of mankind. You are in the same condition spiritually as were bodily the countless persons who were struggling in the primæval flood around the floating ark, after 'Noah had entered, and the Lord shut him in.' There *is*, there *can be*, no safety external to the Church; she is the depository of God's truth, the exponent of His Word, the preserver and distributor of His sacraments, and must ever be so, else would God be without trustworthy witnesses in this world. It is by virtue of the grace of apostolical succession that a due order of ministers has been preserved throughout the Christian ages, and without such qualified and authorized ministers the sacraments could not be administered, which sacraments, as the Church has diligently taught you, are 'generally necessary to salvation—that is to say, baptism and the supper of the Lord'—by the first of which you were 'made a member of Christ, a child of God, and an inheritor of the kingdom of heaven,' and the second is that in which 'the Body and Blood of Christ are verily and indeed taken by the faithful, and by which their souls are strengthened and refreshed,' as are our bodies by the bread and wine. It is by accepting these propositions as absolute facts, without cavil or dispute, that you can ever attain peace. Dark bewilderment, confusion, chaos, anxiety, mental distress, *must* ever follow all attempts to decide by 'private judgment.' Intellect, however great; purity of intention, however sincere, even when combined, are fallacious guides. Uncertainty, discrepancy, schism, are the results. Ponder on the conclusions of the men for whom and for whose writings you have to high an esteem. How different, how discrepant are their opinions on holy things! Observe the honest philosopher Faraday joining himself to a small obscure sect calling themselves 'Sandemanians' (the latter part of the name very suggestive), while on the very opposite pole of thought and feeling we see Darwin and Tyndall, almost deifying *matter*, and the marvellous mathematician Clifford pouring scorn and censure on 'Christianity' as the destroyer of 'civilizations.' Even the greatest of all great scientists, Sir Isaac Newton, forewent the creed of his fathers, and accepted, as I fear you do, the negations of a cold and sterile Arianism; and almost sadder still, the pure-minded Matthew Arnold, one of the great leaders of 'Oxford thought,' the eloquent advocate of 'sweetness and light,' denies the existence of any God who 'thinks and loves,' and has in elegiac strains thus described the hopes and aspirations of the followers of Jesus (as, indeed, you have before related):

> That thorn-crowned Man!
> He lived *while we believed*.
>
> While *we believed*, on earth he went,
>   And open stood his grave.
> Men called from chamber, church, and tent
>   And Christ was by to save.

Now he is *dead!* far hence he lies
  In the lorn Syrian town,
And on his grave with shining eyes
  The Syrian stars look down.

* * * * *

Ah, o'er that silent sacred land
  Of sun, and arid stone,
And crumbling wall, and earthy sand,
  Sounds now one word alone!

From David's lips that word did roll,
  'Tis true, and living yet:
No man can save his brother's soul,
  Nor pay his brother's debt.

Alone, self-pois'd, henceforward man
  Must labour, must resign
His all too human creeds, and scan
  Simply the way divine.

Such, yea, such are the sad results of 'private judgment.' I have referred to these men (although scores may have been taken from other departments of human science) because they belong to a class whose special training and pursuits you yourself honour, to show that there is no logical resting-place between scepticism and an implicit adoption of all the dogmatic teachings of the Catholic and Apostolic Church. The scores of wild sectarians demonstrate this to be a truth. Out of consideration to your views, I have named men accustomed to investigate facts, and to weigh evidence—Faraday, Darwin, Clifford, Tyndall, Newton, and Arnold—and have shown to what different conclusions they have come in religious opinions or convictions. I selected these men of science as being less prone to be swayed by the feelings, less disposed to be credulous, or what, perhaps, you might term fanatical, than others ; had I looked for ordinary individuals anxious respecting their spiritual state and their future life, the divisions would have been almost endless. There are more than two hundred places of meeting for religious worship in England and Wales certified to the Registrar-Genaral on behalf of persons calling themselves by different names, such as 'Believers in the Divine Visitation of Joanna Southcote,' 'Sandemanians,' 'Inghamites,' 'Old Baptists,' 'Strict Baptists,' 'King Jesus' Army,' 'Ranters,' 'Humanitarians,' 'Recreative Religionists,' and the like. To avoid all this awful confusion, there is but one resource to cleave to, and implicitly to follow—the ' one Catholic and Apostolic Church ' appointed by Christ when He said unto Peter, ' Blessed art thou, Simon Bar-jona : for flesh and blood hath not revealed it unto thee, but my Father which is in heaven. And I say also unto thee, That thou art Peter, and upon this rock I will build my church ; and the gates of hell shall not prevail against it. And I will give unto thee the keys of the kingdom of heaven : and whatsoever thou shalt bind on earth shall be bound in heaven : and whatsoever thou shalt loose on earth shall be loosed in heaven.' Into that Church you have been baptized, and from which you have not openly seceded, although you have been culpably negligent of some of her most important rites; and to her I now invite you to come penitentially. As a faithful although unworthy servant of that Church; as a priest to whom the Holy Ghost has been given by the imposition of apostolic hands, for the special purpose that I should thereby become a faithful dispenser of the Word of God and of His holy sacraments, and to be enabled to forgive or to retain sins, I implore you to lead a new life, and henceforth to walk in holy ways by partaking *habitually of that Holy Sacrament which has been specially ordained 'to preserve thy body and soul unto everlasting life.'* This is my last, my most urgent appeal to you as your pastor and priest. '*Liberavi animam meam.*' And may the merciful God, to whom the Church ever prays to have mercy upon all Jews, Turks, infidels, and heretics, take from you all ignorance, hardness of heart, and contempt of His Word, and bring you fully home to His fold, the Church, so that you may be saved among the remnant of the true Israelites, and not be among those unhappy ones who, not 'holding the Catholic Faith whole and undefiled, shall without doubt perish everlastingly.'

Parishioner. I thank you very much. Your

arguments and your words, touched with such deep emotion, would have operated powerfully upon me some years ago—as, indeed, they now would upon hundreds who are willing to accept of an external authority rather than have to think and study and pray for themselves. But your pleadings, kindly meant as they are, *necessarily* fail to produce a like sudden effect upon a mind which, possessing the Berean spirit, inquires 'whether these things *were so*,' and more especially on any one who had accepted the teachings of the Divine One who, instructing His disciples on teachers and 'rabbis' and 'masters,' said, 'Call no man your father upon the earth.' Were I, my dear Vicar, to adopt your arguments, I could not seek the 'fold' you represent, but should forthwith repair to the older, more consistent, and more logical Church from which 'the Church of England' has seceded. To the 'Berean'-like mind, under such appeals as you have made to me, there comes the inevitable inquiry, *Whence is* this 'authority' derived? Such an anxious soul, if in any degree cultured or educated, at once seeks information from the *earliest* records of the Christian life—the sayings ('*logia*') of Christ and the 'Acts of the Apostles'—and in these he cannot find an 'atom' of 'authority' for the dogmas you inculcate and the 'creed' you enforce with such appalling conditions. On the contrary, as I have so profusely shown—from the Old Testament, from the Gospels, from all the Epistles, and even from the Apocrypha itself, or the book of Revelations—the Scriptures in their integrity sustain my opinions and condemn your own, participated in although they are by nearly all the sectarians of the kingdom. Minorities are almost always in the right, and therefore I will not use—what I might to parallel your argument—the fact that Monotheists exceed in number the Trinitarians, taking the world at large, and in the great Church of Rome there are as many who believe by 'authority' in the Immaculate Conception of the Blessed Virgin as in the Church of England believe by a like authority that the Father is God, the Son is God, the Holy Ghost is God, and yet there are not three Gods, but one God. I yield to your entreaty when you can show me a single authentic scriptural statement in which Christ as clearly *indicated* that He was God—as plainly, I mean—as He declared that He was *not*, in the words, 'Why callest thou me good? there is none good but *one*, that is, God: but if thou wilt enter into life, keep the commandments' (Matt. xix. 17); and, in the words recorded by Mark as to the coming of the Judgment day, 'But of that day and that hour knoweth no man, no, not the angels which are in heaven, *neither the Son*, but the Father'; and again, 'If ye loved me, ye would rejoice, because I said, I go unto the Father: for my Father is greater than I'(John xiv. 28). 'To sit on my right hand, and on my left hand, is not mine to give, but it is for them for whom it hath been prepared of my Father' (Matt. xx. 23). There stands also the historic fact, that even the 'false witnesses' did not charge Jesus with saying that He was God, but only that 'this fellow said I am able to destroy the temple of God and to build it in three days,' which false asseveration Jesus treated with silence. How eloquent is that fact, that Jesus never called Himself God. The Trinitarian doctrine, all essential, as you declare, to salvation—without holding which in one especial form of words, you declare that a man, 'without doubt, shall perish everlastingly,' is, I repeat again, absolutely *textless*, and without an atom of authority either from the words of Jesus or the Epistles of His disciples. My position, therefore, remains unshaken, based upon the infallible words, 'The testimony of the Lord is sure, making wise the simple' (Psalm xix. 7), but it would also remain unshaken if tested by the records of the first century of the Christian Era, before the pure and simple faith of the primitive Christians had become corrupted by intercourse with pagan scholars, or contaminated by the influence of wealth and earthly power. The active research of scholars and philologists of all schools of thought, 'secular' as well as 'divine,' penetrating remote and ancient places, convents and libraries, is often bringing to light MSS., tablets, monuments, mural inscriptions, and the like, which inform us of the theories and practice of the immediate Apostolic Age. One of the most valuable of these MSS., published by the Metropolitan of Nicomedia, Philotheos Bryennius, and which was discovered by him in 'The Jerusalem Monastery of the most Holy Sepulchre at Stamboul,' and called the 'Didache ; or, The Teaching of the Twelve Apostles,' gives us the 'beliefs' and the devotional practices of the Christians soon after the martyrdom of 'James, the Lord's brother,' even if not of an earlier date. Professor Schaff calls it 'The Oldest Church Manual,' and it describes the holy rite to which you invite me, and which I long to participate in, but am shut off by awful disquisitions of 'very God of very God,' 'one substance with the Father,' and such like 'scholastic' and 'philosophic' terms, which, while they transcend my powers of comprehension, shock my moral sense and baffle my understanding.' In 'The Oldest Church Manual,' that rite, 'The Agape and the Eucharist,' are not preceded by any such paradoxical and perplexing propositions of belief as are included in the 'Nicene Creed,' nor accompanied by priestly variegated robes, candles, lighted or *unlighted*, eastward positions, elevations, and frequently repeated 'genuflexions'; but the disciples, in all humility one with another, met in their respective homes and 'continued steadfastly in the apostles' doctrine and in breaking of bread, and in prayers' (Acts ii. 42). The 'priest' was then unknown at this rite, and I think that I have somewhere read that even Bishop Lightfoot believes 'that this introduction was probably of *heathen* origin, though seeking support in Old Testament analogies.' In that 'Oldest Christian Manual,' with its second title, 'The Two Ways, the Way of Life and the Way of Death,' we are instructed as follows: 'Now as regards the Eucharist (the Thank-offering), give thanks after this manner—First for the Cup: We give thanks to Thee our Father for the holy vine of David Thy servant, which Thou hast made known to us through Jesus, Thy Servant: to Thee be the glory for ever.' And for the broken bread: We give thanks to Thee our Father, for the life and knowledge which Thou hast made known to us through Jesus, Thy servant: To Thee be the glory for ever. 'As this broken bread was scattered upon the mountains and gathered together became one, so let Thy Church be gathered together from the ends of the earth into Thy kingdom, for Thine is the glory and the power through Jesus Christ for ever. But let no one eat or drink of your Eucharist, except those baptized into the name of the Lord; for, as regards this also the Lord has said: Give not that which is holy to the dogs.' Then is added the following simple command, 'Now after being filled give thanks after this manner: We thank Thee, Holy Father, for Thy holy Name which Thou hast caused to dwell (tabernacle) in our hearts, and for the knowledge and faith, and immortality which Thou hast made known to us through Jesus Thy Servant, to Thee be the glory for ever. Thou, O Almighty Sovereign didst make all things for Thy Name's sake; Thou gavest food and drink to men, for enjoyment that they might give thanks to Thee; but to us Thou didst freely give spiritual food and drink and eternal life through Thy servant. Before all things we give thanks to Thee that thou art mighty; to Thee be the glory for ever. Remember O Lord, Thy Church to deliver her from all evil, and to perfect her in Thy love; and gather her together from the four winds, sanctified for Thy kingdom which Thou didst prepare for her; for Thine is the power and the glory for ever. Let grace come and let this world pass away. Hosanna to the God (Son) of David. If any one is holy let him come, if any one is not holy let him repent. Maranatha. Amen.' Such is the beautiful Service in its entirety. Simple, scriptural, touching. There is some difference of opinion among critics as to whether the word

'God' or 'Son' 'of David' is the more correct. The MS. contains τῷ θεῷ (God), but even Bryennios, the discoverer, thinks it *may* have been an error in the writer for τῳ υιῷ (Son). It cannot be of great moment either way, but most persons unbiassed would, I think, agree with Professor Schaff, that it would be much easier to account for the change of θεῷ into υιῷ than *vice versâ*. But, oh! my dear Vicar, what would I not give to join such a service in your Church! I should spring to your tender invitation, and 'habitually partake of that Holy Sacrament,' but, alas for me! the holy rite has 'been made of none effect by your tradition.' The preliminary confessions demanded of the recipients shut me off as completely as did the 'Cherubims and a flaming sword which turned every way,' shut off the sorrowing Adam from the tree of life.' But for this loss, and also for consolation and guidance in all controversy, I return, in these my last words, to Him who is 'The Way, the Truth, and the Life,' to the 'true Light which lighteth every man that cometh into the world,' who hath given us 'power to become the sons of God,' in whose name, and by whose words, I have been enabled to meet all your admonitions; because, through antecedent circumstances, education, and priestly office, you have all unconsciously been 'teaching for doctrines the commandments of men' (Mark vii. 7). Moreover, from the same great Teacher

I have learnt the gratifying fact, that there is sent to each earnest, anxious, prayerful mind, a Power, a Spirit which 'will guide you into all truth.' I have already shown that even such profound divines as Butler and Hooker admit that the 'private judgment' of the individual— that is, the reason of the enlightened conscience— must be the deciding power in the ultimate appeal of the course to be pursued. It was so even with Cardinal Newman. Although he has since crushed into abject slavishness the highest attribute of humanity, and his reason now lies prostrate under the Papal toe, yet was it by this very faculty that he detected (assumed he detected) and adopted the Romish Church as the infallible guide and source of all 'authority' in spiritual things. Having abandoned his own prerogative of inquiry, the Cardinal (as the fox in Æsop's Fables, when deprived of his tail, expatiated on its inconvenience and uselessness, and urged upon all other foxes to deprive themselves of such distinguishing appendages) now denounces all inquiry in matters of faith as impious, and, in reference to his adopted Church, writes, 'Let a man cease to inquire, or cease to call himself her child.' But let this pass. In 'my mind's eye,' as Hamlet said, the opinions of even Butler and Hooker, still more the abject utterances of Newman on this point, pale and fade away before these words of the great

Nazarene, 'When he, the Spirit of truth, is come, he will *guide you into all truth*'; 'The Comforter, which is the Holy Spirit, whom the Father will send in my name, *he shall teach you all things*'; and all these sublime statements are confirmed by the Apostle who spoke latest in this world of all the immediate disciples of Christ —even the 'disciple whom Jesus loved'—who told his Christian followers, 'Ye have an unction from the Holy One, and ye *know all things.*' '*Know* all things'—these are his words; not *think, opine, speculate, infer,* but '*know.*' Such Christians need not, therefore, the councils of 'pope,' 'priest,' 'monk,' 'father,' or 'confessor,' to guide them through the labyrinths of paradoxical creeds—creeds by which monk and priest alike err in '*teaching for doctrines* the commandments of men' (Matt. xv. 9). '*Know all things*' *necessary to salvation.* Blessed, thrice blessed, is this revealed truth. The 'Holy Spirit' is indeed the 'Comforter' also to weary and anxious souls; yea, the Comforter as well as the one sole, safe, and steadfast Light which, amid the mists of doubt and the waves of perplexity and trial, shines with unclouded ray to guide them safely to their home of everlasting rest. The words of the beloved disciple, my dear Vicar, will still sustain me, because they tell of '*the Comforter,*' and declare that 'the anointing which ye have received of him *abideth in you,* and ye need not that *any man* teach you: but as the same anointing teacheth you of all things, and is truth, and is no lie, and even as it hath taught you, ye shall abide in him' (1 John ii. 27). Under *such* teachings, forms, ceremonies, 'vain oblations,' 'incense,' 'appointed feasts,' 'beggarly elements,' 'new moons,' 'the calling of assemblies,' 'even the solemn meeting,' take a subordinate position. The spirit-illumined soul is 'made a priest to God' by an '*anointing*' more sacred than the 'laying-on of hands' of any pontiff, prelate, or pope, and may therefore fearlessly cast aside the metaphysical jargon of an alleged Athanasius, or any mere human 'dogmas,' and disregard the threats of all who in sacerdotal garb are, to use the words of Jesus, '*teaching for doctrines the commandments of men.*' Accepting in all their tenderness, their beauty, and their holiness the teachings of its Divine Master, clasping the sacred truth, that 'this is life eternal, that they might know Thee THE ONLY TRUE GOD, and Jesus Christ, whom THOU HAST SENT' (John xvii. 3). The Soul may well smile at the anathemas of those who declare that unless it accept their paradoxical and irrational creed, 'whole and undefiled, it shall without doubt perish everlastingly.' The Soul taught by that Spirit which Jesus told His disciples the Father would send to them, 'the Comforter, which is the Holy Ghost, He shall teach you all things,' *knows*, yea verily *knows*, '*the Lord our God is one Lord*' (Deut. vi. 4). It has read and cherished the unchangeable words, 'Unto thee it was showed that thou mightest *know* that the Lord HE IS GOD; THERE IS NONE ELSE beside HIM' (Deut. iv. 35). Yes, the Soul upon whom 'the sun of righteousness has arisen,' reverently listens to the words and accepts the teachings of its Divine Master, as given to the woman of Samaria—'the hour cometh, and now is when the true worshippers shall *worship the Father* in spirit and truth: for such doth the Father seek to be his worshippers' (John iv. 23, 24). Enough. '*Sic itur ad astra.*' Farewell.

INDEX.

A.

Alexander, Pope, VI., 'double nature,' 132.
Alford, Dean, on Paul to Titus, 65.
Allegory used by the Fathers, 62.
Apathy of Parishioners, 21-23.
Apostolic testimony to Divine Unity, 179-182, 183.
Arnold, Matthew, Poem by, 445.
Article 18, Church of England, Sternness of, 343.
Assyrian Sculptures, 48.
Athanasian Creed, Anti-biblical, 230.
Athanasian Creed, 7-13.
Athanasian Creed and Church of England, 11.
Audi alteram partem, 196.
Authority, Church, Necessity of, 258.

B.

Baptism, Rite of, no support to doctrine of Trinity, 251-252, 253.
Baptismal formula and doctrine of Trinity, 247-249.
Baptism, Infant, 345, 346, 347.
Baxter, Richard, on Witchcraft, 285.
Besant, Mrs., and Dr. Pusey, 375-379.
Bible subordinate to Church Authority, 257.
Bible Society disapproved by Popes, 257.
Biblical errors in Natural History, 302-307.
Bibliolatry, 267, 282, 283, 319, 320, 323.

Bibliolatry leads to Scepticism, 268.
Blanco White, 432, 434, 439.
Browne, Rev. Harold, and Revisers of New Testament, 415.
Browne, Sir Thos., on Witchcraft, 287.
Bright Service, A, 212, 213.
Bryennios, P., Discovery of the 'Didache,' 100.
Burgess and Bull on text in St. John's Epistle, 89, 90.
Burgon, Dean, on chapter in St. Mark, 93, 94.

C.

Cabalism and Fanaticism, 120.
Canonical Books, 295, 297, 300.
Canticles, Book of, 296-299.
Catholic Unity, 334.
Chalcedon, Council of, 131.
Character and Form, 425, 426.
Chichester, Bishop of, and Revision of New Testament, 415.
Chillingworth's Aphorism deplored, 250.
Church, The, as Ark of Noah, 444, 445.
Church, The, and Fathers as Authorities of Faith, 246.
Church of Rome and Athanasian Creed, 5.
Church of England and Athanasian Creed, 5-13.
Church of England, Inconsistency of, 108, 109.
Church of England, Cardinal Newman on, 219.
Church of England and Doctrine of Trinity, 202.

Church of England, Practical Errors of, 121.
Church of England as an Authority, 41-51.
Church of England Dissensions, 15.
Church of England a Paradox, 203.
Church of England as Interpreter of Scripture, 257.
Church of England: a personal Appeal, 115.
Church of England Prayer Book, 27, 28, 29.
Church of England Commination Service, 4.
Church of England Communion Service, 126.
Clarke, Dr. Samuel, on Nicene Creed, 144.
Clerical Intolerance and Cruelty, 378-380.
Colenso on Genesis, 277.
Colenso, Persecution of, 382, 383.
Coleridge, Lord, on Differences of Opinion, 428.
Comforter, The, 455-459.
Conception, Immaculate, 155-159.
Conclusion, Final, 458, 459.
Credulity and Creed, 228, 229, 232.

D.

'Dangerous,' the Bigot's cry, 146.
Darwin on Transmission of Propensities, 143.
Delegated honour and power, 136.
Denison, George Anthony, and Convocation, 414.
'Didache,' The, 100.
Durham and Westminster, Deans of, on the Athanasian Creed, 109.
D'Oyly and Mant on the Serpent, 304.

E.

Ecclesiastical Authority adverse to Freedom, 123.
Ecclesiasticus, Book of, 296, 298.
Ellicott, Bishop, Pastoral Epistles, 66, 67.
Ellicott, Bishop, on I Timothy iii., 16,
Eldon, Lord, Prejudice of, 95.

'Emmanuel,' 154, 155.
'Equal with God,' Philippians ii. 5, 260.
Erasmus on Epistle of St. John, 83.
Errors, Textual, Numerous, 257.
Essays and Reviews, Persecution of Writers, 380-383.
Eucharist, Vital Importance of, 117.
Evangelical Teaching of the Past, 328-331.
'Even as' delegated Honour, 186.

F.

Facts and Faith, 227, 301-307.
Falsehood and Forgery, 80-87.
Fanaticism and Cabalism, 120.
Fanaticism, Cruel, 370-373.
Farrar, Jowett, Colenso, 278.
'Forgiveness of Sins' and Divinity, 137-139.
Form and Character, 425, 426.
Fox, George, as a Reformer, 289.

G.

Galileo, Imprisonment of, 123.
Gregory, St., on Councils, 32, 33.
Green, Rev. Sheldon, on Texts in Titus and Timothy, 65, 256.
Griesbach on Spurious Texts, 90.

H.

Habit, Force of, 139, 140.
Hale, Chief Baron, on Witches, 283.
Harvey's Discovery of Circulation of Blood, 327.
Havernick on the word 'Elohim,'
Hayward, Archdeacon, on the Trinity, 114.
Hear the Church, 41, 42, 444.
Hereditary Influence, 22, 23, 24, 139, 147.
Hooker, the Scriptures and doctrine of Trinity, 201, 400.
Homoousian, 9.
Horace on Differences of Taste, 428.
Human and Divine Nature of Christ, 132.

INDEX. 463

I.

Inspiration of Humanity, 308-313.
Inspiration of Scripture, 281-296.
Intolerance of Cardinal Newman, 430, 432.
Intolerance of Rev. J. Keble, 394.
Intolerance of Dr. Pusey, 375-377.
Intelligence, General effect of, 288.

J.

James, St., Testimony to Divine Unity, 182.
Ideas, Persecution of, 391.
Jesus, Delegate of His Father, 103.
Jesus as a Reformer, 238, 289.
Jesus disclaims supreme Godhead, 106, 107.
Jesus, Testimony to Divine Unity, 129.
Jewel, Bishop, on Witchcraft, 284.
John, Epistle of, 31.
John, Epistle of, Spurious Text in, 78-80, 81.
John, Testimony to Divine Unity, 185.
Jowett, Professor, on spurious Text, 90.
Jowett, Professor, as a biblical Interpreter, 278.
Judgment, Private, Evils of, 445, 447.
Judgment, Private, Final Appeal, 40-44, 449.
Justin Martyr on Virgin Mothers, 164.

K.

Keble, John, Scripture and the Trinity, 113, 201.
Keble, John, on Baptism, 347.
Keble, John, Character of, and 'Christian Year,' 249-354.
Keble, John, Seclusion and shyness of, 353-357.
Keble, John, charitable in Gifts, 356.
Keble, John, Home and early Environments, 358, 359.
Keble, John, Affection for his Sisters, 359, 360.
Keble, John, Religious Intolerance of, 361-363.
Keble, John, prejudicial Bias, 365-395.
Keble, John, dislike to intellectual Research, 395-399.
Knowledge, Progressive, 402-403.

L.

Lachmann on Spurious Text, 90.
Legends of Miraculous Births, 162-164.
Lichfield Cathedral and Rev. J. Keble, 395.
Liddon, Canon, on Text to Titus, 66.
Liddon, Canon, on Divinity of Christ, 188-194.
Liddon, Canon, and Rev. J. Keble, 197.
Lightfoot on Spurious Text, 90.
Liturgy, The, 342
Locke on the Trinity, 76, 144.
Lowell, Russell, Hon., Anecdotes by, 19.
Luther on 'Elohim,' 55.
Luther on Witches, 284.
Luther, Fanatic Cruelty, 373.

M.

Macaulay on Christianity and the Church, 59.
Manual, Church, The oldest, 452.
Mark, St., concluding verses, 96, 97, 98.
Martineau on Duty of Inquiry, 233
Mechanical Prayers, 142.
Melville, Rev. H., on the Trinity, 34, 35.
Melville, Perverse Bigotry of, 320, 321.
Melioza, 332.
Meyer on our Text of St. Paul, 69.
Miller, Hugh, on Geology and Genesis, 277.
Milman, Dean, on the Trinity, 10.

INDEX.

Milton, John, on the Trinity, 75, 144.
Milton, John, on Schism, 199, 200.
Milton, John, on Popular Beliefs, 152.
Mind and Materialism, 439-444.
Misuse of Words, Mischief of, 418, 419.
Modern Miracles v. Trinity, 228, 229.
Mohammedans adverse to the Trinity, 73, 74.
'More Light,' 195.
Moses, Errors of, in Natural History, 303.
'Mystery of Godliness,' 255.
Mythic Legends, 162.

N.

Nahushtan, 443.
National Church, The, 205-211.
National Church, The, Cardinal Newman on, 219.
Nature, Double, The, of Christians, 131-135.
Neander on the Trinity, 82.
Newman, Cardinal, on the Trinity, 201.
Newman, Cardinal, Character of, 220-240, 423.
Newman, Cardinal, on the Deaths of Pious Men, 433-438.
New Testament, Greek, 245.
Newspapers, 'Religious,' 17.
Newton, Sir Isaac, 77.
Newton, Sir Isaac, on Arianism, 144.
Newton, Sir Isaac, on the Incarnation, 161.
Numbers, Fallacy of, as Test of Truth, 122, 144, 145, 179.

O.

Oberlin, John Frederic, 423.
Oehler on the word 'Elohim,' 55.
Oldest Church Manual, 452.
Organization and Thought, 425-429.
Origen on the Trinity, 101.
Origen on the Canticle, 296.

Oude, Queen of, on the Trinity, 75.

P.

Pagan Triads, 46, 59.
Parmenides and Biology, 401.
Parties in the Church of England, 15.
Parishioners, Apathy of, 17-20.
Passive Piety, 232.
Pauline Epistles, 260-265.
Paul to Timothy and Titus, 64, 65, 70.
Paul on Doctrine of Divine Unity, 179, 182.
Paul, Lucidity of, 71, 74.
Paul receding before Christ, 328.
Paul, Spiritual Development of, 386, 387.
Pearson on Text in St. John's Epistle, 83.
Penn, William, on the Trinity, 86-88.
Peter, St., Testimony to the Divine Unity, 182-184.
Petition of Laity against Athanasian Creed, 110.
Polycarp, 92.
Porson on Spurious Text in St. John's Epistle, 84.
'Poor in Spirit,' 'Pure in Heart,' 237, 238.
Prayer Book, The, 27, 28, 29.
Praying Wheels, 142.
Preaching the Gospel, 338, 339.
Priestly Fanaticism, 372-377.
Private Judgment, Thirty-fourth Article on, 198.
Private Judgment, 444, 445.
Progress, Modern, 170-174.
Prophecy and Inspiration, 317, 318.
Pusey, Dr., and Mrs. Besant, 375-379.

Q.

'Quicunque vult,' Cardinal Newman on, 112.
'Quicunque vult,' Pusey and Denison on, 113.
Queen Elizabeth and Witchcraft, 287.

R.

Raising the Dead, 177, 178.
Reason and the French Revolution, 148.
Reason, Warburton, Bishop, on, 148.
Reason, Tillotson, Archbishop, on, 149.
Reason, Coleridge, Taylor, on, 149.
Reason, Gladstone, Ewart, on, 150.
Reason, Bishop Butler on, 150.
'Religious' Newspapers, 16, 17.
Religious Intolerance, 388, 390, 431, 434.
Religion and Science, 403, 409, 414, 438.
Reverence, Want of, 420.
Reverence, Feeling of, 422, 423.
Reverence, Feeling of, in Cardinal Newman, 423.
Revisers of New Testament, 414.

S.

Sacramental Grace, 337.
Sacramentary System, 345, 346.
Scepticism and Bibliolatry, 268.
Scepticism, Spread of, 269-275.
Scepticism and Evangelical Teaching, 323.
Schism, 199.
Scholz on Spurious Text, 90.
Science and Religion, 405-414.
Scripture interpreted by the Church, 45.
Scripture Authority slight in support of the Trinity, 201
Scripture as a Final Appeal, 265.
Scripture and Geology, 276-279.
Sculptures of Assyria, 47, 48.
Search the Scriptures, 232.
Sects, numerous, The, 447.
Seneca and Mahomet, 291.
Sensuous Services, 214-217.
Serpent of Scripture, 303, 365.
Smith, Rev. Vance, Reviser of New Testament, 414, 416.
'Son of God,' Appellation of, 104, 105.
Speculation and Fact, 146.
Spirit of Truth, The, 449-456.
Spiritual Service Distasteful, 214.
Spirit, Holy, as Teacher, 39-44.

Spurgeon, Rev. C., on eternal Torment, 322.
Spurious Texts, 80-91.
Stanley, Dean, on Councils, 32.
Stanley, Dean, Noble Conduct of, 382-384.
Stanley, Dean, Defence of Religious Liberty, 415-417.
Steadfastness, Christian, 111-118.
Sternness of Eighteenth Article, 343.
'Stubbs, Dr.,' on the Trinity, 5.
Subtlety of Church of Rome, 215.
Supremacy of Jesus over Councils, 126, 127.
Symbols of the Trinity, 49-63.

T.

Teaching of the Twelve Apostles, 100.
Tenacity of Early Belief, 48.
Tertullian on Divinity of Christ, 8.
Tertullian on Symbols of the Trinity, 62.
Texts in Defence of the Trinity, 54-57.
Textual Error, Difficulty of Avoiding, 259.
Theory of Trinity Textless, 239, 240.
Theophilus on the Trinity, 57.
Thirlwall, Bishop, on Athanasian Creed, 119.
Thought and Organization, 425-429.
Thomas, St., Exclamation of, 241.
Tischendorff on Spurious Text, 90.
Toleration, Duty of, 429.
Torment, Eternal Doctrine of, 321, 323-341.
Torture Employed on Witches, 285, 286.
Transmission of Propensities, 143.
Tregelles on Spurious Text, 90.
Trinity, The, Practically Textless, 239, 240.
Trinity, Doctrine of, 36, 37, 38.
Trinity recognized by Pagans, 46.
Trinity, Egyptian, Grecian, and Assyrian Symbols of, 49-54.
Truth *versus* Numbers, 122, 123.
Truthfulness of Jesus, 133, 134.

Tyndale on a Text of St. Paul, 67.

U.

Unbelief and Evangelicalism, 325, 327.
Unity, Divine, described by Jesus, 129, 130.
Unity and Supremacy of God, 102.
Unknown Tongue, 234.

V.

Valpy's Greek Testament, 92.
Virchow on Theory and Facts, 302.
Virgin Mothers, 162-165.

W.

Webster's and Wilkinson's Greek Testament, 92.
Wesley on Witchcraft, 285.
Wette, De, on a Text of St. Paul, 65.
Whately, Archbishop, on Man's Dislike to Investigate Religious Truth, 141.
Wheels, Praying, 142.
Whittier, J. G., on Priestcraft, 371.
White, Blanco, Sufferings and Faith, 432-439.
Winer on Text of St. Paul, 68.
Wisdom of St. Paul, 151.
Wisdom of Solomon, Hosea, Jesus, 151.
Wisdom, John Milton on, 152.
Wisdom *versus* Church Authority, 158.
Witchcraft, 284-287.
Words, Torture of, 29.

www.ingramcontent.com/pod-product-compliance
Lightning Source LLC
Chambersburg PA
CBHW022100300426
44117CB00007B/525